# THE SON IN MY EYES

# *The* SON *in* MY EYES

*Seeing the Light
of Jesus
in Vietnam*

## MAI SPENCER
WITH DIXIE PHILLIPS

THE SON IN MY EYES

Deep River Books
Sisters, Oregon
http://www.deepriverbooks.com

ISBN-978-1-935265-66-5
ISBN-10-1-935265-66-0

Library of Congress 2011925528

Printed in the USA

Cover design by blackbirdcreative.biz

If you would like to know more about the ministry of Dennis and Mai Spencer or if God speaks to your heart to help financially support the ministry in Vietnam to see His Kingdom expand there, please contact us by email or visit our website:

Dennis and Mai Spencer
Jesus in Vietnam Ministries
E-mail: camonchua@comcast.net
Website: www.Jesusinvietnam.com

⌒⌒

We are a Private Foundation with tax-exempt status under §501(c) (3) of the Internal Revenue Code and all contributions are tax deductible.

*Expect great things from God. Attempt great things for God.*

WILLIAM CAREY, MISSIONARY TO INDIA

⌒⌒

*Special Thanks*

First, to the love of my life – my best friend and husband, Dennis, thank you for not giving up on me or our marriage when I was so steeped in grief. You showed me Jesus' love and I will be eternally grateful. I look forward to growing old with you.

Second, my spiritual godmother, Marge Pitchford, your love for and obedience to God not only changed my life forever, but instilled in my heart a deep desire to share Jesus with other "lost souls". Thank you, Grandma Margie. When I grow up I want to be just like you.

And last but not least, my eternal friends, Anthony and Denise Barnett. I know our friendship was orchestrated by Divine appointment. I love you and can never repay you for the kindnesses you have extended to me and my family.

# TABLE OF CONTENTS

# INTRODUCTION

*O the love that sought me,*
*O the Blood that bought me,*
*O the grace that brought me to the fold,*
*Wondrous grace that brought me to the fold.*

❧

## MERCY REWROTE MY LIFE

The powerful lyrics of this old hymn tell my story. It was His love that sought me, His blood that bought me, and His wondrous grace that brought me to the fold. I was a poor Buddhist girl born and raised in Vietnam. My future was bleak, but Jesus knew my name, and He dipped His pen into a well of mercy and rewrote my life. As I share my story, you will see I was steeped in great darkness, but the Light of the World shone His love into my soul and brought me out of that black pit. Corrie Ten Boom once said, "There is no pit so deep that God's love is not deeper still." I have personally experienced the lifting power of God's love and encountered what the psalmist David wrote about in the fortieth Psalm.

*He brought me up also out of an horrible pit, out of the miry clay, and set my feet upon a rock, and established my goings.*

PSALM 40:2 KJV

❧

## HIS GRACE STILL AMAZES ME

*Amazing grace how sweet the sound.*
*That saved a wretch like me.*
*I once was lost, but now am found.*
*Was blind, but now I see.*

*T'was grace that taught my heart to fear.*
*And grace, my fears relieved.*
*How precious did that grace appear*
*The hour I first believed.*

*Through many dangers, toils and snares*
*We have already come.*
*T'was grace that brought us safe thus far*
*And grace will lead us home.*

*When we've been there ten thousand years*
*Bright shining as the sun.*
*We've no less days to sing God's praise*
*Than when we've first begun.*

The first time I heard *Amazing Grace,* tears filled my eyes. There was such a revelation in the depths of my soul. I realized God was extending an invitation to me. The true God who created this vast universe desired that I be the recipient of His amazing grace. As each verse of John Newton's timeless hymn was sung, I was immensely aware of how big God's love was for me. As I basked in His presence, He seemed so large and I seemed so small. His love overwhelmed me. I pondered this glorious truth. The King of kings died for a sinful soul like me. Gently and tenderly, He charmed my broken heart. Never once did He condemn me or mention the mistakes I had made. His holy presence swept over me, and for the first time in my life, I knew I was forgiven. He looked beyond all my faults and saw my great need of a Savior. I will never forget the day He reached down and lovingly picked me up. His blood cleansed me from all unrighteousness. My life has never been the same since Jesus came into my heart. I became a new person in Christ Jesus.

> *Therefore, if anyone is in Christ, he is a new creation; the*
> *old has gone, the new has come.*

2 CORINTHIANS 5:17

Maybe you feel hopeless today. Possibly you are looking for a new lease on life. I believe God has placed my story in your hands. If God is able to transform a Buddhist girl and make her a true believer in Jesus Christ, He can transform you. His Word declares if we truly confess our sins, He will not only forgive us, but cleanse us from all unrighteousness. Oh, it's so wonderful to be clean.

> *If we confess our sins, he is faithful and just to forgive us*
> *our sins, and to cleanse us from all unrighteousness.*

1 JOHN 1:9 KJV

Satan may lie to you and try to convince you it is impossible for you to change. You don't have to change yourself. God changes you from the inside out. His Word promises nothing is too difficult for Him. We must doubt our doubts and believe the Word of God.

> *Jesus looked at them and said, "With man this is impossible, but*
> *with God all things are possible."*

MATTHEW 19:26

## GOD IS NO RESPECTER OF PERSONS

To grasp the miracle that took place in my life, you must know more about my story and the stronghold Satan had on my family. We were Buddhist for many generations, but Jesus passed by and changed our beliefs. No longer do we bow to false gods. We now bow our knees before Jesus and boldly proclaim, "Jesus Christ is Lord!" What He has done for me, He will do for you. He shows no partiality. His Word makes this promise.

*Then Peter opened his mouth, and said,*
*Of a truth I perceive that God is no respecter of persons.*

ACTS 10:34 KJV

*Indeed, the very hairs of your head are all numbered.*
*Don't be afraid; you are worth more than many sparrows.*

LUKE 12:7

Jesus took the stumbling blocks in my life and transformed them into stepping stones. He made something beautiful of my life. I have experienced what Isaiah proclaimed: beauty for ashes, the oil of gladness for mourning and the garment of praise for the spirit of despair.

## MAI'S HISTORY

In every generation, there are circumstances that shape the destiny of a soul. For those of us who have experienced war in our homeland and seen firsthand the havoc it wreaks on individuals, families, communities and the entire country, we realize there are no winners in war, only losers. The question is not who won the most, but who lost the least.

As I reflect back over my life, I realize now that I had several factors against me. First, I was born in severe poverty with no way out in sight. Second, I never knew my biological father. Third, I was born and raised during the Vietnam War. Just one of these negative influences could guarantee a life filled with despair and hopelessness, but the One whose eye is on the sparrow was the One watching me.

*...and provide for those who grieve in Zion—*
*to bestow on them a crown of beauty*
*instead of ashes,*
*the oil of gladness*
*instead of mourning,*
*and a garment of praise*
*instead of a spirit of despair.*
*They will be called oaks of righteousness,*

*a planting of the Lord
for the display of his splendor.*

Isaiah 61:3

Oh, if you don't know my wonderful Friend, won't you consider inviting Him into your life? He will make something beautiful out of your life. That's exactly what He did for me!

# FOREWORD

✑

To appreciate the following pages, I believe it is important for you to know how strategic God's plan was for Mai and Dennis Spencer. After all, He is the Master Architect, seeing every detail meets His expectations. He is able to bring every purpose and plan into fruition. Out of the soil of obedience, I moved my family from Los Angeles, California, to Tucson, Arizona during Memorial Day weekend, 1991. We were excited and cautious at the same time. But why? What's in Tucson? Where is Tucson? Coming from Los Angeles, why would anyone in their right mind want to leave the Pacific Ocean – great weather, cultural venues, amusement parks, Trojan football, a plethora of great dining establishments, churches and family—to relocate to Tucson? We didn't wake up one morning and say, "Hey! I think I'll move to Tucson." The desert? Well, you will be surprised at the lengths God went through to get us here. The genesis started with God dealing with my heart; dissolving self-will and replacing it with His. In my foolishness, I made dumb statements like, "I would never live in those apartments!" and "I'd never live in the desert!" Funny, both of those statements came back at me. Life's issues dictated otherwise; the very place where I had made the apartment statement, I ended up renting. The desert? Well, I'm here. It reminds me of what the Spirit told Peter in the Book of Acts.

*The next day as they were still on their way and were approaching the town, Peter went up to the roof of the house to pray, about the sixth hour [noon].*

*But he became very hungry, and wanted something to eat; and while the meal was being prepared a trance came over him,*

*And he saw the sky opened and something like a great sheet lowered by the four corners, descending to the earth.*

*It contained all kinds of quadrupeds and wild beasts and creeping things of the earth and birds of the air.*

*And there came a voice to him, saying, Rise up, Peter, kill and eat.*

*But Peter said, No, by no means, Lord; for I have never eaten anything that is common and unhallowed or [ceremonially] unclean.*

*And the voice came to him again a second time, What God has cleansed and pronounced clean, do not you defile and profane by regarding and calling common and unhallowed or unclean.*

ACTS 10:9–15 AMP

Do not call anything impure God has made clean. That is, though you don't understand it, though it is contrary to your tradition and judgment, the Lord requires you to be in a specific place, at a specific time, for a specific purpose. Like Peter, I was obedient, not understanding God's plan. Understanding His plan was not important; obeying His directive was. So, we made the move. A few months after arriving, my wife and I met Mai. She had previously met our children, but not us. It was her opinion that our children were polite and exemplified good manners. She reasoned, "Perhaps they can help me with the issues I face with one of my children." That one encounter led to more discussions. She began to pour her heart out to us, even though we were complete strangers. As she told her many stories, we could see the discontent, confusion, emotional pain, hurt, disappointment and emptiness. Oh, the pain she described. The disappointment and hurt of her deceased children. And the pain brought on by a disobedient and wayward daughter's life seemed to be a major question mark. This was a life full of events like a connect-the-dots puzzle, but what image was it outlining? After scores of prayer and counseling, Mai gave her life to Jesus. What a transformation! Soon after Mai's salvation, Terri, her oldest and wayward daughter who was terminally ill, also gave her life to Jesus. Did Terri's illness rock her faith? No, it energized her faith! She believed God for her salvation and healing. God used that illness to bring her family closer together. Terri gave her heart to Jesus, and through the pain of cancer and gave up this life for her residence in Heaven. Through every trial, Mai tried to see the hand of our Father in it. The questions were many; Questions about faith in Christ Jesus and questions of purpose. We met with Mai often. Her family quickly became our family. Those were the beginnings of her spiritual walk with Jesus. Yes, Mai was, and is, tenacious. Her desire to know the Bible was insatiable. We began to see this neophyte grow and blossom. There was fruit on the tree, and others began to rest under her shade and feed among her branches. God was working in her family. Following in her footsteps, her husband, Dennis, renewed his relationship with God; Terri's daughter Cherée received Jesus; and soon Mai's family in Vietnam belonged to the family of God. Wow!

Mai started a clothing manufacturing business. Before the work day began, her mornings were a time set aside to seek the Lord's favor through prayer with her employees. Those who wanted to participate did. Others respectfully waited for work to begin. Her employees were exposed to the Word of God via the Bible on tape throughout the day. Amazingly, most, if not all of them, gave their lives to Jesus. Forced? Not at all. Compelled through love and the Word of God? Absolutely!

Several years ago, after a trip home to Vietnam, Mai shared her heart's desire to build a church in Binh Chau, Vietnam. She did not know how to do it, but do it she must – and that she did! God has allowed us the privilege to be a part of her spiritual development and support for the propagation of the Gospel in Vietnam through Jesus in Vietnam Ministries. Mai's heart for the salvation of people in Vietnam is limitless. She constantly prays and invites her family and friends to do the same. Her heart burns passionately as we ask God's favor in breaking yokes of bondage, fear, avarice, suspicion, arrogance and pride in the hearts of governmental officials and others. The following pages chronicle the acts of God in a life submitted to the will and call of God. May you be blessed and challenged as you read the pages of her journey, may it ignite your heart and soul to do great things for God, in His sight, for His Glory! Remember, the Scripture declares:

*...but the people who know their God shall be strong, and carry out great exploits. And those of the people who understand shall instruct many.*

DANIEL 11:32b, 33a NKJV

— Anthony & Denise Barnett

# Chapter One

# Humble Beginnings

❧

"Mai, go pick some of my marigolds." Grandmother barked the order to me. "Hurry up! I want some for our table and also would like you to prepare some for the altars."

Even though I was just a little girl, I was very familiar with arranging special offerings for the Buddhist altars in our home. Grandmother had several statues of Buddha in strategic parts of the house. Phat Ba Quan Am was a statue elevated high in the center of our home. She was sometimes called the "Lady Buddha." We were taught to call on her when we were having a difficult time, and she would help us. We had Ong Dia, who was known as Happy Buddha. We believed he would bring us good luck. Ong Tham Tai was the god of money. He was supposed to increase our wealth. Ong Tho Dia was the land god. We would pray to him to bless the land we lived on. Ong Tao was the stove god. He sat on the stove in our tiny kitchen and was privy to our family's most private business and intimate secrets for the entire year. Then, on January 23, he was to go to Heaven and report to the Jade Emperor, informing him of how we were doing, and hopefully, he would bless us.

## Breaking of a Generational Curse

We were a superstitious family. We were always looking for something to bring us good luck or change our dire circumstances, but it never seemed to work. In fact, as you will soon discover, our family was under a generational curse. In accordance with Vietnamese culture, my grandmother told us children that we were the children of the dragon (Con Rong), and she believed our ancestors were fallen angels (Chau Tien).

If any Vietnamese people believe this today, they are still under this generational curse. I thank God for opening my eyes to see I am not a child of the dragon and my ancestors are not fallen angels. God reveals in His Word that I am made in His image and I am a child of God.

*Then another sign appeared in heaven: an enormous red dragon with seven heads and ten horns and seven crowns on his heads. His tail swept a third of the stars out of the sky and flung them to the earth. The dragon stood in front of the woman who was about to give birth, so that he might devour her child the moment it was born.*

REVELATION 12:3–4 NIV

*Then God said, "Let us make man in our image, in our likeness."*

GENESIS 1:26A NIV

*The LORD God formed the man from the dust of the ground and breathed into his nostrils the breath of life, and the man became a living being.*

GENESIS 2:7 NIV

*Yet to all who received him, to those who believed in his name, he gave the right to become children of God.*

JOHN 1:12 NIV

This generational curse has been broken. I now realize there is only one antidote for this curse we were under: the precious blood of Jesus. Yes, His blood was the only power that could break the curse. Oh, how thankful I am today to be forgiven and free from the horrible darkness and worship of false gods. The Word of God is truth. There is only one name under heaven by which we can be saved, and that name is Jesus Christ.

*Salvation is found in no one else, for there is no other name under heaven given to men by which we must be saved."*

ACTS 4:12

My family did not know any better than to worship false gods. Our understanding was darkened. I can not remember any Christians in our village. I do remember some Catholics, and I had heard them speak of Jesus, but never once did I realize a person could experience a personal relationship with Him. My Buddhist ways did not stop Jesus from loving me. His plan was to call me to Himself and deliver me from the false teaching of Buddhism. He kept His hand upon my life and even protected me from being killed on numerous occasions. How thankful I am He never gave up on me, even when I was worshipping false gods. Now that I know Him, it seems so appalling that I believed such heresy, but at the time, I thought it was truth. I didn't know any better. I was like a blind man groping in the darkness. I was ignorant of Jesus' love for me. I had not yet read the words found in the fifth chapter of Romans.

*But God demonstrates his own love for us in this: While we were still sinners, Christ died for us.*

ROMANS 5:8

## ANCESTRAL WORSHIP

My family had a mixed religion. Not only did we worship Buddha, but we also took part in ancestral worship. Grandmother had two altars in her home set up for her deceased parents, and every time another family member died, she set up more altars in honor of their memory. We would place offerings of fruit or flowers on the altars and pray we would be kept from danger.

In the center of our front yard was Ong Troi, the altar for the universal God. We recognized the infinite space over our heads was Heaven or Troi. We felt there was a Supreme Being in Heaven who was the Creator, but that was the only bit of truth in our darkened theology.

After I was saved and began to dig into God's Word, I read the story in Acts 17 about Paul the Apostle preaching to the men of Athens at the altar of the unknown God on Mars' Hill. As I read those verses, I thought of how my family worshipped Ong Troi, the Supreme Being in Heaven. How ignorant we were, but God had a plan.

*Then Paul stood in the midst of Mars' hill, and said, Ye men of Athens, I perceive that in all things ye are too superstitious. For as I passed by, and beheld your devotions, I found an altar with this inscription, TO THE UNKNOWN GOD. Whom therefore ye ignorantly worship, him declare I unto you. God that made the world and all things therein, seeing that he is Lord of heaven and earth, dwelleth not in temples made with hands; Neither is worshipped with men's hands, as though he needed any thing, seeing he giveth to all life, and breath, and all things; And hath made of one blood all nations of men for to dwell on all the face of the earth, and hath determined the times before appointed, and the bounds of their habitation; That they should seek the Lord, if haply they might feel after him, and find him, though he be not far from every one of us: For in him we live, and move, and have our being; as certain also of your own poets have said, For we are also his offspring. Forasmuch then as we are the offspring of God, we ought not to think that the Godhead is like unto gold, or silver, or stone, graven by art and man's device. And the times of this ignorance God winked at; but now commandeth all men every where to repent: Because he hath appointed a day, in the which he will judge the world in righteousness by that man whom he hath ordained; whereof he hath given assurance unto all men, in that he hath raised him from the dead. And when they heard of the resurrection of the dead, some mocked: and others said, We will hear thee again of this matter. So Paul departed from among them. Howbeit certain men clave unto him, and believed: among the which was Dionysius the Areopagite, and a woman named Damaris, and others with them.*

ACTS 17:22–34 KJV

How thankful I am that I have had a personal encounter with the one true, universal God. The world declares, "You must know who you are if you want to discover your divine destiny." But I have found it's more important to know whose you are. When you know this precious truth, you can't help but discover your divine destiny. My knees have bowed and my tongue has confessed that Jesus Christ is Lord. Have yours? You can have a personal encounter with the universal God today.

> *And being found in appearance as a man,*
> *he humbled himself*
> *and became obedient to death—*
> *even death on a cross!*
> *Therefore God exalted him to the highest place*
> *and gave him the name that is above every name,*
> *that at the name of Jesus every knee should bow,*
> *in heaven and on earth and under the earth,*
> *and every tongue confess that Jesus Christ is Lord,*
> *to the glory of God the Father*

PHILIPPIANS 2:8–11

## TEA OFFERINGS

Every morning Grandmother would ask me to prepare a pot of hot tea. She always had three tiny cups that held about an ounce of water. At each altar, Grandmother would have one plate and one of the tiny teacups. It was my job to empty the old tea from the day before, and fill the teacup with the fresh brewed tea. Once again Grandmother would follow me, inspect my work, and light incense at each altar. Every evening before she went to bed she would pray to her idols, and once a month, she would fast from animal flesh. She practiced this religious ritual her entire life.

One of the more humorous traits about my grandmother was her temper. As Buddhists, we were taught to be gentle and humble towards people. Good works were expected to get you to Heaven. We had not heard the truths the Bible teaches about works in the second chapter of Ephesians.

*For it is by grace you have been saved, through faith—and this not from yourselves, it is the gift of God—not by works, so that no one can boast.*

EPHESIANS 2:8, 9

Grandmother was extra kind to the people in our town who held any position of honor. She would bend over backwards greeting them, but at home, she was just the opposite. When she lit her incense and prayed at the altars, her countenance appeared quite solemn and humble, but woe to us children if we made the slightest noise. Her religious piety was thrown out the window, and she would scream at us and even threaten to spank us if we didn't hush. Don't misunderstand. We knew Grandmother loved us. She worked so hard to make ends meet. Every day she would cook us delicious meals. Food was scarce in Vietnam during this time, but Grandmother always tried to keep our tummies from growling with hunger. As I reminisce, I can see the sacrifices she made for us, but I also realize we children were a constant source of irritation to her. It probably had something to do with her age. Taking care of all of us was probably the straw that broke the camel's back. The financial load she carried was heavy enough, but then add several young children to the mix, and it sent her over the edge. I hold nothing in my heart against her even though she spanked me quite frequently. If I had to endure all the sufferings she did, I probably would have screamed and handed out some spankings along the way, too.

Grandmother never had the opportunity to know Jesus like I do. She never knew how good God is. All she was exposed to were the false religions of Vietnam. She was born on a farm and raised in the jungle. She was surrounded by a handful of poor, illiterate souls who had experienced much of the same war-ravaged existence she had. It was a way of life and was all she knew. Very few citizens in her village had a decent education, and the ones who could read and write usually moved to the city and worked for the government.

An example of my grandmother's rigid rules would be the times she had me be her errand girl. Whatever she needed, my young legs would run and get it for her. One day she asked me to pick up something at the store. The minute I started out the door, she began timing my trip. She gave me no wiggle room to stop and play or visit a neighbor's house. She made sure she kept tabs on me, and when I ran an errand for her, I was to perform my duty in record time. If I didn't, I would be punished. However, if I pleased her with my speed and a job well done, there was to be no applause or compliments. It was what was expected of me. She set the standard high, and I was required to meet that standard.

She constantly stressed that, as a young girl, I was never to sit with my friends and gossip. In order for my family to survive, I had to work. I realize now, as an adult, I probably was worked too hard, but God has blessed me to see the bright side of it. Because of the hardships I endured as a child, I have a tremendous work ethic. I might not have been able to experience deep friendships and a carefree childhood because I was too busy working from dawn to dusk, but I learned the art of surviving in the most dire circumstances. Once again I see God's hand in this.

# Chapter Two

# LIFE IN THE JUNGLE

❧

n 1958, I was eight and lived with my mom and grandmother, my two uncles, their wives and four cousins, my retarded sister, Luom, and my baby sister, Nga. My two sisters and I had already experienced enough rejection to last a lifetime.

Luom was the oldest. My mother married very young and was only seventeen when Luom was born. Her father abandoned her and my mother when Luom was just an infant. They never heard from him again. Luom was sickly and had seizures for the first three years of her life. There was no money for doctors or medications to treat her. My mother and grandmother did the best they could with the cards they had been dealt. They worked very hard taking care of Luom at home.

Nga was born in 1954. Her father deserted the family, too. There was always speculation that he was in Hanoi. We never knew for sure what happened to him, but we did know he probably wouldn't return.

Every morning my mom and I woke around four o'clock. We ate rice and dried fish for breakfast. Then we packed a lunch of whatever was left over from supper the night before, added some more rice and dried fish, and headed off to work. We hired a few Montagnard People to help us. The Montagnards were hard working folks, but lacked formal education. Most of them were illiterate and lived a very simple lifestyle. Many were bound by their addiction to rice liquor, and some practiced witchcraft and voodoo. The Montagnards, Mother and I traipsed about eight miles by foot deep into the jungle and located the best Dauchai trees. Our work station, which housed the Dauchai trees, was three miles in diameter. We trimmed the mature trees by cutting and shaping the bottom three feet of each tree. Then we cut a one-foot trench or gutter into this area. After a while, the sap oil flowed down the tree into the trench. Then we lit a fire that caused the sap to boil. When it was time to go home, we extinguished the fire, and the sap continued to flow. Five days later, we returned to the jungle to harvest the oil from the trees. We filled the buckets and carried them to drop points about every mile or so. We emptied the oil into ten-gallon containers, carried it back to our village, and sold it to farmers and fishermen in the village. It was a precious commodity for many of our citizens. They used the sap oil to seal boats and as fuel for lanterns. They even rolled the pasty substance inside palm branches, then lit the branches and used them as torches to give light as they worked in the fields at night.

It was important when we arrived in the jungle to locate a spot where we could set up a campsite. This would be the meeting place where we'd take lunch breaks and enjoy short power naps. There were no clocks or watches in the jungle, but we were able to tell when it was time for lunch by looking at our feet. If there was a shadow around them, we knew it was noon and would stop working and take an hour lunch break. If there was no shadow, we kept working.

## I HATE BUGS

There were many mosquitoes and gnats in the jungle. The bugs thrived in the moist climate and were constantly biting me. In an attempt to drive them away, I started smoking cigarettes. At nine I became addicted to nicotine. My mother and grandmother didn't want me embracing this nasty habit, but I was surrounded by the Montagnard People. They all smoked, and I just mirrored what I saw. When I came home from working in the jungle, there were times I craved a cigarette, but I knew my mother and grandmother would be angry if they saw me smoking. I mastered the art of sneaking behind their backs so I could satisfy my nicotine craving.

## NO CHILD LABOR LAWS

My grandmother loved me, but she could be quite cruel. I don't think she meant to be, but if I didn't do everything exactly as she wanted, she would scream at me and many times it escalated to a point of violence. Because I was one of the oldest children, she expected more from me than the others.

Anything could set off her explosive temper. So, to avoid conflict, I bent over backwards to try to please her.

My mother and I had a different relationship. She only spanked me a few times, but neither she nor my grandmother were affectionate people. It just wasn't the custom of the Vietnamese women to shower love on their children back then. While I was growing up, I never received hugs, kisses or words of affirmation, but I did experience numerous whippings, and I was repeatedly scolded. After I was grown, I thought often about my upbringing. Since my emotional love tank was constantly empty, I feel it made me vulnerable in relationships with the opposite sex in my early adult years. I was constantly searching for love and acceptance in all the wrong places.

There were no child labor laws in Vietnam when I was growing up. My family was like most families in our village, trying to survive in any way we could. Because my older sister was retarded, most of the workload fell on my young shoulders. The welfare of my younger cousins and siblings became my job description. I worked like an adult, even though I was only nine. I knew how to wheel the water out of the wells, fill up the large vases and carry them to wherever they needed to go. Every day it was mandatory for us to have six vases filled for showers, drinking, cooking and watering the garden. After supper, it was my job to wash and dry the dishes. Then it was my responsibility to bathe the younger children. At this time there were six children under the age of five. I poured the water from the vase into Grandmother's giant bowl. I placed the children one by one into this homemade bathtub and scrubbed them down and then rinsed them off. There were no towels, so the little ones were trained to shake the excess water off, and then I'd help dress them.

Because of my family's severe poverty, I was forced to work diligently even though I was just a child myself. Even with me working we could barely make ends meet. I only had three sets of clothes. Two sets were my work clothes, and one set was what I wore when I went to market. It never occurred to me that life could be any different. All the families we knew were poverty-stricken.

## FATHERLESS

My father abandoned my mother before I was born. For years I had questions about him and wondered where he came from and what he was like. A neighbor lady, who was about my grandmother's age, understood my curiosity and one day answered some of my questions. According to her, my father was from Hanoi and worked for the government. He was educated and originally from the North. She remembered his frequent temper tantrums and my mother receiving cruel blows from his hands because of his jealousy. He would often slap my mother if he discovered her chatting with her male cousin, who lived next door. When my mother was pregnant with me, he gave her one final beating. She could no longer endure the physical abuse. She ran away to my grandmother's house, which was about thirty miles away, in the middle of the night. It was quite a journey for a young pregnant woman fleeing for her safety. After a few months, my father grew tired of waiting for my mother to return. He moved away, and we never heard from him again. After he left, my mother heard a rumor around our little village that he had returned to Hanoi, but she never knew if it was actually true.

Please don't feel sorry for me because my father abandoned me. God's Word promises, if the biological father forsakes his children, the Lord will watch over them. As I look back over my life, I see how the Lord kept His Word. God had His eye on me.

*When my father and my mother forsake me, then the Lord will take me up.*

PSALM 27:10 KJV

## FATHER'S EYES

There is a story about a little girl who never knew her biological father. As she walked through her small village, some of the people would whisper behind her back. She heard cruel comments like, "Who do you think her father is?" and "Her mother is no good."

It brought so much pain to her young heart. One day she met an elderly Christian woman who discerned her pain. Hot tears spilled down the young girl's cheeks as she poured out her soul to her newfound friend. "They keep whispering behind my back, trying to figure out who my father is. Some say they know, and others say terrible things about my mother. It hurts so bad." The compassionate woman listened as the little girl continued, "I feel like God wants to use me, but can He use someone who doesn't even know who her biological father is?"

The woman's gnarled fingers lifted the little girl's tiny chin. Their eyes met. "Now, you listen to me, I know who your Father is. When I look into your eyes, I can see Him – your heavenly Father. You have His eyes. I can see Him every time I look at you. You can be anything He wants you to be."

This little story has helped me so much. I may never know this side of Heaven who my biological father is, but that isn't as important to me as it once was. What matters to me now is that my life reflects my Heavenly Father. I pray, when others look at me, they will see my Father. I hope I have my Father's eyes.

## AMBITIOUS GRANDMOTHER

My grandfather passed away years before I was born. My grandmother remained single and raised my mother and my two uncles. There were many incidences in Vietnam of widows without a male as the head of the house being taken advantage of. My grandmother was determined to not let this happen. Although she didn't have much of a formal education, she was street smart. She had been educated by the most prestigious university of all: the School of Adversity.

My grandmother was ambitious when it came to her children. She hoped my mother would marry someone in a high position or with powerful status. When she discovered my father was a government official, she put pressure on my mother to marry him. She had an ulterior motive. She knew, if they married, it would benefit our family financially. At that time in Vietnam, the government wouldn't let the farmers sell extra produce in the next village. There was a food shortage, and the government insisted whatever produce was grown in a certain village should be sold to the citizens of that same village. Grandmother grew plenty of bananas and had a crew to harvest oil from the Dauchai trees. Because of this ordinance, Grandmother wasn't allowed to sell her produce. This created more financial strain on our already struggling family.

My mother had been trained since she was small to obey her elders and submit to their authority. Even though she never loved my father, she married him because of my grandmother's insistence.

## THE LETTER

A few months after my father left, my mother became involved with a married man. Soon after their affair, she discovered she was pregnant with his child. He was from the city and came to our hometown of Bao Tron. According to the Vietnamese culture, this sexual indiscretion brought great shame to our family. My mother was humiliated. In an attempt to escape any more public embarrassment, she ran away to Saigon with some of her friends and cousins. She left without telling any of us where she had gone. I thought she had missed her bus ride home. For several days, I waited for the evening bus, hoping to catch a glimpse of her. I waited at the bus stop week after week, but there was so sign of my mother. She was gone. Three months later, Grandmother handed me a letter and asked me to read it. My heart beat wildly in my chest when I saw the letter was from my mother. I didn't want to cry in front of my grandmother as I read it to her. Afterwards, I excused myself and went into the bedroom and sobbed uncontrollably, but whenever I was in my grandmother's presence, I tried to stay composed. As young as I was, I realized she must be hurting, too. I didn't want my tears to cause her more pain. It felt like my heart was being ripped in two. Even though my mother wasn't affectionate, I dearly loved her. My heart ached for her. The grief was suffocating.

A few more months went by, and my grandmother came up with a plan to bring my mother home. She went to Saigon to find her. Grandmother reassured my mother that her place was at home with all of us children. Mom listened to my grandmother and returned home.

## IT'S A GIRL

In Vietnam, when the time comes for the mother to deliver her baby, she cannot give birth inside the family's house. They believe the woman is unclean, and you cannot have anything unclean walking around the idols. So the family builds a little shack about 10 feet by 12 feet beside the family's house for the pregnant woman. She will give birth to the baby and live in the little shack for 30 days after the baby is born. After this time, she can rejoin her family in the main house.

During the time my mother lived in the little homemade shack, I stayed with her. I was so happy to be reunited with her and never wanted her go away again. She gave birth to her fourth daughter, Nam. Instead of living in that shack for 30 days, as was the Vietnam custom, we stayed for five months.

I never felt Nam's father loved our mother. He only used her during the time he was away from his wife. Mother was his mistress, and he didn't take any responsibility for his newborn daughter.

I'm not sure why my mother had so many relationships with different men. Sometimes I feel it was because my grandmother was not sensitive to my mother's emotional needs. Grandmother worshipped my two uncles but neglected my mother. It's typical of that generation to spoil their sons and treat their daughters with an attitude of indifference. I think my mother felt unloved and unwanted. To fill the hole in her soul, she sought love in all the wrong places. Oh, if only someone could have shared with her the story of the woman caught in the act of adultery. I'm sure her broken heart would have melted when she saw the way the Master treated the adulterous woman with no condemnation.

*Jesus straightened up and asked her, "Woman, where are they? Has no one condemned you?"*

*"No one, sir," she said.*

*"Then neither do I condemn you," Jesus declared. "Go now and leave your life of sin."*

JOHN 8:10, 11

My mother's sinful pattern continued. She didn't know any better and walked on in the darkness she was accustomed to. When Nam was five months old, a different man came into our mother's life. Grandmother was so excited because this new man's father was a government official. Her desire for our family to have a little power and honor got the best of her. She went to my mother and insisted my mother marry him. My mom agreed, and my three sisters and I had a new stepfather. We moved about a mile down the road from my grandmother's house.

When my mother was married, my grandmother didn't give her any wedding presents. No dishes, pots, pans, blankets—not one gift. I don't know why my grandmother did this, but it is just another indication of how neglected my mother must have felt. We didn't even have a chopstick to eat our food with. My grandmother had over two hundred dishes in her house. People in the village would come and ask to borrow some of her pots and pans when they had a wedding or special occasion in their family because they knew my grandmother had plenty of kitchenware. For some reason, she wouldn't share one dish with her daughter. Since we lived so close, I could walk to my grandmother's house. My mother ordered me to stand behind a bamboo bush in her yard. I wasn't supposed to let Grandmother see me. I would wait until I saw one of my aunts, and then I would plead with her to give me a cooking pot, some bowls and chopsticks. I have never understood why my grandmother wouldn't share with her own daughter when she had more utensils than she could use.

Luom and Nga continued to live with my grandmother, while Nam and I moved in with our mother and new stepfather. The honeymoon was soon over, and the domestic violence began. One night my stepfather went berserk and beat my mother. I was standing in the front yard watching. Suddenly, I began screaming at the top of my lungs. My mom ordered him to leave, but he wouldn't listen. Fortunately, one of my uncles came to her rescue. My stepfather left in a huff and never returned.

Nam was still a baby and needed milk. There was no formula in those days like there is now. I would sometimes cook rice and mash the milky liquid out of it and put it in a bottle and give it to her. Other times I found a wet nurse, and she would nurse Nam until her little tummy was full.

# THE MOVE

n 1959, my mother became reacquainted with an old friend from high school. They had known each other as teenagers, but as the years marched on, they went their separate ways. He became a businessman with his own bus that carried people from one town to the next. He already had a wife and five children, but that didn't stop them from reconnecting. As they spent more time together, they began to have feelings for one another. It wasn't very long until my mother discovered she was pregnant with his child. My grandmother and uncles were furious. They were adamantly against the relationship and insisted that she end it. My mother couldn't stand their opposition and decided she wanted to move away to escape the scrutiny of their watchful eye. She reasoned, too, this would allow her to spend more time with her new boyfriend. Thinking this would free her from interfering relatives, she started making plans to move. During this time, the government decided to relocate 60 families from the mountains to the valley town of Som Thuong. My mom saw this as her opportunity to escape my grandmother's and uncles' disapproval. The government agreed to provide a house for us. I moved with my mother, and we opened a store to sell dry goods. We sold rice, salt, oil, crackers, cookies, candy, liquor and the sap oil from the Dauchai trees. Mother and I were thankful we no longer had to traipse into the jungle in the wee hours of the morning to harvest the sap. The Montagnard People did all the hard work, and we purchased it from them and sold it in our store.

My mom continued her relationship with the married man. She willingly accepted her place as his second wife. It was part of the culture at that time. The mistress was to take the role of the second wife.

I was able to attend school in the mornings and babysit Nam in the

35

afternoons. As I reflect on this time in my life, I count it as some of my family's more stable days. I loved the store and the fact our lives seemed happier, but it was just the calm before the storms that were ahead for us.

## BARLEY

Americans helped the South Vietnamese government purchase materials to build houses and dig wells. They also supplied clothing and food for the families until they could get established. One staple the Americans provided was barley, but all the Vietnamese were afraid to eat it. There were rumors throughout the village that the Americans wanted to harm us. Some of the Montagnard People were convinced if they ate the barley it would stunt their growth and possibly even cause them to shrink.

My family fed the barley to the chickens and pigs. There were times we were so hungry, and if we weren't so bound by our suspicions, the barley would have been a great blessing in our lives. Instead we would go into the jungle and find wild yams and mix them with corn to eat.

## TOO MUCH LIQUOR

Montagnard People loved their liquor. At our family store, we sold liquor that looked like tequila. It was made from sweet rice, and it was quite potent. A few swigs and you were drunk. I wasn't even ten, and my job was to suck the rice wine out of the vase. Every evening the people would come with a bottle to purchase wine for dinner. I had to suck the liquor out of the vase with a plastic tube. Sometimes I would accidentally swallow it. Three or four times a week I would become intoxicated. My mother knew about it, but she lacked the knowledge to understand this could be harmful to me. Once again, it was just normal living for us. I was drunk many times the year we had the store. I realize now it had to be the hand of the Lord protecting me from becoming an alcoholic or damaging my liver.

I remember one time I became extremely drunk. The jug was full, and I sucked the tube. The liquor came out, but then dropped back into the vase. I had to keep sucking. That night I was vomiting profusely. My mother knew all about it, but she didn't know any better. All the people we knew lived like this. We were a pitiful group in need of a Savior.

## Mushrooms Galore

As a child, I had two dogs as pets. I enjoyed taking them for long walks in the jungle. They would run for miles, and I would tag along behind them, trying to catch up. One morning they took off, and I followed them. They wouldn't stop, so deeper and deeper into the jungle we ran. At some point during our adventure, I looked up and saw that a large tree had fallen. Around that tree were boo coos of fresh oyster mushrooms. I took off my shirt and started piling as many mushrooms as I could inside of it. Then I realized there were a lot more mushrooms I could collect if I just had a container to put them in. It didn't take me long to come up with a plan. I stripped off my pants and tied up the legs. It was a perfect bag for my new-found treasures. I only had a minor problem: I was naked. I started streaking through the jungle with the mushrooms in my arms. It must have been a sight to behold. As I got closer to home, I knew I was in trouble. I had to cross a highway. There was a large oak tree near the highway. I hid behind the tree and waited until I didn't see anyone coming. Then I zipped across the road and arrived safely at home. My mom saw me and grinned really big. When she saw all the mushrooms, she lovingly patted me on the shoulder. She was so proud of my creativity in finding some way to bring home mushrooms for our family—even if it meant taking off all my clothes. I remember how thrilled I was when she patted my shoulder. I wasn't used to any type of affection or affirmation from my mother. I don't remember her kissing me or holding me on her lap very often when I was little. I still look back on my mushroom find as a very happy memory in my life. It's good I had this happy experience because life as I knew it was about to change forever.

# YEAR OF TRAGEDY

*I* will never forget the traumatic events that happened to my family in July of 1960. One evening we heard voices outside. We peered out our windows to see who was making all the racket. Terror gripped our hearts when we saw some Viet Cong walking up and down the highway. One of them was carrying a megaphone yelling, "We have come here to visit your village. Whoever shows themselves and supports our views, we will honor them, but whoever shows rebellion, we will kill them. We will shed their blood to pay the price for their rebellion against the Viet Cong government."

I remember my mom, her girlfriend and I were riveted with fear. After a little time elapsed, we heard screaming. We ran down to a tunnel that was under our house and continued to run under our backyard. Bullets were whizzing through the air. As we hid in the tunnel, our hearts were racing. The gunfire stopped, and then it seemed to get very still. I was the first to climb out of the tunnel. I tiptoed to the front door to see if it was safe for the others to come up. As I looked out the door, I didn't see any more Viet Cong, but I heard a familiar voice. I hurried back to the tunnel and motioned for my mom to come. My mom and her friend followed me back to the front door. They heard a woman's voice wailing. I bolted out the door and ran down the highway barefooted. I recognized the voice. It was my aunt. As I got closer, I saw my aunt huddled over the body of her dead husband. The Viet Cong had killed my uncle Mai Van Duong. It was mid-evening, and a neighbor brought out a lantern. As he brought the light closer to my uncle's body, I saw his face. Blood was everywhere, and his left eye had been shot out. Waves of grief swept over me. All of us fell to the ground and sobbed. We were so shocked we couldn't even make an attempt to console my aunt. All we could do was lament with her.

Precious memories of my favorite uncle flooded my mind. He was the youngest in his family and only 27 when the Viet Cong killed him in cold blood. I was especially attached to him because he always made time for me. He would give me rides on his bicycle. Many times we would ride his bike over 20 miles to the market just so we could eat a bowl of noodle soup together. He left behind a beautiful wife, a daughter, Mai Thi Thanh, who was two, and a son, Mai Van Nay, who was one.

It was surreal. We couldn't stop crying. We couldn't believe this had happened to our family. As we sat stunned and grieving on the ground, another man ran up to us and screamed, "Your other uncle is dead, too."

Panic seized me. I jumped up and ran to my grandmother's house, which was a mile away. When I arrived, I saw the lights inside the house were on. I could hear my grandmother weeping. Then she was completely silent for several seconds. I didn't understand why she was so quiet, but when I arrived at her side, I saw she was in a state of shock. She lost consciousness for a few seconds, and when she came to, she began crying again. Someone followed me into the house and informed Grandmother her youngest son had died, too. It was too much for her. She fainted. I looked around but couldn't see my older uncle's body anywhere. I asked where he was. Someone pointed to an extension house that was beside Grandmother's house. This was a building where we stored grain and would house animals or sometimes create a guest bedroom. I ran to the extension house, but I couldn't see his body. I stepped inside, and a sticky liquid squished between my toes. I thought I had stepped in some cow urine. I moved a little farther and tripped over something. I looked, and it was my Uncle Mai Van Ho's body. He was only 35. It seemed like time stood still. How could this be happening? I glanced down at my feet and realized the wet, sticky substance wasn't cow urine, but my uncle's blood. A chill ran down my spine. My thoughts were interrupted by my mother's voice asking me if I had found his body. I told her I had. Neighbors came pouring out of the village. We also learned from some of the villagers that two other men had lost their lives that night. One was my second cousin, and the other was my grandmother's adopted son.

Even though I was only ten, my childhood ended that night. Those tragic events would cause me to never look at life the same again. I wasn't the only one in deep mourning. After my uncles died, my grandmother wasn't able to stay at home for extended periods of time. It was too difficult for her to be in the familiar surroundings where she had seen her boys on a regular basis. She began to travel to see her sisters and would stay with them for months at a time. She suffered from severe depression and attempted to escape her anguish by traveling to some of her relatives. This was a double whammy for me because not only was I in grief, but my grandmother was gone most of the time. Even though she was set in her ways, she was a stabilizing force in our lives. It was Grandmother who kept our home clean and every day made delicious meals for us.

Oh, how I wish my grandmother could have known Jesus during this time in her life. The Holy Spirit could have brought her comfort in the midst of her pain. I know Christian missionaries came to Vietnam for many years, but there were none in my hometown. The only religious individuals we knew at that time were Catholics, Buddhists and those who practiced witchcraft, but we needed someone who could touch the Lord for our hurting family. We didn't know anyone then, but God had a plan to reach my family. It was only a matter of time.

## ANOTHER BABY ON THE WAY

My mom and I visited with my stepfather to see if it was possible for us to move back into Grandmother's house. He was a compassionate man in his own way and was willing to share my mom with my grandmother again. The only hindrance to us moving right away was the fact that Mom was pregnant again. After much discussion, we decided to wait until after the baby was born to move in and help my grandmother.

During this waiting period, my mom was trying to think of some new ways to make more money. She was frequently gone, pursuing other financial possibilities. This left me in charge of my sisters and managing the store. Before she left, Mom gave me strict orders: none of the Montagnard People were to take anything from the store unless their bill was paid. It was a wise business decision, but I was a softie. Mom tried to help me see that if they didn't pay their bill, we wouldn't have any revenue for more inventory. I understood my mother's rules, but they were too difficult for me to obey because the Montagnard People lived in such severe poverty. Their houses had palm leaves for walls. They usually only had one or two pots to cook with, and their eating utensils were made from bamboo. Many of them were sick and hungry. I have vivid memories of them coming to the store and begging for food. It would break my heart and I would give them some rice because I felt so sorry for them. The store had to close because of my generosity.

Even though I wasn't a Christian at this time, God had placed a compassionate heart deep within my soul. I know this is a gift from my heavenly Father. Almost every day, I thank Him for giving me a heart that can empathize and sympathize with humanity. I often think when I reach the end of my life I will never be sorry for providing food for someone who was hungry, but I would be full of regret if I didn't feed someone who was hungry. Jesus had compassion for people. The Bible tells many stories of Him helping those in need. We are His body. We are His hands reaching and helping those in need.

*Jesus had compassion on them...*

MATTHEW 20:34a

I didn't realize at the time that I was obeying a biblical principle. If we see someone who is hungry, we should feed them. How thankful I am for a compassionate heart.

*When the Son of Man comes in his glory, and all the angels with him, he will sit on his throne in heavenly glory. All the nations will be gathered before him, and he will separate the people one from another as a shepherd separates the sheep from the goats. He will put the sheep on his right and the goats on his left.*

*Then the King will say to those on his right, "Come, you who are blessed by my Father; take your inheritance, the kingdom prepared for you since the creation of the world. For I was hungry and you gave me something to eat, I was thirsty and you gave me something to drink, I was a stranger and you invited me in, I needed clothes and you clothed me, I was sick and you looked after me, I was in prison and you came to visit me."*

*Then the righteous will answer him, "Lord, when did we see you hungry and feed you, or thirsty and give you something to drink? When did we see you a stranger and invite you in, or needing clothes and clothe you? When did we see you sick or in prison and go to visit you?"*

*The King will reply, "I tell you the truth, whatever you did for one of the least of these brothers of mine, you did for me."*

*Then he will say to those on his left, "Depart from me, you who are cursed, into the eternal fire prepared for the devil and his angels. For I was hungry and you gave me nothing to eat, I was thirsty and you gave me nothing to drink, I was a stranger and you did not invite me in, I needed clothes and you did not clothe me, I was sick and in prison and you did not look after me."*

*"They also will answer, Lord, when did we see you hungry or thirsty or a stranger or needing clothes or sick or in prison, and did not help you?"*

*He will reply, "I tell you the truth, whatever you did not do for one of the least of these, you did not do for me."*

MATTHEW 25:31–45

## IT'S A BOY

Early one morning, Mom woke me up. She said she was in labor and I needed to run and fetch the midwife. I ran past my grandmother's house, straight to the midwife's house. She was sound asleep. I woke her, and we ran back to my mom. It was a great honor for me to be present at the birth of my little brother Hoa. I actually helped deliver him. I had never seen anything more sacred in my entire life. As I watched my mom endure such intense labor pains, my love for her increased.

After Hoa was born and my mom regained her strength, we kept our word and moved back to help my grandmother. When I think about it now, I'm sure we were a diversion for Grandmother. There were five children at this time: Luom, Nga, Nam, Hoa and myself. We meant well moving in to take care of Grandmother, but I have a hunch it was really Grandmother taking care of us.

## ORPHANS

When my older uncle Mai Van Ho died that fateful night, he left behind a little boy, Mai Van Tru, and a little girl, Mai Thi Cong. Tragedy struck again a few years later, when these two children became orphans. Their mother succumbed to tuberculosis. Mai Van Tru and Mai Thi Cong needed someone to care for them, so they came to live with my grandmother.

I was especially fond of Mai Thi Cong. Every time I ate, I gave her the first bite. Grandmother would take rice paper and sprinkle it with sugar. It was a simple snack, but all of us children thought it was delicious. I always rolled up the rice paper and gave Mai Thi Cong a bite. Once again my heart of compassion, which God blessed me with, took over. I was aware of her dire circumstances. She was fatherless and motherless. I wanted to make a difference in her life. Because of my love for her, we bonded in spirit. I knew when she hurt before she even told me.

I remember one day I went to work in the jungle with my mom. We didn't return home until around four o'clock in the evening. My great uncle came for a visit. He brought a bag of tangerines to my grandmother. Mai Thi Cong especially loved fruit and watched him as he set the bag down. She ran toward the fruit. Her feet somehow got tangled, and she fell. She smacked her head between her eyes. It immediately began to swell, and her nose started bleeding. There was no medical help available. My grandmother and uncle took some loose tobacco and bandaged her wound. Meanwhile, I was on my way home with my mom, and out of the blue, I began to experience intense anxiety. I knew something was wrong, and I started to hurry home. In my haste, I tripped and ripped one of my toenails completely off. When I walked into the house, my cousin saw me and started crying. Even though I was in pain, I picked her up, took her to the hammock, and started singing to her. I loved her so much and constantly watched out for her even after she grew up. She was diagnosed with breast cancer and passed away eight years ago, leaving behind three children. They still live in Vietnam with their father.

## GOVERNMENT MOVE

In 1961 and 1962, the South government would not let us stay in Bao Tron. In order for them to keep an eye on us, we had to move. The government strategically placed us around their village so that if the Viet Cong attacked we would be struck first. They placed civilians around the military camp. We were their human shields.

Early one morning, the Viet Cong ambushed the soldiers' camp that was just thirty yards from our house. They threw grenades and shot bullets when they saw any military personnel walking around outside. It didn't take long for the soldiers to realize what was happening. They put a defensive plan into action. The gunfire sounded like popcorn popping. My grandmother and I stood on our porch trying to grasp what was going on. The fighting seemed to be coming closer and closer. We heard more gunfire and dropped to the floor of our porch. We looked around, trying to make sure that all the children were safe. We shooed them into the tunnel, but after we did a head count we discovered one child was missing. It was eight-year-old Tru, my uncle's son. We looked outside and saw him caught in the middle of the gunfire. He must have gone outside to play when grandmother and I were preoccupied. We heard him wailing, and we screamed to him, "Lie down in the ditch!"

He started bawling and stood frozen with fear. I couldn't take it any longer. I loved Tru and favored him because of all the hardships he had experienced. Visions of the Viet Cong murdering his father filled my head. I would do anything to keep history from repeating itself. I bolted from the porch and ran out into the midst of the dangerous gunfire. I was not afraid. All I wanted was my little cousin to be comforted and safe. I ran for probably 50 to 60 feet, grabbed him, and we rolled into the ditch together. The ditch was probably three feet deep. He whimpered as I shielded him. I tried to console him. As soon as the gunfire ceased, we ran back to Grandmother's house. She threw both of us in the tunnel. Our hearts were beating wildly in our chests. We heard a plane overhead, and then there were large explosions. The plane had dropped bombs around the camp that was about five hundred yards from our house. A fire broke out from the explosion. Grandmother ordered us out of the tunnel just in case the back of our house caught fire. She feared we could be trapped inside and die from smoke inhalation. It was utter chaos. There were many people who died that day. After the bombs and gunfire ceased, we walked outside and saw dead cows and water buffalo. Three days later, the stench of rotten flesh permeated the entire village. Blackbirds circled over our heads, waiting to nibble on the dead carcasses. For an entire month, no civilians were allowed to go into the jungle for fear of landmines. The soldiers only permitted the civilians to walk on the streets. Once again I felt dazed by the horrors of war, but I was so thankful Tru was alive and safe.

# Chapter Five

# THE VISION

⬦

Early one morning, I walked to my grandmother's house in Bao Tron to water her banana trees. Across my shoulders, I was carrying a yoke that held ten-gallon buckets on each end. It was my job to go to the well, fill these buckets, carry them back to the banana field, and water the young bananas. I had a rest stop at the halfway point because I didn't have the strength to carry the heavy buckets all the way. When I reached the rest stop, I sat down and attempted to catch my breath. While I was sitting there, I had a vision. I had never had an experience like that before, but I saw my future husband walking towards me. He was very handsome and light-skinned. No words were spoken in the vision, but somehow, it was conveyed clearly to me that this man did not drink and was very kind and loving. I saw two children and the house we lived in. It was a beautiful home with a red roof. There were beds with crisp, white linens. My kitchen had fancy pots and pans. You must realize, at this point in my young life, I had never traveled very far from home. The items I was seeing I had never seen before. There wasn't a single soul in my hometown who owned any material goods as fancy as that. Years later when I married my husband, Dennis, I knew he was the man I had seen in my vision.

## OFF TO WORK WE GO

Now that I am grown, I sometimes giggle to myself when I hear children complain about having to make their beds or take out the trash. As a child, I put in ten- to twelve-hour days, working from sunup to sundown. I never really thought much about it. It seemed normal to me. It was necessary for me to work like an adult or our family might not survive. Some nights I would come home after working in the jungle, and it was my job to cook and tend to my younger siblings and cousins. Most days I was in charge of the laundry. After my work was done, I would fall asleep and wake up early the next morning and start all over again. It never occurred to me other people didn't live this way. It was just how life was in Vietnam. I thought this was the way everyone lived. I never really complained about working, but I do remember I disliked walking six or seven miles from my house to my grandmother's banana field. I'm sure I probably grumbled about that long walk. I was just a child of 11 or 12 and would have to walk and work completely alone. There were some days I forgot to take any food along, and I would try to find a piece of fruit along the way. I realized watering the banana trees was top priority because, in the summer, we hardly had any rain.

## AGENT ORANGE

Another day when I was out in the banana field watering the young bananas, I heard a plane engine roaring in the sky. I looked up as the aircraft was circling over my grandmother's hometown. There were streaks of orange smoke spewing out of the plane's tail. I watched as it circled two more times. A few minutes later, an unusual aroma filled the air. Then a sticky substance floated through the air and covered everything. I couldn't figure out what it was. After the plane disappeared, I continued watering the trees. Around mid-afternoon I noticed the trees started to droop. I hurried to Grandmother's house and told her about the plane and the orange smoke. My mom chimed in and said she saw it, too. Some of the townspeople had also seen the plane, but not one of them knew what the sticky substance was. The following day, we went out to the banana field and couldn't believe our eyes. All the trees from our house to the banana field were withering up and dying. I continued to water the banana trees, hoping to save them, but nothing helped. They were drooping and looked pitiful. By the third day, the leaves turned yellow, and by the fourth day, all the trees looked like autumn had arrived. Then every tree lost all their leaves. One week later, all the vegetation and trees for miles and miles had died. Every tree in the jungle was dead. We didn't know our entire village had been sprayed with Agent Orange.

Agent Orange was the code name for an herbicide developed for the American military, primarily for use in tropical climates. The purpose of the product was to deny an enemy cover and concealment in dense terrain by defoliating trees and shrubbery where the enemy could hide. Agent Orange was a code name for the orange band that was used to mark the drums the herbicide was stored in. It was very effective against broadleaf foliage, such as in the dense jungle-like terrain of Vietnam.

A few months after I was exposed to Agent Orange, all my hair fell out. My bones ached, and I was unable to eat and lost quite a bit of weight. I was extremely skinny. Nobody knew what was wrong with me. My grandmother and mother thought I had some type of virus. We never considered the fact I had been exposed to toxic herbicides. There were no doctors, drugs or shots for me. Grandmother attempted to doctor me with natural herbs. I was violently ill for three months, and then slowly but surely, I began to mend and gain strength.

My mother experienced three miscarriages after her exposure. I am convinced my sickness and my mother's miscarriages were because of our exposure to the toxic chemicals found in Agent Orange.

## BUDDHIST TEMPLE

During the time I was so sick, our little village pulled together and built a Buddhist Temple two miles from our house. They called for the elders, including my grandmother, and asked if different families would ban together and help erect this temple. All the people were thrilled to have a place to worship Buddha. Some of them actually believed Buddha was God. My family jumped on board and helped in any way they could. The temple was 12 feet wide and 20 feet long. There were all kinds of statues and altars inside. There was one giant statue of Buddha. My grandmother was a devout member of this little group. For some reason, my mother wouldn't join. Every night my grandmother would make me ride my bike down to the Buddha Temple. There was a shortage of workers, and we didn't have a monk assigned to the temple in our village. This meant my family had the responsibility of taking care of the temple. Once I arrived, a man would meet me, and I was supposed to help him prepare for the idol worship ceremony. He would light incense and chant. He taught me how to chant. I was to say the same lines over and over again. I never understood what I was saying. He didn't take the time to explain it to me, but I did what I was told.

Oh, how thankful I am for the Word of God and His voice of Truth. Now I sing His praises and know I am exalting the Name that is above every name.

## WOUNDED SERGEANT

My family experienced firsthand the uncertainty of life. With the Viet Cong's frequent appearances, we realized violence could break out at any moment. Soldiers from the South were patrolling around our village when suddenly they were ambushed by the Viet Cong. We heard grenade blasts and airplanes overhead dropping bombs near our home. My stepfather looked out and saw some of his cattle had been killed. After the gunfire ceased, he went to assess the damage. He noticed the Viet Cong harassing a wounded soldier. Something had to be done or they would kill this young man. My stepfather began to plead with the Viet Cong.

"Let me take this wounded soldier into my house and bandage his wounds." He continued, "Your good name will spread among the people, and they will know you treat people fairly."

His words seemed to appease them. They agreed to let my stepfather take the injured soldier home.

We learned his name was Tu Hay. He stayed with us for a few days. My job was to cook for him and feed him. When he was strong enough, the South government sent a helicopter to escort him back to the hospital.

I thought I would never see this man again, but I was wrong. We would meet again, and our little act of kindness may have saved my life.

## FOOD SHORTAGE

With all our fruit trees and vegetation destroyed, we had a severe food shortage. Mom and I would delve deeper and deeper into the jungle looking for food and sap trees. Because of the devastation caused by Agent Orange, we were forced to march fifteen to seventeen miles into the jungle before we could find any sap trees that were alive. Even though these trees were alive, they still weren't as healthy as the trees we had harvested oil from before. Mom and I were just not physically able to carry the workload. We hired three men from our village, but we needed even more help. Most of the men from our village had left, seeking employment in the next town. This put us in a dilemma. There was a group called the Independent Viet Cong. They did not agree with the South government, so they fled into the jungle. They lived with some of the Viet Cong, but did not take part in the war. They seemed to mind their own business and didn't carry any weapons. We hired four of the Independent Viet Cong along with the three men from our village to help us harvest the oil from the sap trees. We realized this was taking a risk should the South government find out about it, but our backs were against the wall. We had no other choice if we wanted to survive financially.

One day my mother sent me to the jungle with our work crew that included the Independent Viet Cong. Mom was unable to go that day because she and one of her friends would often return favors. It was my mom's turn to take care of her friend's little girl, Ket. When Mom and Ket were drawing water from the well, they noticed a group of soldiers from the South government headed in the same direction in which I had just taken our work crew. There was only one narrow path, and the soldiers saw our footprints and became suspicious about what we were doing. Mom realized immediately they could kill us if they discovered we had hired the Independent Viet Cong. She whispered to Ket, "Run and warn Mai and the others about the soldiers coming."

That day I carried the water for our crew to drink. I accidentally fell and spilled the water. I had to replenish it, and the men went on ahead of me. I joined them later. After working for a couple of hours, I looked up and saw Ket running toward me. She screamed, "The soldiers from the South government are coming! They are on their way here! You've got to send the crew home immediately!"

My work crew looked at each other and scoffed, "Those soldiers aren't going to come here. We are too far back in the jungle for them to come looking for us." They refused to stop working.

I could tell by the horror in Ket's eyes that she was quite traumatized by whatever she had seen. I tried to come up with a game plan to appease both sides.

"I'll go back to the lunch camp. Ket, you stay here with the crew. If the soldiers do show up, you can tell them what we are doing, but whatever you do, don't tell them that the Independent Viet Cong are working for us."

One of the men came with me. He was not an Independent Viet Cong. We headed back to the lunch camp. It was about a mile from where we were working. My knees went weak when I looked up and saw the soldiers from the South government waiting for us. They began to interrogate us. "What are you doing in the jungle?" the soldier barked.

I swallowed hard and answered. "We are harvesting sap from the Dauchai trees."

One of the soldiers waved his finger in front of our faces and asked, "How many people do you have working in the jungle?"

I was petrified so I lied. "Three men and myself."

He looked at the lunch packets and growled, "Why do you have eight lunch packs?"

The man with me began to get nervous. He started spilling our secret. He informed them that my mother and I had hired the Independent Viet Cong to work for us. He offered to take them to where they were working. The soldiers assumed they had weapons and followed him to the campsite. When they arrived, they shot and killed one of the Independent Viet Cong. They returned to the lunch camp where I was and began to harass me. Just as one of the soldiers lifted his weapon to strike me, I looked up and recognized the sergeant. It was Tu Hay. Our eyes met, and he began to defend me.

"Leave her alone. She's just a child. It's not her fault. It was her mother who hired them."

I trembled as they threatened to head back to the village and arrest my mom. I started crying because I didn't want them to hurt her. I assured them it was my fault. I insisted I had authorized the entire work crew, attempting to protect my mother. All my negotiating backfired because since one of the Independent Viet Cong was shot, their group felt my mom set them up to be killed by the South government. From that time on, the South government kept a watchful eye on us. We continued to live in fear.

At this time, the war was in full swing. A couple of times a week, the Viet Cong would come into our town at night and raid people's homes. The local government in that town made some mandatory rules for the civilians who lived there. Each family had to have one person come out and make some sharp bungee sticks and stick them down into the ground in a ditch that was six feet wide by six feet deep. These sticks were to prevent the Viet Cong from coming over. We had no men in our home, so my mom sent me to find the sharp sticks, place them in the ground, and carry the sticks into the ditch. We worked for six days and then that day had to perform our "mandatory" volunteer work for the government. This lasted for six or seven months. It was a difficult year because of the food shortage, and there were very few ways to make a decent living.

## LIFE IN A WAR ZONE

At that time, the American military had a plane the Vietnamese called "the spy plane." It was a small plane and had a quiet engine. The military always sought information and used this spy plane to snoop and uncover any suspicious activity. The cameras on this plane would take pictures and send them back to the base.

There were many occasions when we were working in the jungle and the spy plane would fly overhead very slowly, surveying the landscape. Sometimes we would hear the plane early and put out the fires and hide under the bush, but other times because of the noise created by the fire in the jungle, we would not hear the plane until it took off very quickly to leave the area. As soon as we heard it take off, we would drop everything and run as fast as we could away from that area because we knew the aircrafts that carried bombs would show up very soon. When we returned to that area, everything would be destroyed by the bombs. This happened on numerous occasions since that jungle was heavily controlled by the Viet Cong.

One time while we were working in the jungle boiling the sap oil, we were unaware that a spy plane was flying above us. They saw the smoke and felt this warranted further investigation. We, of course, didn't hear the plane's engine and were oblivious to what was going on. They thought we were the

Viet Cong and sent a message back to the base ordering a larger aircraft to come and drop bombs on the exact spot where we were working. When the bombs started to explode, we ran for cover. We didn't know what to do or where to hide. The explosion caused a huge fire in the jungle. I was caught in the middle of this dangerous warfare three times.

There were rocket missiles that were fired at us, too. The South government forces were trying to kill the Viet Cong in that area. The missiles were fired from miles away, and you could hear the whine of the rockets as they approached. When we heard the rockets, we would immediately find a place to hide. Many times we hid under the giant trees in the jungle. The rocket attack usually ended after seven or eight missiles had exploded. When it was all over, we would come out of our hiding places. There would be pieces of shrapnel from the rockets stuck in the trees.

One time I was working with two other ladies in the jungle when bombs starting exploding. We dove under one of the giant trees. After the bombing stopped, we emerged from our hiding place and saw the bomb shell. I didn't know how we survived. After I became a Christian, I knew it was God's saving grace. I believe, beyond a shadow of a doubt, He protected me because He has a work for me to do in the remaining years I have on this earth. It was a true miracle I survived these intense bombings. The aircrafts were so high-tech and precise. The bombs landed exactly where we had been working, but God intervened and protected us. We would run one way and two minutes later, there would be another explosion. Then we would run the other way. Just a few minutes later another bomb was dropped. There were a few men with us that day, too. They did their best to try to point us all to the safest place to hide. This was the most terrifying day I had ever experienced.

Bomb attacks were a way of life for those in Vietnam. In the beginning, we were fearful, but they were such a common occurrence, we became desensitized. Even though I was just a young girl, I became pretty brave. I was acclimated to life in the war zone. My mom knew the plane was dropping bombs right where I was in the jungle, and she didn't panic either. When I returned home after an attack, Mom would ask me where I hid when the bombs were going off. It was the talk around the supper table.

# MY FIRST GLIMPSE OF AN
# AMERICAN SOLDIER

he food shortage continued, and our family was forced to make another move. Instead of moving to the city, we moved to the outskirts of town, to a section the South government referred to as "Enemy's Territory." There were no guards in our new neighborhood. The fact that my stepfather's family lived on one end of town influenced our decision to move there. My stepfather liked the convenience of this arrangement. If he wanted to come for a visit he could just drop over, but if we lived in a big city, it would be difficult for him to see my mother and his children. When we moved from our house, we didn't let the government know where we were moving. They might have assumed we joined ranks with the Viet Cong and begin to harass us. At that time, Binh Chau was under Communist control, and there were soldiers walking up and down the street during the day. My stepfather bought a house near the ocean. We had to think of a way to make a living. Our resources were limited, but we decided to open another store and sell juice.

Our new house was very small. By this time we had another addition to our growing family: my sister Hiep. We only stayed in our new home for two months. My mom, Luom, Nga, Nam, Hoa, Hiep and I were forced to move again.

Early one morning, I heard engines roaring in the sky. I ran outside and saw five helicopters. As they hovered in the air, they dropped blue paper with instructions written on each piece to the ground. A man's voice announced over an intercom, "Evacuate immediately! If you're in the fishing trade, you are to relocate to Long Hai and continue your fishing there. If you are a farmer or business owner, you are to relocate in Xuyen Moc."

People ran out of their houses to see what was going on. I glanced towards the ocean and saw three Navy ships. I ran into the house and called my mother. She instructed me to grab the radio and go hide under the house. My siblings were at Grandmother's house, so I had to hide all by myself. My mother knew the soldiers would soon be on patrol. She had seen enough death and devastation and feared for my life. I knew this was a serious situation and I had better obey my mother's orders. I wrapped our radio in a blue shirt, tucked it under my chin, and crawled under the house. My mother promised to let me know when it was safe to come out. I peered out from my hiding place. I couldn't tell what was going on, but after a few minutes, I saw several American servicemen's boots. I had been brainwashed by the Viet Cong, who had warned us time and again the Americans wanted to take over our country, steal from us, kill our people, and rape our women. I had heard all their propaganda, but my young eyes had never seen what an American looked like. For an instant, my curiosity got the best of me. I scooted to where I could get a better peek. There stood a tall, white creature. His hair was a strange color, and I thought, "That has to be the ugliest human being I have ever seen." I was in a state of shock. I quickly ducked back inside my refuge. After a few minutes, my mom called and told me it was safe to come out. The American soldiers had come on a mission to help evacuate our entire village of one thousand families. Mother acted like we could trust them, so we packed our belongings and headed to Xuyen Moc.

## XUYEN MOC

When we arrived in Xuyen Moc, we only had a piece of land and no house to live in. The soldiers had dumped all our belongings in a heap on the ground. Each family was given a few sheets of aluminum to make a tent until the building materials arrived for us to begin constructing our new homes. A few weeks went by, and then the families were called into the office. We were each given five hundred Vietnamese dong, five hundred pounds of oatmeal, and building materials for our new homes. The rumors began to circulate again. We were warned the oatmeal would give us ulcers. We would flip back and forth in our opinion of the Americans. We trusted them enough to move us here, but we weren't sure about eating oatmeal.

There were a few days when we were starving, so we would add a bit of oatmeal to our rice. However, most of it went to the pigs and chickens.

One of my humorous memories is of my grandmother experimenting with oatmeal. She combined oatmeal, water and sugar and made a patty and fried it. It looked like an oatmeal pancake. I thought it tasted pretty good, but the real oatmeal "discovery" was made by a group of Chinese in our area. A group of them came from the city to our little village. They went from door to door offering payment for any leftover oatmeal we could give them. They had a "patent" on the oatmeal cookie in our neck of the woods, and it was a hit! It was kind of sad because when they came to our house, we just shook our heads and pointed out back to the pigs and chickens. We had fed the entire coveted commodity to them.

## Light Bulb Moment

When I was thirteen, everywhere I looked, I saw the generosity of Americans. They provided clothes, food and even the materials to build our homes. It was the beginning of a "light bulb" moment for me. I couldn't understand why the Vietnamese continued to believe Americans were evil and just wanted to steal our land. As I look back on those days, the only conclusion I am able to make is the fact we were just caught up in the only life we knew. We hadn't been exposed to different cultures, and we were trapped in our isolation and ignorance. What made matters worse was the fact we believed our superstitions more than the kindnesses shown to us, but all that was about to change for me. I was beginning to see life a little more clearly.

One night a few months after we moved to Xuyen Moc, my grandmother, my two sisters, my two cousins and I had just fallen asleep when several rockets were fired into the village by the Viet Cong. They were aiming for the South Vietnamese soldiers who were about a quarter mile from our house, but they missed their target. We could hear many of the rockets hitting close by and exploding. Suddenly we heard a rocket getting louder and louder as it bore down on our house. It hit with a loud thud in our back yard, but did not explode. We then heard two more rockets coming closer to us. One hit in our front yard, and the next one actually hit the wall between my grandmother's bedroom and my bedroom. Both these rockets failed to explode also. After a while the rockets stopped coming, but we were afraid to go outside to see what had happened. The next morning, we realized we had three unexploded rockets laying in our yard. Later that morning, a helicopter landed in our back yard, and an American soldier got out of it. This was the second time I had seen an American. The American soldier, with the assistance of some South Vietnamese soldiers, defused the rockets and took them away in the helicopter. One family not too far from us had been killed in the attack. Looking back, I realize it was only by the grace of God that all our lives were spared that night. I didn't know Him, but He had His arms around me. His Word tells in the Psalms of His divine protection.

*The Lord will protect him and preserve his life; he will bless him in the land and not surrender him to the desire of his foes.*

PSALM 41:2

## MOVING AGAIN

My mother had a tremendous work ethic. She didn't have a lazy bone in her body. She was always coming up with creative ways to make money. This meant she would be away from us the majority of the time. During her absence, I stayed with my grandmother. Those were difficult days for me. My heart ached from lonesomeness. For some reason, as my grandmother grew older she became more unreasonable and stricter with me. In my early teen years she had unrealistic expectations of me, and when I failed to meet her demands, she whipped me. It was so strange because, most of the time, I was blamed for situations that weren't my fault. As Grandmother became more rigid, I felt my spirit shutting down. She was determined to keep me in line by enforcing even harsher discipline.

To complicate the situation, my mother was consumed with making a living. It really wasn't her fault. In order for us to survive, she had to work very hard, but this meant limited time to meet the needs of each of her children. My mother didn't intentionally mean to neglect us, but because of her absence, our needs were overlooked. My stepfather was busy supporting his first family who lived thirty or forty miles from us. There just wasn't enough time or money to give to both families. This required the second family to do without. My stepfather simply refused to help us financially. Instead, he requested money from us. There were many times I saw my mother and grandmother, who barely had enough to keep us afloat, give him money. One memory I don't have is seeing my stepfather give money to my mother or grandmother. One time my mother was asking him about repaying some money he had borrowed from her. He exploded and hit her. The next day, I saw the bruises on my mother's swollen face. I asked her what had happened. She lied and said she had awaken in the middle of the night, stumbled and ran into a pole.

Because the time with my mom was limited, I became quite jealous of anyone who stood in the way of my relationship with her. I remember craving her attention and longing for her to focus on us children, but she didn't have a clue. She was consumed with pleasing my stepfather and making a living. There were many days when my stepfather would show up at our house and I secretly wished he would go away. I just wanted my mom to be a mom and love us. I never told my mother of my feelings, because I knew it wouldn't help the situation.

In 1965, we moved to Long Hai to be closer to the city. My mom built a grass house for my grandmother and all of us. We opened a small store where we sold juice drinks. Inside this store was a room where we had two pool tables.

My mother wanted to be near my stepfather who was living in Vung Tau to work in his taxi business. He owned four horses and one buggy. People would pay him to pick them up and give them a ride to their destinations. Most of his customers were American soldiers. I stayed with Grandmother for a while, but then my mom and stepfather requested I come and help in their business. My new duties included harvesting the hay and straw in the rice fields and bringing it back to the house. One morning after I had finished my chores, I came home and my stepfather was beating my mother. I had seen him hit her before, but this time he was taking his fists and pounding her face. The next day, her face was swollen and bruised. I couldn't wait to get to Grandmother's house. I informed her about the physical abuse. I moved back in with my grandmother, but she was meaner than ever. She made more unrealistic demands of me. I spent a lot of time crying. Little did I know, there were more tears to be shed in the days ahead.

# Chapter Seven

# THE WHIPPING BOY

rom Xuyen Moc to Long Hai, there was a highway. The Viet Cong had blown up a bridge and miles of the road. No motorcycle, car or bike was allowed to travel to Xuyen Moc. The food supply was cut off, too. The only people who had food were the soldiers, policemen and government workers. The civilians didn't have any food. The citizens of Long Hai put their heads together and tried to come up with some sort of solution. We decided to take food to them. I would get up at three o'clock in the morning, place 40 pounds of food on each side of my yoke, and walk about 15 miles. I traveled with other people who had food to sell, too. We had to carry our supplies on our shoulders and cross over where the bridge had been demolished. It was very dangerous. We would sell green beans, bananas and peanuts. The money was excellent, but it didn't appease Grandmother. Even though I worked hard and traveled back and forth three times a week to sell my supplies, when I arrived home, I would be screamed at and whipped again.

## WEARING THE YOKE

When my family needed clean water to drink, I placed a yoke around my neck and hiked to the mountains to get fresh water. I carried ten gallons of water on the front and ten gallons of water on the back of the yoke. There were people in the village who would pay me to carry water for them, too. I also gathered firewood to help make some extra cash. I went into the jungle with my yoke and stacked firewood on it and brought it home. There were many days I was unable to carry the wood all the way home because of how heavy it was. I would stop and rest for a while. After I caught my breath, I carried the wood the rest of the way home. One day a neighbor lady saw me and mentioned to one of the other women in our village what a diligent worker I was. She shared with her how sorry she felt for me because I worked so hard. She said she would love to have me for her daughter-in-law, but I wasn't allowed to date or have a boyfriend. My grandmother was very strict when it came to my relationship with boys.

Grandmother had two pool tables in her store. This attracted a lot of teenage boys. I was oblivious to the opposite sex, but they seemed to be attracted to me. Grandmother would spank me for any attention a boy who came into the store gave me. Sometimes it was necessary for me to go back into the kitchen to pick up something and one of the boys would follow me. If Grandmother saw that, watch out! She had a big stick and would hit me with it. I was so depressed, and I didn't understand what I was doing wrong. I saw other girls my age and marveled at the freedom their parents gave them. I had absolutely no friends, no social life, and no clue as to why my grandmother was so upset with me all the time. She saw to it that I was under her thumb every waking minute. In my despair, I was befriended by another neighbor lady who was a distant relative of our family. I was only able to visit her for a few minutes at a time. If I didn't make myself known to my grandmother throughout the day, she would be very angry with me. This neighbor lady saw how hard I worked and the abuse I endured. She seemed to take an interest in my life and would ask me a lot of questions. She expressed how sorry she felt for me because of my grandmother's harsh treatment. One day she began to inquire if a rich man came to our village and asked me to marry him, if I would consider it. I was so emotionally drained from all the spankings I told her I would consider such a marriage proposal. Just thinking about a way of escape caused me to fantasize about a life without whippings. I could hardly wait for my new life.

## THE BIG SPILL

My grandmother sent Luom and I about a mile across Long Hai to a factory to pick up some fish sauce and carry it home. We carried ten gallon buckets on our yoke. My sister carried the one at the front, and I carried the one at the back. There is an art to carrying the yoke. The person in the back carries most of the weight, but the person in the front must be very careful about the way she walks or she would scrape her heel on the container and hurt herself. Luom was struggling and I felt sorry for her. I pushed more of the yoke back so I would carry the heaviest part of the load. On our way home, there were some children playing hide-and-seek. Luom and I didn't see them, but they jumped out and surprised us. We spilled some of the fish sauce. I knew I would be in trouble when we got home. I was right. Grandmother flew into a rage and started screaming at me and hit me. I was glad Luom didn't receive any punishment. I was so upset and ran crying to the neighbor lady who had befriended me. She felt sorry for my circumstances and tried to come up with a plan to rescue me from this continual abuse. One of her friends had a son, Hai, and she wondered if my grandmother and mother would give their permission for me to marry Hai. (It is a Vietnamese custom that the groom's family approach the bride's and makes sure the couple has their blessing.) Shortly after our visit, a knock came to our door. It was Hai's mother requesting permission for Hai to marry me. My mom didn't answer right away, but focused her attention on me. She asked me if I was sure I wanted to marry him since I was just sixteen and he was six years older than me. My fantasy of escaping all the whippings and heated verbal exchanges made this marriage arrangement such a temptation. I asked my mom what she thought. She said she really liked Hai, but she would feel more comfortable about the situation if we had three months to become better acquainted. This would also give her time to plan a wedding. I agreed to this arrangement.

## COURTSHIP

Hai showed up at our house the next day, and we began our courtship. We started to learn more about each other. He was the only son in his family. In Vietnam, the only son receives lots of attention and is usually quite spoiled. If his mother passed away he would inherit everything. My mother and grandmother liked that aspect. He came over every day and worked around our house. He would initiate conversation and smile at me, but every day after he left, Grandmother took out her big stick and beat me. One day after she kept hitting me over and over, I was emotionally depleted. I thought if she hit me one more time I would explode in anger.

I continued to work at Grandmother's store during this three-month engagement. Other young men continued to come and play pool and sometimes they wanted to chat with me, but Grandmother was very protective. If she caught me visiting with one of them, I was in deep trouble. Most of the time, she had me working in the back kitchen. One day one of the boys came back there to smoke and talk to me. Grandmother saw us talking. After the boy left, she threw a temper tantrum. We were in a very narrow hallway, and I was trying to quickly slip past her in an attempt to dodge the spanking. I accidentally brushed against her and caused her to fall. I felt bad that she fell, but I didn't understand why she was so mean to me. I was completely innocent of any wrongdoing.

The fall infuriated her, and she sent for my mom to come and whip me that night. My mom came and tied me from my feet up to my shoulder to a pole. Hai heard what was going to happen. I think he did care for me because he stepped in between my mom and me in an attempt to absorb the blows. After Mom hit him a few times, she stopped. I really think it would have been much worse if he hadn't been there. I was so confused and didn't understand why my mother and grandmother were doing this. My heart was broken. I realized I couldn't bear another whipping. Even though I didn't love Hai, I married him in an attempt to escape the constant conflict I was forced to endure.

## HONEYDOOM

I had no honeymoon, but I did have a "honeydoom." It was not a pleasant experience for me. My new home was directly across from my grandmother's house. The first night, I was unable to stop crying. Even though I had endured my grandmother's spankings and constant scolding, deep down I knew she loved me and I loved her. As I wept through my "honeydoom" night, I realized my grandmother did the best she could with what understanding she had. My heart yearned to be at home with my grandmother rather than living in a strange house and married to a man I didn't love. I wanted to move home where things were familiar, but I realized it probably wasn't going to happen. The more my mind dwelt on home, the harder I cried. I ended up crying myself to sleep.

The next morning when I woke up I was informed of my new duties. It appeared to me that my arranged marriage was a marriage of convenience. I wanted a way out, and my in-laws wanted a slave. They made it clear that my job was to serve my new husband's family. I was to be their maid. No task was too menial. I had traded serving my grandmother for serving strangers.

## DATED JEKYLL – MARRIED HYDE

My mother-in-law was very sweet to me when my husband was around, but the minute he left she treated me cruelly. One day she asked me to run to town and purchase 50 pounds of rice. I misunderstood and returned home with only 25 pounds. She went berserk. I begged for forgiveness, but she made me feel so ignorant. When my husband returned from work, she told him what had happened and accused me of sassing her. I was cooking dinner in the kitchen. She wouldn't stop complaining about me and insisted I had no appreciation for all they had done for me. My husband raised his fist to strike me to satisfy his mother. I covered my face with my hands. I pleaded, "Do you remember just a few weeks before our wedding, when I told you, if I ever did something to upset you, not to hit me? I cannot stay here if you treat me this way."

He thought I didn't mean what I said, but I was dead serious. That night I snuck over to see my mother. I was crying so hard. I begged her to let me live with her. She realized it would be impossible for me to live anywhere near my in-laws. I explained to her about my husband threatening to hit me. It seemed to strike a chord in her compassionate mother's heart. She told me about her cousin who was planning to leave for Da Lat and suggested I leave town with her. We began to make plans for my escape. I knew I couldn't pack anything because my in-laws might become suspicious. The plan was for me to leave on a bus from Long Hai and ride to Long Dien. My cousin would follow on another bus at six o'clock in the morning. We would meet at Long Dien, where I would get on her bus, and we would travel the rest of the way to Da Lat together. My cousin had instructed the bus driver to honk the horn three times. This would be the signal for me to get on the bus, and this bus would take us to Saigon. I was waiting in Long

Dien for my cousin's bus to arrive. A bus pulled up, and the driver honked his horn three times. I boarded the bus and it headed for Saigon. I looked for my cousin, but she was not on the bus. I wasn't quite sure what to do, but about 30 minutes later a man came around to collect my ticket. He looked at mine and informed me I was on the wrong bus, but everything would be OK because the bus I was on was still headed to Saigon. Finally the bus stopped and the announcement was made over the intercom, "We are in Saigon."

I got off the bus. I was petrified because of all the horrible stories I had heard about Saigon. I found a bus employee and explained where I was supposed to go. He laughed and said there are many bus stops in Saigon and I had exited at the wrong bus depot. He put me on another bus that took me to the central part of Saigon. I wasn't there very long when I looked up and saw my cousin. She was shouting my name. We were both relieved to be reunited. We stayed one night with relatives in Saigon. The next day we left for Da Lat, where we lived for the next six months.

I was fortunate to find a decent job in Da Lat. There was a wealthy Chinese family who hired me to work in their kitchen. My skills were limited, but this family was very kind to me. They took the time to teach me how to cook new recipes. All their children attended school in Saigon, and once a month they would come home. I wasn't able to keep my job because after six months I became homesick. I had never been away from my family for that length of time. I decided it was time for me to take a little road trip and see my family again.

## ROAD TRIP

My mom was the first one to see me when I arrived in Vung Tau. She wasn't happy I had returned. She had been under the stress of dealing with my in-laws. They blamed her for my disappearance and insisted she reimburse them for the cost of the wedding. My mom told them she didn't have the money to pay them. They were angry and demanded I immediately be returned to them. I told my mom I wasn't willing to go back. Once again my mom felt my pain. She agreed to let me stay for seven days. During that week, I watched as my mother slaved for hours in the rice field. I winced as she carried the heavy bundles of hay for the horses. Finally, I convinced her to allow me to help. I did my best to relieve her of the strenuous manual labor. My heart went out to her because she was expecting her ninth child and working too hard for a woman of her age and condition.

During the time I stayed with my mom, I saw my stepfather take advantage of her. The domestic violence was increasing. I learned he was sending his first family to the superior schools, but he was grossly neglecting his second family. This made me so sad. I wanted to change my family's circumstances and say something to my mother, but in the Vietnamese culture the children are never to lecture the parents. If I had a differing opinion, I was allowed to speak gently, but I was so angry with my stepfather that I knew I wouldn't be able to speak kindly. What he was putting our family through just didn't seem fair to me. I knew if I opened my mouth and attempted to speak about the delicate situation it wouldn't be pretty. I had already received a spanking because I spoke my mind. I was intimidated and decided it would be better if I didn't say anything.

## PLAN B

I was very concerned for my mother's well-being. Knowing it was best to not confront the situation head-on, I decided to come up with "Plan B." I remembered when we moved to the edge of town in Vung Tau we lived near a big airbase. We thought we would find work there, but we didn't. At this airbase, they used many kitchen supplies. They would throw away their garbage near the back of a hill close to our house. My mom's first cousin would wait for the garbage truck. As soon as it left, she waded through the trash looking for food. She picked out old hot dogs, fried chicken and ham. She would take it home, wash it and sell it. There were many times she gave us some of the food because we had nothing else to eat. We would fry up the hot dogs for breakfast, lunch and supper. I know God protected us because we were eating spoiled food, but we never got sick.

Mom's cousin was very poor all her life. Like so many of the men in our lives, her husband had abandoned her. Inside her house was a huge statue of Buddha. She put all kinds of candles, incense, flowers, bananas and other fruit on the altar. Whenever I went there, I stared at that statue.

A suffocating feeling of hopelessness would overwhelm me. It was like a dark depression. I felt an emptiness inside. It was a dark time in my life. I think that was the first time I began to have questions about Buddha. I was sitting with my cousin staring at Buddha when I asked her, "How long have you had that statue? Do you believe in Buddha? Have you dedicated your life to him?"

She looked at me and said, "I do believe in him but I cannot dedicate my life to him because I would have to make a vow to eat only a vegetarian diet. I wouldn't be able to eat fish or meat."

She told me some of her friends had a Buddha statue in their homes, so she wanted to have one. She said she prayed to him to bless her because she needed help. There was one point she made that haunts me to this day. Even now as I write about it, I get shivers up and down my spine. She said she had noticed most of the people who worshipped Buddha statues were usually very, very poor. I was shocked and asked her why she had one if it makes you poor. She said she didn't know why, but she was afraid to get rid of it because it was supposed to bless her. Even when I moved to America her statement haunted me, but Buddha was all I had ever known. So when I took a trip to Mexico, I purchased a Buddha statue for our home. I also had an altar and put oranges, apples and flowers on it, but every time I lit the incense, I remembered her words. I didn't know how to find truth. My Buddhist traditions were all I'd ever known. Everyone in my circle of friends worshipped Buddha; so I did, too.

## DECISIONS

My mother gathered all the money she could, even borrowing from her friends to make a way for me to leave. After she gave me the money I started walking towards the highway. I saw my stepfather coming in from work. He wished me good luck and told me to go to Da Lat and be good. He assured me when things quieted down, I was welcome to come back. I started walking to the bus station about three miles away. I was tormented about leaving my family. When I reached the bus depot, I didn't want to get on the bus. I looked around. Then I sat down and tried to get some direction. I just couldn't bring myself to get on the bus and leave. Oh, how I wish I had known Jesus back then. How I wish someone would have told me I could call upon His name and He would rescue me, but I didn't know Him. I continued to walk in great darkness, and it was about to get even darker.

# Chapter Eight

# THE MAKEOVER

s I sat at the bus depot in Vung Tau, I saw a horse and buggy carrying an American soldier through the streets. It was a reminder of my stepfather and mother. Waves of grief began to swallow me. I didn't want to leave all that was familiar. I was very naïve. My mother and grandmother had sheltered me from the ways of the world. As a girl, I was never allowed to go to Vung Tau except to purchase food and supplies, and when I did go to town, I always went with my mother.

As I sat drowning in despair, I looked up and down the streets and noticed all the bars. My mind started buzzing.

"Maybe I could get a job at a bar right here in Vung Tau," I reasoned. "That way I wouldn't have to be far from my family. I could make some money and help support my mother and grandmother."

It was settled in my heart. I was not getting on the bus. I was going to stay in Vung Tau. At that very moment I looked up and saw a bar girl walking with a soldier. I knew she was a bar girl because she looked very different from the average woman in Vung Tau. Her hair was styled and she wore heavy makeup. Her lipstick and nails were bright red, and she wore stylish high heels that matched her fancy clothes. A few minutes later, I saw two more bar girls pass by. I didn't have enough nerve to ask if they could help me get a job, but I determined in my heart that I would approach the next bar girl who walked by and speak with her about job possibilities. Finally a fourth girl walked by. I took at deep breath and walked up to her. I asked her if I could work with her at the bar. She just stared at me. I even offered to be a simple housekeeper. She continued to stare at me. I felt like I could read her mind. I had absolutely no pizzazz. I was a plain Jane who had worked in the jungle. Fortunately, she didn't tell me what she was thinking as she looked me over. Finally, she asked me where I was from. I didn't want her to know I was from Vung Tau because she might not hire me if she thought my parents would show up. I lied without batting an eye. I've often heard people say, "Desperate people go to desperate measures."

I was desperate and in need of work. My new friend took me to her home and introduced me to another gal who worked at the bar. They looked me over from the top of my head to the soles of my feet. Together they discussed how they could give me a makeover. First, they threw me in the shower and scrubbed me clean. Second, they took me to the beauty salon and gave me a fresh hairdo. Then they applied makeup and dressed me in one of their fancy outfits. I looked in the mirror and hardly recognized who was looking back at me. They took me to the bar owner and told her I needed work, but that I didn't have any nice clothes. The owner loaned me some money, and my new friends took me to the market and bought some pretty material and made some nice outfits. The next day, I went to work as a bar girl with my new friends.

Inside the bar it was very dark. There were long counters and booths along the wall. I would sit in the booth and stare out the window. Whenever I saw a horse and buggy, I was afraid it might be my stepfather. I feared my secret would soon be discovered.

## LEAVING ON MY MIND

Many of the soldiers, who came into the bar, wanted to pay me to accompany them to a movie or dinner. I refused because I didn't want to leave the confines of the bar in case someone might recognize me. My boss disapproved of my unwillingness to accommodate the customers. She knew it meant less money for her. Once again my nomadic spirit kicked in. I felt I needed to leave Vung Tau after just working there a few months.

## GREEN BERET

There was a violent, military group in Vietnam called the Green Beret. They fiercely fought the Viet Cong. Every so often they would show up in Vung Tau. All the businesses, especially bar owners, were intimidated by them. The Green Beret were jealous of the American soldiers, and in revenge would think nothing of throwing a grenade into a bar, hoping to maim or kill some American soldiers. One night a group of Green Beret showed up at the bar where I was working. They stormed in and looked the place over. One of the men chose me to be his companion for the evening. I told him I couldn't sit with him. He flew into a rage and slapped me. I winced in pain. Everyone in the bar froze in terror. I remember, from that point on, something changed in my heart towards life. I had seen and endured so much abuse. His cruel slap caused a hardened crust to glaze over my heart. No longer would I be the sweet, tenderhearted girl. My language and lifestyle changed.

## HEART TRANSPLANT

When I think back on those days, I have a gratefulness that wells up in my heart for all Jesus has done for me. My girlfriends gave me a makeover on the outside, but when I gave my heart to Jesus, He gave me a makeover on the inside. I cannot thank Him enough for the love and mercy He has shown me. When He saved me, He gave me a heart transplant!

*A new heart also will I give you, and a new spirit will I put within you: and I will take away the stony heart out of your flesh, and I will give you an heart of flesh.*

EZEKIEL 26:36 KJV

Before I knew Jesus, I had a stony heart, and life in the bar desensitized me even more.

I was deeply affected by the slapping incident. My girlfriend Mai and I decided to leave Vung Tau. Mai had much more bar experience than I did. I was just a rookie. She was constantly telling me what to do.

## SAIGON

Mai and I found a hotel in Saigon and rented a room. It didn't take us long before we were employed at another bar. American soldiers were housed in a hotel next to where we lived. I met one of those soldiers, and he asked me if he could see me on his next day off. I could only speak simple phrases in

English but agreed to go out with him. We spent a couple of days together. We went back out one week later. He handed me a bag filled with cash and told me the money was mine and I could buy whatever I wanted. I knew there was no way a soldier made this kind of money. He had to be involved in something illegal. I figured out he was deep into the black market. I had never had access to that kind of cash in my life. The dollar signs started swirling in my head. The first thing I wanted to do was go home and see my mom. I wanted to share my wealth with her, but I quickly dismissed the thought because there was a possibility she would find out I was working in a bar, and I knew she would be very displeased.

I began to see the American soldier on a regular basis. One day he called and informed me we were going to rent a house together. Every two weeks he would bring me a bag full of cash. There was approximately $800 in each bag he gave me. He insisted I was not to ask any questions about where the money came from. He also insisted I was never to ask for his military paycheck. It would always go back home to America. He seemed like a good man, but he was involved with the black market. I stayed with him about three months. Then he went to the States on leave for four weeks. He promised, when he returned, we would purchase a home in Saigon. While he was gone I decided to go home and see my family. I left my hometown an innocent, tenderhearted child, but returned hardened by sin. My mother knew I was not the same. Something had drastically changed. Even though I attempted to hide my dark secret by wearing decent clothes and styling my hair like common people, she recognized immediately I was a barmaid. I intentionally did not wear any heavy makeup, but my mom had a mother's heart. Questions started pouring out of her about my new life. She bluntly asked me if I was employed at a bar. There was no way I could tell her the truth. I was ashamed and knew it would break her heart, so I lied. I convinced her I was working for Americans at the PX, a place where the military families purchased food and supplies. I told her I was doing very well and even gave her a large sum of cash. I told her I wanted her to buy the piece of property she had always wanted and build a new house on the land. We talked about her starting a new business that would require less manual labor. My mom thanked me over and over again for the financial blessing.

I stayed for two more weeks and promised to help her in any way I could. My boyfriend returned from his trip to America shortly after I returned to Saigon. He acted strangely and refused to come inside our home. I asked him what was wrong, and he told me he had heard how I was cheating on him. A girlfriend had come to him and said they had seen me leaving town immediately after he left. I pleaded with him, assuring him I had not been unfaithful, but he wouldn't listen. He was convinced I was running around with other men. I tried to figure out where this vicious rumor came from and finally came to the conclusion my girlfriend Mai, who lived with another soldier, was jealous because of the large amounts of cash I was receiving. I believe she came up with these false accusations in hopes of ending our relationship.

## HIGH-CLASS BAR MAID

My life continued to be unstable and had absolutely no direction. I was bouncing from one thing to another. I received word that my mom's cousin had invited me to come and live with her. I accepted her offer and found a high-class bar to work at. This was a far cry from the cheap lifestyle I had experienced before. I began to bring in large amounts of cash. I had a certain monetary standard I wanted to live up to now that I was making more money. I craved success and purchased designer clothes and expensive cosmetics. I learned quickly how to apply my makeup so I would look sophisticated. The bar owner was running a top of the line operation. My good looks and experience made this job a Cinderella slipper fit for me.

One morning it was my turn to open the bar early. I woke up and hurried to get ready for work. I hopped on my motorcycle, turned the key, and groaned when I discovered the engine was dead. A neighbor was sitting on his porch sipping a cup of coffee. In the weeks previous, Son had made futile attempts to take me out, but I wasn't interested. I was desperate and needed help because my employer had some very strict rules. If you were late, even one time, you could lose your job. I looked up and saw Son walking toward me. He looked over my motorcycle but couldn't seem to fix the problem. He asked if I needed a ride to work. I was thankful and accepted his offer.

The bar was located in downtown Saigon. Most people would drop you off at the front door, but not Son. He knew the reputation of the bar and dropped me off a block or two away. He asked what time my shift was finished and offered to pick me up. I was determined not to be involved with a Vietnamese man. I had already been slapped and threatened by one. It could mean trouble for me if I dated Son and he discovered my involvement with American men. I didn't want to have to deal with that. Most of the women who worked at the bar came from broken homes. We were a hurting bunch. It was much easier for us to deal with foreigners than to have to expose our painful past to someone who knew where we had come from.

After my shift, Son came to pick me up, but I had left work early. He waited quite some time for me, but I was already home. A knock came at our door, and my cousin answered. I was hiding in the other room. I heard my cousin tell him I wasn't home, but what I didn't know was she was pointing toward the room I was in, indicating with her hands that I was home. I kept wondering why Son wouldn't leave. After a lengthy time, I realized there was no way out. I had to face him and apologize for my rude behavior. Embarrassed, I appeared from my hiding place and attempted to explain my bizarre behavior. He was very kind and forgiving and invited me to see a movie with him. Something about his gentleness charmed my heart. Son was the first Vietnamese man I had met with such gentlemanly qualities. It became evident, after our misunderstanding was cleared up, we were falling in love.

Son came from a well respected family. His father was a pharmacist and all of his relatives were high ranking officials. In Vietnam, the culture is very particular: The wealthy marry the wealthy; the poor marry the poor. It is never accepted for the educated to wed the uneducated. Son's mother knew I worked in a bar. She was kind to my face, but I knew in my heart she did not approve of our relationship. It didn't seem to matter to Son. He was deeply in love with me. In all my life, I had never met a kinder Vietnamese man. I had fallen in love with him, too. I took him to meet my mother and the rest of my family. I wanted my mother's permission to marry him. My mother and grandmother immediately approved of Son. We began to plan a wedding. It was during this time his mother began to whisper her disapproval behind my back. I personally felt it was because he was making good money and no longer giving any to her, but he was sharing it with me. She became quite vocal and insisted no son of hers was going to marry a barmaid. She even threatened to commit suicide if he continued our relationship. The culture in Vietnam emphasizes honoring your parents. You are looked down upon if you don't. Son was 18 at the time. We had been together about six months, and looking back, I probably didn't realize the extreme pressure his mother was putting on him.

The war was going on. It was mandatory every young man appear at the local police station and register. Son was worried about joining the military. He feared he might be sent to a dangerous place and would never return home again. Coupled with the fact his mother wanted him to end his relationship with me and move to his grandmother's hometown, he couldn't take the pressure any more. He left without saying goodbye. I was left wondering where he was and what had happened to him. The first 24 hours he was gone, I thought the police had picked him up and assigned him to some military unit where he had to fight in the war. I was upset and couldn't stop crying. Finally, one of his friends came and saw I was visibly shaken. He recognized the mental anguish I was in and had mercy on me. He told me Son had left Saigon and moved to Can Tho, near his grandmother's hometown. This friend had been the one to take him to the boat. The mystery was solved. I finally knew where he was. I ran and grabbed a bag and started packing my things. One of my girlfriends went with me to help me find him. When we arrived at the house where Son lived, my girlfriend went up and knocked on the door. She found Son and told him I was waiting for him down by the river. He came to find me. When I looked into his eyes I could see he was as sad as I was. He began apologizing and told me he was forced to move on. We visited a while and then he took me and my girlfriend to a motel where he rented a room for the three of us. Son and I slept very little. We stayed up most of the night discussing our situation. We tried to come up with a magical solution, but we came to the conclusion our problems couldn't be solved. I assured him I didn't want him to be disobedient to his parents' wishes. He asked me to go up North with him, but in my heart I knew his mother would never accept me. It just wasn't meant to be. With heavy hearts, we said our final farewell.

## BABY ON THE WAY

I returned to Saigon with my girlfriend and went back to work at the bar. As the weeks went by, I discovered I had conceived a child the last night I spent with Son. Abortions are commonplace in Vietnam. I didn't know abortion was wrong, so I considered it, but thank God He intervened on my baby's behalf, and I decided to not terminate my pregnancy.

As my tummy grew, the owner of the hotel saw it was quite awkward for me to be a barmaid. She made some arrangements for me to be hired for a new position. I recorded all the customers who rented rooms in the hotel. I kept the books and informed the police station who came to the hotel, what time they arrived, and what time they left. I held this position for four months.

One day my cousin came by. She saw I was alone and pregnant. She felt it was her duty to find my mother and inform her of my condition. The news of my pregnancy prompted my mother to come looking for me. I had warned all my coworkers at the hotel, "If anybody shows up here and asks about my whereabouts, don't tell them anything!"

I worried Son might find out I was pregnant. I didn't want him feeling trapped into marrying me. I realized his mother now had ammunition that could be used against us. Any hopes of a future between Son and I was looking quite bleak.

## THE LOST IS FOUND

My mother showed up at the hotel carrying my picture in her hand. The owners did as I had requested. They told her they didn't recognize the young woman in the picture. My mother was quite emotional and determined to find me. They held their ground and insisted they didn't know me. Mom returned to my cousin's house defeated. When I arrived at the hotel and heard my mother was there trying to find me and how upset she was, I felt terrible. I could no longer hide from her, knowing she was concerned about my welfare. I went to find her. When our eyes met, we were overjoyed to see each other, even though I was seven months pregnant. Mom asked me to come home with her. I agreed, and the next day we packed all my belongings and I moved home. Mom took care of me until my daughter Dai Trang was born. I stayed with her for six months.

Looking back, I realize I was a young girl of only 18 with a broken heart. There are so many memories of this time in my life that evoke painful emotions. I was severely depressed because the man I loved had abandoned me and I was forced to go through the pregnancy alone. I couldn't fault Son because he didn't know I was expecting. We had no contact after our final night together. I would dream of Son coming back and rescuing me, but he never came. After a few months, word spread I was pregnant, and some of Son's friends informed him about my condition. Even though he knew, he never came to find me. This rejection left deep scars in my heart.

## TENDER LOVING CARE

While I was pregnant, my mom gave me tender loving care. She made sure I didn't perform any strenuous duties or overexert myself. I knew it was her way of showing me she was sorry for past mistakes. I will never forget her kindness to me during my pregnancy.

Many times people cannot understand the deep love members of dysfunctional families have for one another. I understand. Families often mirror the examples they have seen. I know my mother and grandmother didn't have easy lives. They did the very best they could for me and my siblings with the knowledge they had.

Mom knew my body left home but my heart was never far from my family. While I worked in Saigon, I would send her money every month. She used the money to purchase a piece of land in Vung Tau, and she also bought a vehicle.

After experiencing labor pains for two full days, my water broke. I went to the clinic and started crying for Son. I still longed for him to come and be my knight in shining armor, but he never came. My mom was there to comfort me. She never left my side, and my precious grandmother was there, too. Grandmother lit incense, went out to the front yard, bowed down and prayed to Ong Troi, the universal God. She asked Him to be merciful to me and to please let the pain ease up. My cousin hurried to the clinic to see me. On her way, she passed my house and saw my grandmother placing fruit and flowers on the altar in the front yard. Afterwards, my grandmother told me she prayed around eight o'clock that I would give birth to the baby very soon, and my little girl, Dai Trang, was born on October 18, 1969, two hours later. I stayed in the clinic for three days and then came home. Our house only had one bed at the back of the house. Mom had me walk around to the back of the house. I wasn't permitted to go in the front of the house because they believed a woman who had given birth was unclean for 30 days. Mom gave me her bed so I could get the rest I needed. I have often thought of her sacrifice.

Even though I didn't know Jesus and I was steeped in darkness, the desire of my heart while I was laboring to give birth to Dai Trang was to have a mother and a father for our baby. I kept wishing Son would be there to welcome our baby into the world. Somehow deep in my heart, I had a conviction about the importance of both a father and mother. When God gave me Dennis, He gave me His very best. Jesus was able to heal all my hurts from the abandonment I had experienced with Son. Dennis supported me from the day I conceived until the day our baby was born. He would come home from work and put his ear on my tummy and listen to our baby's heartbeat. Every time the baby moved, Dennis was thrilled. It was a joyous occasion. And when the day came for me to give birth, it was Dennis who took me to the hospital, and he didn't leave my side until the baby and I were safe. My sorrow was turned to joy because God gave me a beautiful husband in Dennis. My heavenly Father knew the inner healing I needed. He did as He promises in the Psalms: He heard my cries and fulfilled the desires of my heart. He truly blessed me beyond what I ever imagined. Even though I was shackled by the bondage of sin and didn't know Jesus, I cried out to God in my heart, and He heard me.

*He fulfills the desires of those who fear him; he hears their cry and saves them.*

PSALM145:19

## A TIME TO BE BORN – A TIME TO DIE

*There is a time for everything, and a season for every activity under heaven: a time to be born and a time to die.*

### ECCLESIASTES 3:1-2a

The same year Dai Trang was born, my sister Luom died. She was only 23 when she passed away. It was especially traumatic for my mother and I because neither of us was home when she died. I was living in Saigon and Mom came to visit me. Luom was home in Vung Tau with Grandmother and my other siblings. My grandmother's cousin came to visit the night before Luom died. He had a special bond with Luom because he had visited Mom the day she gave birth to her. In fact, he delivered her. He had since moved away and never returned for a visit until the day before Luom died. We went to his house from time to time, but he never came to ours.

Luom was carrying water one morning from the well in the back of the house. She was on her way to the kitchen when she collapsed. She couldn't be revived. We don't know if the fall caused her death or if she simply died and fell down. In those days, the calendar of the Buddhists believed there were "good days" and "bad days" to bury your deceased. If you buried someone on a bad day, a curse would come upon the family. My grandmother's cousin looked on the Asian calendar and found the day Luom died was a good day, but the next five days were bad days. Their decision to bury her on the good day was totally based on superstitions. Luom died in the morning and was buried by three o'clock that afternoon. No one thought of sending someone to contact Mom or me because of the distance involved and the time it would take for us to return home. Mom left Saigon and went home a few days later and discovered Luom was dead and buried. I didn't find out until three months later because when Mom left Saigon we had a terrible disagreement. I moved and didn't tell her or anyone in my family where I was. Three months later, I returned to Vung Tau to find my beloved sister was gone. It was such a sad and painful day for me. I grieved because I did not have the chance to say goodbye. The last time I had seen Luom was several months before she died.

## PRECIOUS MEMORIES, HOW THEY LINGER

Memories are a gift from God that death cannot destroy. I have many precious memories of Luom. She was blessed with a sunny disposition and loved to sing. You could always find her singing a song or sipping on coffee, her favorite drink. She had a good appetite and was a little chubby. Grandmother would give us children the same portions of food. I would always save part of mine and share it with Luom. As a loving gesture, she would tickle me and make me laugh. I knew it was her way of saying thank you. Her skin was lighter than the rest of us, and I always thought she was very beautiful. God gave Luom an amazing gift of organization. She was a tremendous help around the house because she loved to clean. She and I would wash dishes together and prepare tea for Grandmother's statues. We bonded during these times. Luom loved to collect things: buttons, razor blades, rubber bands and needles. She would take thread and string them all together in one long strand to keep from losing them.

We have no pictures of Luom, but her face has remained etched in my memory. I still love her so very much. She had the mind of an innocent child and never heard the name of Jesus, but I know Jesus loves her very much. What a joyful celebration it will be when we meet again in Heaven. Luom left our family a legacy of love. This poem is a tribute to her life.

## LEGACY OF LOVE

*You've left us for awhile,*
*We'll miss your lovely smile,*
*But death cannot erase*
*Sweet memories that took place,*
*Although you've gone away,*
*In our heart you'll always stay,*
*Our gift from God above – Our legacy of love.*
*Your work on Earth is done,*
*Life's final war you've won.*
*This one thing we know,*
*You've left "footprints" in our soul,*
*We'll keep marching on,*
*We'll keep singing all your songs*
*Until we reach Heaven above,*
*To see our legacy of love.*
*Your legacy of love with us will remain,*
*Echoing the truths your life did proclaim,*
*The torch has now been passed, we raise it unashamed,*
*You're with Christ above, and Christ is here with me,*
*We're really not apart, there's just a veil between,*
*You will always be etched in our memory – Our legacy of love.*

—DIXIE PHILLIPS

# MEETING DENNIS

After Dai Trang was born, I returned to Saigon to live with my cousin. We lived close to Son's house, and I continued to work at the bar. I maintained a friendly relationship with Son's family because of Dai Trang. They seemed to care for her.

Because I had to work so much, I had to take Dai Trang to my mother's house for weeks at a time. I was so lonesome for her, but I knew I had to make a living, and there was nothing else I could do. As I sat at a fruit stand in front of my house, I was so sad and grieved for my baby girl. About this time, a handsome American soldier came out of Son's house. Son's sister had married an American, and the handsome soldier was his good friend Dennis Spencer. He spotted me, and later told me he was immediately attracted to me. He never mentioned it to anyone until the next day, when he asked his buddy, "Who is that girl?"

His friend explained I was Son's ex-girlfriend. Dennis expressed an interest in wanting to be introduced to me. His friend came and asked if I would be willing to go to the zoo with Dennis. I agreed to go. I could speak very little English, but we seemed to communicate with our hearts and through our eyes. There was an immediate chemistry between us, even though we had a language barrier. As we walked hand-in-hand through the zoo, we would stop complete strangers and hand them our camera. They would take our picture. We enjoyed each other's company. I knew I was falling in love with this fine gentleman.

## CHARMED

Dennis charmed my heart on our very first date. Three high school girls, all dressed in their uniforms, came up to us. They said some man had stolen their purses and ran away. They were frightened because they didn't have enough cash to pay a taxi to drive them home. Without hesitation Dennis pulled out his wallet and gave them five dollars. His random act of kindness gave me a glimpse inside his big heart. What blessed me even more was the fact he knew there was a good possibility these young girls were lying to us. Many times in Vietnam people play on the sympathy of others. Dennis was no dummy. Yet he still showed compassion. I knew he would rather err on the side of mercy.

It was apparent from the very beginning of our relationship that we cared deeply for each other. After the visit to the zoo, we went to see *Romeo and Juliet*. Afterwards, Dennis had to go back to work but came to visit me the next day after he found out where I worked. When Dennis came to see me at the bar, he noticed how sad I was and decided to cheer me up. He carried in his pocket a box with a coiled fake snake in a hidden compartment. When you first opened the box you saw just the empty compartment, but when you closed it and opened it a second time, the snake would jump out of the box at you. He told me he could get me to laugh, but I didn't think he could because I was very depressed about being separated from my baby girl. He showed me the box and asked me to open it. I wasn't impressed with the empty box and thought he was a little strange. He asked me to open the box a second time. When the snake jumped out at me, I screamed and jumped about a foot out of my chair. At first I was scared, but then I started laughing. Dennis was so proud of himself and chuckled, "See! I told you I could get you to smile."

I felt so comfortable with him and decided to show him a picture of Dai Trang. I explained to him she was my daughter. It was a very tender moment for both of us. Our hearts were being cemented together with love. He took my hand and walked me to the front of the porch and looked me squarely in the eyes and asked me bluntly, "Mai, I need you to tell me the truth. Do you like me?"

I responded, "Yes, I like you."

It wasn't enough for him. He probed further. "Mai, some girls just say what they think men want to hear. They even lie to them, but I need to know today if you really like me."

I assured him I did like him very much.

We spent the next two days and nights together in my house. During this time, we stayed up and talked into the wee hours of the morning. Even though we faced some language barriers, we could both sense our hearts were being united. In the early morning hours, as I lay snuggled in Dennis' arms, he softly told me he loved me, but I didn't hear what he said, so I didn't respond. About two hours later, I told Dennis I loved him. He was so happy as he held me and ran his fingers through my hair. He then told me he had first said he loved me earlier but was sad when I didn't say "I love you" back. We still kid each other to this day as to which one of us really professed their love first. I had never experienced a love like this. He was so gentle and caring, and we had fallen deeply in love. Dennis proposed to me, and I promised to be his wife. We understood our commitment was for the rest of our lives. I knew he was the man I had been searching for, and he knew I was the woman he had dreamed of.

I am a realist. Fantasy and romance only last for a short while. I realized if I married Dennis it would be a life-changing experience for me. I would not live in Vietnam anymore. I would have to move to the United States. I made plans to visit my mother and grandmother. I wanted their blessing on my upcoming marriage. It wasn't going to be easy to get their approval because they didn't like Americans. We lived in such a remote area and were influenced by the communistic Viet Cong. Even though the Viet Cong had killed my two uncles, we loved Vietnam, and we believed the Americans came to our country to take over our land and control us. I realized it would take some persuading to get my mother and grandmother's approval. I poured out my heart to them. They listened and then expressed their concern. I was shocked when my stepfather spoke up and gave his blessing for our upcoming marriage. I have my own theory about why he wanted me to marry Dennis. I think he didn't appreciate my influence in the family. For years, he had neglected them and drained my mother financially. He was very proud and enjoyed when people admired him, and he didn't want me staying around because I could influence my mom. If I left he would have more control over her. He told her she should be happy I had found a good man who loved me. The fact he was American didn't matter.

If Dennis and I were happy, they should be happy for us. I watched as my mother and grandmother listened to him. They agreed and gave their blessing for our upcoming marriage.

When I returned home, Dennis came out to greet me. We embraced, and I told him I had been given the green light to marry him. We were thrilled. We celebrated by going out to eat.

## TAXI TROUBLES

One day after we were engaged, Dennis and I went to the PX in Cho Lon to buy our monthly supply of food. After Tet of 1968, when the Viet Cong attacked Saigon, the military would not let any Vietnamese go inside the PX except those who worked there. I waited outside the PX while Dennis did the shopping. After a few minutes, I saw Dennis walking towards me carrying two large bags in his arms. Outside the PX were taxis lined up to take the soldiers wherever they wanted to go. Dennis had learned you negotiate the price before getting into the taxi because none of the taxi drivers used the meters. After letting the taxi driver know where we lived and agreeing on a price, we entered the taxi. We were traveling down a main road when Dennis motioned to the taxi driver to turn left onto a smaller street. Instead of turning onto the smaller street, the taxi driver pulled over to the right and stopped his taxi. He mumbled something. Dennis turned to me and asked what he had said.

"He said this is too far for what you are paying him."

Dennis tossed about half of what the agreed price was on the front seat.

I turned to the driver and said, "If you aren't going to take us all the way home, this is all we are going to pay."

We picked up our bags and got out of the taxi. The driver was furious and jumped out. He tried to get in Dennis' face and started screaming. I stepped between them and started arguing with the driver. I explained he had not lived up to the agreement. The argument was taking place on a very busy street and soon a large crowd of over 100 Vietnamese gathered. A truck came by with some fellow soldiers on it. One stopped and asked Dennis if everything was OK and if he needed a ride somewhere. Dennis told him he was all right, and they drove off.

Dennis turned around and noticed I had tied the sides of my ao dai, a Vietnamese dress, up and had taken off my shoes. He asked, "Are we going to make a run for it?"

I said, "No, we are getting ready to fight!"

Many of the people who had gathered were students from a nearby school. When they figured out what had happened, they started defending us, shouting at the driver. The driver was preoccupied with the students. Dennis and I picked up our bags and walked away from the crowd to our house. Looking back, the situation could have had a very different ending, but God's hand of protection was upon us, even though we didn't know it at the time. Dennis enjoys telling this story to his friends, but I always remind him, "Honey, that old Mai is dead. Jesus has given you a new Mai".

## MORE TAXI WOES

We had other strange experiences with the taxi drivers. We took a taxi from the PX. The taxi driver informed us he must first drop off two American soldiers whose clothes were soiled with red dirt. The taxi driver asked Dennis and I if we knew anyone who wanted to buy some cognac. We told him about our landlord who also ran a store. He drove us there, and we asked her if she would like to purchase some good liquor for six dollars a bottle. She agreed to buy it but didn't have any cash on hand. She told me if I'd buy it she would pay me back. I did what she asked and took the cognac to her. The taxi driver left in a hurry. When I brought the liquor to my landlord, she took one look at it and scoffed, "This is nothing but tea and water."

I was shocked. I couldn't figure out why the seal was not broken. I did not like to be played a fool. Here Dennis and I were "stuck" with six bottles of colored water we thought were cognac. I tried to figure out a way to get our money back. I was so upset and insisted Dennis find the taxi drivers who catered to Americans because most of them were con men, and I wouldn't have any regrets if we tried to resell the colored tea water to them. I was ruled by sin. I wanted to get even. Up to this point in my life, I had been surrounded by a corrupt group of hurting people and retaliation was just a way of life.

Dennis sold the cognac to the taxi drivers, but he didn't like being deceitful. He hoped I would just drop it, but I was upset and put pressure on him. He wanted to please me. I didn't want him to go alone because if they discovered the fake cognac, they might beat up Dennis. I sent a boy who was 13 with him. They sold the "tea water" and brought the money back to me. I share this to show how bound by sin I was. Sin will always take you farther than you want to go, and it will make you pay far more than you want to pay.

Looking back, I realize for the first years of my life I was a gentle, sweet girl. Even though my grandmother had to spank me, I knew she loved me and was just trying to make a better person out of me. During those early years, even though I cried and fussed about her discipline, I remained a very innocent child, but when I left home and started socializing with those who were steeped in sin, I mirrored their behavior. I became more angry and frustrated and complained all the time. I became more like the enemy. It reminds me of what God's Word declares:

*Do not be so deceived and misled! Evil companionships (communion, associations) corrupt and deprave good manners and morals and character.*

1 CORINTHIANS 15:33 AMP

When Dennis brought the money back I felt satisfied. Revenge was sweet to me. Oh, how thankful I am to know now about God's love and the laws of His kingdom. I don't know how Dennis could see any good in me, but somehow he did, and I was excited to become Mrs. Dennis Spencer.

## HERE COMES THE BRIDE

In order for us to get married, we had to get permission from Dennis' superiors. He had to meet with several to request permission to marry. Even though no one actually forbid Dennis to marry me, it was obvious they would rather not have him marry a Vietnamese woman. The military always tried to discourage American soldiers from marrying nationals. I believe they felt the longer they could delay a wedding and the closer the time came for the soldier to return to the United States, the more likely he would change his mind and not marry. I thank God Dennis loved me enough to withstand the opposition. He wasn't about to let any delays prevent us from becoming man and wife.

Two months after Dennis' request, the Army informed him they were going to send him home to America four months early and let him out of the Army as part of the United States Troop Reduction in Vietnam. The night Dennis told me the Army wanted to send him home in two weeks was very emotional for both of us. We sobbed as we held each other tightly, wondering if this was the Army's way of preventing us from getting married. I feared Dennis would go back to his country and never return for me. After all, I had experienced abandonment in my life before. Dennis could sense my anxiety and assured me he loved me and would never leave me. He vowed to return for me and Dai Trang.

Dennis went to his superiors to tell them he did not want to go home early or get out of the Army at that time because of our pending wedding plans. He wanted to extend his time in the Army by another six months to ensure we would have plenty of time to get married and have Dai Trang's and my exit visas approved by the Vietnamese government. It took meeting with several of his superiors, but the Army finally agreed to let him stay another six months. The night he came home and told me the Army had agreed to let him stay in Vietnam we were overjoyed, and excitement was in the air. Our marriage was going to become a reality!

Five long months went by and we heard no word from the Army about our permission to marry letter. Every time Dennis would inquire about the status of the important letter, his superiors would say they hadn't received any response yet. After more inquiries, Dennis was finally told we could go to the American Embassy in Saigon and pick up the anticipated letter. When we checked in at the Embassy, we talked to a lady who handled our case.

"Where have you been? How come it took you so long to pick this up?" she asked.

Dennis and I looked at each other and exclaimed, "How long have you had this letter?'

She replied, "For almost six months!"

It confirmed our suspicions. We felt all along the Army was trying to delay our marriage. They must have sensed our resolve and finally realized nothing could prevent us from becoming husband and wife.

We took the letter to the police station and had some papers notarized. The long wait was over. We were now Mr. and Mrs. Dennis Spencer. It was a simple but sacred ceremony for us. We pledged our lives to each other and couldn't wait to start our new life together.

When we arrived home, Dennis picked me up and carried me into the house. I giggled and asked, "What are you doing?"

He told me it was an American custom to carry the bride across the threshold. I giggled and loved him even more for being so patient to teach me his American traditions.

Dennis quickly captured my grandmother's heart, too. When I first met him, he had a very dark tan from being out in the sun for extended hours. He was even darker than me. My grandmother took one look at him and joked, "Mai, with his dark hair and dark skin, he looks like he's Vietnamese." We all laughed, and I knew then Dennis was a permanent member of my family.

It didn't matter to me what nationality Dennis was. I was in love with him and knew I wanted to grow old with him. I made a promise to him that I would be a true and faithful wife. I have kept my promise.

## PROMISE ME

*I promise you, I'll always to be true to you,*
*I promise you, I'll always share your dreams,*
*And as we grow old*
*And our story is told,*
*I'll love you as I've promised you.*
*Promise me, you'll always be true to me,*
*Promise me, you'll always share my dreams,*
*And as we grow old,*
*And our story is told,*
*You'll love me as you've promised me.*

And in just a few years, Dennis and I would make another vow to each other and to God. We promised the Lord we would give our hearts and homes to Him, and we have kept our word.

*Let's promise Him, we'll give our homes to Him,*
*Let's promise Him, a place right from the start,*
*And as we grow old*
*And our story is told,*
*We've loved Him with all of our hearts.*
*I'll love you, as I've promised you,*
*You'll love me, as you've promised, too,*
*We've loved Him as we've promised, too.*

—DIXIE PHILLIPS

# Chapter Ten

# LEFT BEHIND

n August of 1971, Dennis' six months were up and he had to return to the United States. Dai Trang and I could not leave with him because the Vietnamese government had not approved our exit visas. I thought I couldn't bear to be separated from the man I loved, but I was forced to be. Cruel comments were made by people living around me.

Some would say, "Dennis won't write you or keep in touch with you once he gets back to America."

I had already experienced enough rejection in my life. Their words caused my insecurity to kick in full throttle, which drove me to despair. I would try to find comfort remembering past conversations Dennis and I had. They would play over and over in my mind.

"Dennis, when you get back home to America and when you go out with your old friends, will you forget about me?" I whimpered. "Will you still love me?"

Dennis would put his arms around me and reassure me with this soothing promise, "I will never forget about you. I will come back and get you."

Stubbornly I would probe deeper, "What if I won't go with you to the United States?"

Dennis seemed to understand my pain. I didn't mean half of what I said when I was hurting. He knew that and would reply, "I will come back and find you and bring you back to America with me."

I needed constant reassurance because of the distrust clamoring in my soul. I remembered a story Dennis had told me about his father. Questions spilled out of me.

"Do you remember when you told me about your daddy, Dennis, and how he would hit your mom? What if you are like your father. Like father, like son they always say?"

With a twinkle in his eye, Dennis thrust his finger in his chest, "Mai, I am Dennis; I am not Elmer."

I always felt better after we communicated about my fears and insecurities. His patience and sense of humor made me trust him even more.

## PROVISION

Before Dennis left for the United States, he wanted to make sure all my needs were taken care of. He introduced me to one of his buddies, Jerry. Dennis had many friends, but Jerry was the one he chose to watch over me while he was gone. He told him to please provide whatever I needed while he was in America, and he would reimburse him. Jerry was to put Dai Trang and me on the plane and watch us fly out of the Saigon Airport once our passports arrived. Jerry agreed to help me in Dennis' absence. He would always come and check on me and constantly asked me if I needed anything.

After Dennis left, I would use the telephone at the American USO once a week to call him in America. I was able to do this because I had an American-issued ID card stating I was a dependent of a soldier. Every week I would give Dennis an update on the status of our visa requests.

On our last night together, Dennis and I wept bitterly. We knew it was going to be a difficult separation. Dennis attempted to soothe my pain. "Mai, I love you so much. I want to take you to my country to meet my family. They will love you and treat you with respect. Your life will greatly improve. I promise."

I couldn't grasp how much my life would change. I had never been out of Vietnam. All I knew for sure was I loved this man with all my heart, and when he left for America he would be taking half my heart with him. The dreaded day arrived, and I didn't know if we could survive the separation, but we were determined to try.

## GOODBYE

Dennis and I said our final farewells in our home. We were both sobbing. I snipped a lock of his hair and put it in a plastic bag. I kept two of his T-shirts. One I used as a pillowcase, and the other I tucked under my pillow, so every night I could take a deep whiff of his familiar fragrance. It was a comfort to me and made me feel like he was right beside me. Dai Trang and I stayed behind waiting for our passports and visas.

During the month that Dennis was in America, he wrote me a letter every day, but some days I didn't receive a letter from him because it was delayed in the mail for some reason. There were other days when I would pick up my mail, and I would have two or three letters. Oh, I was so excited and couldn't wait to read them. Those letters were a lifeline to our relationship.

While Dennis was in America, he stayed with the Atwoods. These wonderful people had taken Dennis under their wings and loved him through a difficult time in his life. He went to live with them during his parents' divorce. They have been more like family to Dennis than friends. When he arrived back home, they invited him to come and stay with them. He slept on the sofa, strategically placing the telephone next to him so he wouldn't miss my calls.

## SON APPEARS

A short while after Dennis left for America, a taxi pulled up in front of our neighbor's house. I was shocked to see my old boyfriend Son get out of the taxi and walk into his parents' home. I noticed he looked my way and grinned. He spotted Dai Trang playing near me, but he didn't say anything. I loved Dennis, but I was still stinging because Son had abandoned me. We had never had closure from our past relationship. One day he saw me coming out of our house and initiated a conversation. His mother had let him know about Dai Trang and how precious she was. She had also informed him of my recent marriage and decision to move to the United States. He told me about life in the Air Force and expressed his feelings and intentions toward me. I couldn't believe my ears. He wanted me to divorce Dennis with hopes that he and I would pick up where we had left off. It was so strange. I cannot say I didn't have feelings for him, but my love for my husband was much purer and deeper. Even though I wasn't a Christian at that time, I know God had put in my heart a love that was loyal and faithful to my husband. God gave me this gift and enabled me to endure our short separation without weakening.

*Love bears up under anything and everything that comes, is ever ready to believe the best of every person, its hopes are fadeless under all circumstances, and it endures everything [without weakening].*

I told Son our relationship could never be rekindled. I had pledged my love to Dennis. Once Son realized I wasn't changing my mind, he became more concerned about me taking Dai Trang out of the country. This greatly concerned me, and I feared he might attempt to kidnap Dai Trang. I warned my housekeeper and my mother about my fears. They kept a watchful eye on Dai Trang. Son came to visit three or four times while Dennis was gone. I allowed him to see Dai Trang, but I set boundaries and held my ground. I was now a married woman and in love with a handsome American man. My heart was set, and nobody could change my mind.

## IGNORANCE ISN'T BLISS

Even though Dennis and I loved each other with all of our hearts, we had much to learn. As I look back, I have to take most of the blame for our disagreements. I think part of my problem was how I was raised. It's typical of my culture, because of our lack of education, to become part of the problem rather than part of the solution. Because of my ignorance, I was hard on Dennis. I would yell and scream at him in an attempt to control him. It was just like how my grandmother had tried to manipulate me. Dennis loved me even though I was, at times, not very nice to him. I've tried to analyze why I reacted in such an "intense" manner, and the only answer I can come up with is ignorance. I required Dennis' attention all the time. I don't know if it was because I was neglected as a little girl, but I do know in those early years of marriage, I was a "high maintenance" wife. It is only by God's grace that Dennis was patient with me. I would be furious with him over some little thing, and he would come and wrap his arms around me. He seemed to know exactly how to diffuse me. His God-given gift of gentleness is what persuaded me to go with him to his homeland.

## ONLY JESUS CAN SATISFY THE LONGINGS IN YOUR SOUL

There is a beautiful story of a Christian woman who married a godly man. The wife idolized her husband, but after they had been married for a few months, the wife experienced great discontentment. She sought out her mentor and explained the situation. The wife turned to her mentor and asked, "Can you tell me why I am so unhappy?"

The wise, seasoned saint patted the young wife's hand and said, "I think I can. It seems you expect your husband to meet all your needs. That's a heavy load to put on a mere mortal. Only Jesus can satisfy the longings in your soul."

A spiritual arrow pierced the heart of the young woman. She realized the error of her ways and began letting Jesus meet her needs. Her husband was amazed at the transformation that took place.

I was like the young wife, but I wouldn't understand the tremendous demands I was placing on Dennis until Jesus came into my heart. Only then would I experience contentment and receive the inner healing I needed.

*But godliness with contentment is great gain.*

1 TIMOTHY 6:6

## NEW NAME

There is no doubt in my mind Dennis is the man God ordained from the foundations of the world to be my husband. He is the man God showed me in the vision when I was just a young girl. There is a peace in my heart knowing I have married in God's will. It's another indicator of God's great love. Even though Dennis and I weren't Christians yet, God brought us together.

Dennis promised me he would do everything in his power to make me happy. The one pledge he made that deepened my love for him was vowing to be a good father to Dai Trang. He adopted her, and her new name would forever be Terri Lynn Spencer.

## DREAMS

Dennis and I made plans for the day I would arrive in the United States. He was to meet me at the airport and take me to meet his sister in San Francisco. After spending a few days with her, we planned to travel to Missouri to meet his parents. After a few weeks, we were to settle in Apache Junction, Arizona. It was so exciting when we spoke of our dreams for our future. We both expressed an interest in beginning anew and afresh, leaving behind my painful past. We agreed we would not share with people the fact Terri was my daughter from a previous relationship. We would introduce her as "our" firstborn child. We were so naïve, because anyone taking one look at Terri would immediately realize, because of her complexion, eyes and nose that she was Asian. We were determined to convince people she was our biological child. I think we just wanted everyone to treat Terri as our child.

The first item of business on the agenda when Dennis arrived in America was to request his family to always refer to Terri as his biological child and not to mention she was adopted. It was very important to Dennis that Terri would grow up believing he was her father. All of Dennis' family loved and adored Terri, and they kept their promise. As we look back, we see this might not have been the wisest decision we've ever made. Honesty is always the best policy, and we weren't being honest with Terri. At the time it made sense to us, but the Lord wouldn't let us be deceitful. He had a day planned for us to tell Terri the truth, but it would be years down the road. At that point in our lives, all we could think about was being reunited and beginning our new life together.

## GOOD SAMARITAN

When Dennis went back to America, I was given my own personal ID card. This card allowed me to enter American businesses. The first couple of times I used my ID everything was fine, but the third time I showed my ID at the gate I saw two American women standing there. They didn't appear to be military women because they were wearing civilian clothes. After the attack in 1968, it was mandatory for all service personnel to wear their uniforms. One of the women spoke up and said I shouldn't be allowed inside because only Americans were allowed. She was quite adamant and continued her rampage. She pointed out all Vietnamese must obtain permission before they were allowed to enter the premises. It was apparent she didn't know I was an American soldier's wife. She was bold and bossy. She turned to the officer and thundered, "You can't let her go in there. She could be a Viet Cong and set off a bomb and then 'boom' we are all dead."

The officer in charge was very young and intimidated by her forcefulness. He was afraid to let me go in. I attempted to persuade him by saying, "My husband is in the Army."

The woman took my ID card and insisted, "Your husband has been dismissed from the Army. He is no longer in the service anymore. Forget about him. He's already forgotten about you."

They refused to admit me. At this time I didn't know the Lord, but He was watching out for me. He sent a man who had been injured in the war and lost both his legs. He was sitting in a wheelchair. He had a heart to defend the weak. He rolled his wheelchair toward the officer because he overheard the woman scolding me. I'm not sure what all he said, but I don't think it was very nice. He ordered the woman to keep her mouth shut, and then he told the officer he would take full responsibility for me. He insisted they allow me to go inside so I could call my husband. The stranger signed his name on a form that allowed me entrance into the building. I was so affected and hurting from their condescending looks and harsh tones, but God sent this kind man to help a damsel in distress. After I gave my heart to Jesus, I realized this kind man was like the Good Samaritan Jesus spoke about in the Gospel of Luke.

After all the humiliation I went through, this kind man knew I needed something to cheer me up. He took me to the mess hall and ordered a fancy drink with whipped cream on top. He asked me for Dennis' number and even took the time to phone Dennis. It was very unusual for me to have such a helpful friend. I started crying when I chatted with Dennis. He was thousands of miles away, trying to figure out what was wrong with his new bride. I told him I didn't want to live in the United States and pleaded with him to return to Vietnam. He asked me why I had changed my mind. I shared with him about the traumatic incident. He was so sweet to me and replied, "Mai, you ran into a bad person today. Just like in Vietnam, there are some good people and some bad people. You encountered a rotten one, but not everyone is like that."

My spine stiffened, and my stubborn will just wouldn't let go. "No, I am not going. I want to stay in Vietnam because I know the culture of my own people and understand my own language."

My feathers got ruffled, but God gave Dennis a gift for soothing them. God must have known one day Dennis was going to marry one spunky woman. His words calmed my anxious spirit. "Mai, I will protect you. There are wonderful people here. They will like you, and you will like them."

All I needed were his words of assurance. He had, once again, warmed my heart, and I knew I couldn't live without him. If this meant living in a foreign land, then so be it. I was going to be wherever Dennis was.

## FAREWELL

I knew I needed to take a few days to go back to Vung Tau and say goodbye to my grandmother. She was so sad we were moving so far away. She and Terri had spent time together and grown quite attached.

My whole family came and stayed with us a few days before Terri and I left for the United States. The day came for me to go to the airport. Jerry showed up right on time. He fulfilled his promise to Dennis. I was to fly out around eight o'clock. We arrived at the airport in plenty of time. Jerry and I sat and visited. He made some remark that Dennis was probably at the San Francisco airport already. I began to worry. I wondered what would happen if Dennis was late to pick me up. The survival instincts that had been with me in the jungles of Vietnam kicked in. I had to have a Plan B, just in case. I asked Jerry if he had Dennis' sister's phone number.

Jerry laughed. "Don't you worry about a thing, Mai. Dennis will be there. He's so crazy about you I bet he spent the night in the airport to be sure he wouldn't miss you."

Even though Jerry attempted to reassure me, I couldn't rest until I had the phone number in my possession. Once again God was looking out for me.

Terri and I said our farewells to Jerry and boarded the plane. When we arrived in Hong Kong we had a two-hour delay. I couldn't believe my eyes. The airport was enormous and full of people. It was a sight to behold. I had never seen anything like it in all my life. I was mesmerized by what I saw. The old saying is true: You can take the girl out of the country, but you can't take the country out of the girl. I was about to need help, and I wasn't afraid to ask.

When the plane landed in Japan to gas up, a soldier boarded the plane. He sat next to Terri and me. He was so kind to us. He asked me where we were headed. I told him I was going to be reunited with my husband in the United States. Looking back, I realize God was once again watching over me, placing a kind, gentle soul beside me. Back then there were not many Asians who had come to America. I didn't know how to communicate effectively. When Terri and I needed something to eat, I was unsure of how to tell the stewardess what our needs were. The sympathetic soldier spoke for me. I will never forget his kindness to us.

When we arrived in Hawaii, the soldier's wife was there to meet him. He introduced us to her. We said our goodbyes, and Terri and I were off again. This time we were headed to San Francisco.

# Chapter Eleven

# LOST AND FOUND

Terri and I were so excited to finally be in America. I was a little nervous, but knew the minute my eyes caught a glimpse of Dennis, I would be just fine. When we exited the plane, I couldn't find Dennis anywhere. Terri and I found a bench and sat down and waited. I began to realize Dennis and I had had the worst communication disaster of our lives. He thought I was on a certain flight, but I was on a different one. He was waiting at one end of the airport, and Terri and I were waiting at the opposite end. We waited and waited, but there was no sign of Dennis. I started to get really anxious. When Dennis had sent my plane ticket, he tucked in a hundred dollar bill. I gave all but two dollars of it to my mom, thinking I wouldn't possibly need that much money. After two hours, Terri asked for something to eat. A kind woman was seated next to us on the bench. She watched Terri, while I went to the food court and bought a hamburger and drink for her. She was starving and gobbled it down. I didn't know what to do, but I found a stewardess and asked her to call Dennis. She tried, but couldn't reach him. After a little more time passed, I remembered I had my new sister-in-law's phone number. I hurried to the phone booth and picked up the telephone. Jerry had given me instructions on calling collect. I kept dialing the phone number over and over, but it wouldn't go through. An operator kept coming on the line. I told her I was trying to reach my sister-in-law Lois, but she didn't seem to understand me. Finally, after about the tenth attempt, she realized I was from a different country and needed assistance. She reached Lois, and I was so thankful. Lois explained to her I had just arrived in America from Vietnam. I was relieved when Lois assured me Dennis was at the airport. She suggested we page him.

I smiled as the announcement came over the intercom, "Mr. Dennis Spencer, would you please call your sister?"

Lois gave me specific instructions. "Mai, don't you go anywhere. Dennis will come and pick you up. Stay put."

I might not have been able to understand much English, but I understood her important instructions. I was determined to obey them implicitly.

## DAMSEL IN DISTRESS

The simplest tasks were difficult for me because I had never had exposure to all the luxuries of America. After the phone call to Lois, I attempted to put the phone back on the hook, but it kept slipping off. I would pick it up and try again to place it back on its cradle. It dropped off again. I was so embarrassed. I watched when other people finished talking. They just hung up the phone. I tried to copy them, but I couldn't figure it out. I was smart enough to realize I couldn't just leave the receiver dangling in midair. Humility is a virtue. I decided I needed help. It always seemed to work for me in Vietnam. About that time, a janitor walked by. I motioned for him to show me how to hang the phone up. With a single swoop of his hand, he hung up the phone. I couldn't believe my eyes. He turned and walked away. I went to the phone and tried to figure out what I did wrong. I immediately saw my problem. I was trying to hang the phone upside down. The janitor smiled. He knew I was the new kid on the block and took pride in helping a damsel in distress.

While I was learning the art of hanging up telephones, Dennis was calling Lois to find out exactly where Terri and I were. Dennis walked up behind us, but he didn't see us. He was carrying a big teddy bear. My heart started to race.

"Dennis!" I screamed.

He couldn't hear me. I'm sure I was the only Asian woman in the airport. I kept hollering, "Dennis! Dennis!"

Finally, he spotted us. He ran over and hugged us. We wept for joy. We were so happy to be reunited.

When Terri saw Dennis, she hung on his neck and looked like a little monkey. She grabbed his hand and hopped on his lap. She wasn't afraid to be close to Dennis because of the nurturing love he had showered upon her. Once again, I thought of my childhood. I never knew my father, and my little girl was so blessed to have a caring father watching over her.

After we greeted each other, we took our luggage to the car. He walked us past some old clunker and he'd tease, "This is our new car."

In Vietnam they don't have many cars, but the ones they have are nice and clean, even if they are old.

"I thought you told me you had a new car," I replied.

He would just laugh. He has always had a great sense of humor.

Finally we walked toward a new Ford Mustang. "This is our new car," Dennis said. I knew this time he was telling the truth. We got in, and it felt so right. We were finally together as a family, just like we had dreamed.

We drove back to Lois' house. We stayed three days with her. She welcomed me and treated me with the utmost respect. Her husband J. D. was so funny and friendly. He didn't know how to eat anything except Spam and hamburger. I fixed Asian food, and his taste buds were transformed. He began to enjoy a variety of foods. To this day, whenever we go to their home for a visit, he always puts in his menu request. He loves it when I make Asian food.

As I met my new family, I couldn't help but compare my experience in Vietnam with Son's sister. I really can't say she was mean to me, but she certainly didn't treat me with love and respect like Dennis' sister did. A warm welcome was extended to me. I knew they accepted me like family. We stayed with Lois for a few days. They managed an apartment complex. They had a vacant apartment where Dennis, Terri and I could stay while we were visiting.

## TOGETHER AGAIN

Dennis and I were overjoyed to be reunited. It was like a second honeymoon for us. We had a lot of catching up to do, and we didn't take being together for granted. How thankful we were to be a family again.

Terri was just as excited as I was to be reunited with her daddy. When Dennis left Vietnam, Terri was about two. I thought she might need some time to get reacquainted with him when we arrived in America, but she just picked up where their relationship left off. When Dennis was still in Vietnam, he would ride a motorcycle home from work around six o'clock. When Terri heard the engine, she ran and opened the door. When Dennis came into the house, he would pick her up, kiss her and carry her around. It did get a little confusing for Terri's toddler mind when she heard other motorcycles. She would squeal, "Daddy's come home!" She'd run to the door to try to catch a glimpse of him. When she didn't see him anywhere, she'd hang her head and sigh. "Oh, Mommy, Daddy not come home."

## NOSEY NEIGHBOR

During our visit with Lois and her family, we noticed one of their neighbors always had her drapes closed. From time to time, we would see her peeking through the pulled drapes, watching our every move. There were a few times I saw her staring at me with a strange look on her face. It made me feel uncomfortable. Even though I wasn't fluent in English, God had blessed me with an internal antenna. At times it would warn me of danger, but this time, I knew this woman was prejudiced. My feelings were confirmed when I heard Lois and Dennis talking. Lois shared how this neighbor had voiced her opinion about how terrible she thought it was of Dennis to bring me to a strange land. She felt, no matter how hard I tried, I would never fit into American society. She went on to say how it would have been better, if Dennis wanted to marry an Asian girl, if he lived with her in Vietnam. Of course Dennis protected me from her poisonous venom. He didn't let me know all she had said.

## MRS. ATWOOD TO THE RESCUE

When we left Lois and her family, Dennis was excited to travel to Apache Junction, Arizona and introduce me to Mr. and Mrs. Atwood, the couple Dennis lived with when his parents were going through their divorce. When I walked into the Atwoods' home, I was immediately surrounded with love and acceptance. Mrs. Atwood welcomed me with open arms. She taught me more in our short time together than I had ever learned from anyone else in my life. I wanted to learn how to cook American dishes, and it was Mrs. Atwood to the rescue. She even gave me helpful hints on taking better care of Terri and Dennis. I will never forget the loving way she mentored me.

## WEDDING RECEPTION

Dennis was born in Missouri, and his mother and many other relatives still lived in Lexington. After our visit with the Atwoods, Dennis took us there. When we arrived, we were amazed. His grandmother and mother prepared a beautiful wedding reception and invited friends and relatives to come out and congratulate us. They worked hard and made us feel so special. People showed up with armloads of presents for us. When we arrived in Missouri, we only had a suitcase or two filled with clothes and necessities, but when we left, our car was loaded down with presents. In fact, we even had to ship the gifts we didn't have room for back to Apache Junction. We didn't need to buy anything for several months because of the generosity of Dennis' family.

## MY FIRST CHRISTMAS

We chose to settle in Apache Junction. We lived off our savings and were in desperate need of a job. The Lord was so faithful to us even though we didn't have a personal relationship with Him. He provided a wonderful job for Dennis. We had to pinch pennies because some weeks there wasn't enough for us to pay all the bills, but we were so thankful Dennis had employment. I wanted to send gifts home to Vietnam to my grandmother and family, but in the early years of our marriage, I couldn't because we were just getting established. In Vietnam, there is an assumption that all Americans are prosperous. Family members expect presents. In those early years, we didn't have anything to send back. I tried to not let it bother me because I knew, once we were financially able, we would send money and gifts to my family.

Our first Christmas in America was in Apache Junction. It was an experience I will never forget. I said goodbye to the Dauchai trees of the jungles in Vietnam and hello to the beautiful, white artificial Christmas trees.

Dennis' mother and sisters sent us boxes of presents. We opened package after package. We giggled as we opened one gift after another. Even little Terri had numerous gifts. I was in awe of how simple presents could make me feel loved and welcomed into the family. What a stark contrast to the poverty and rejection I had felt in Vietnam. As I opened each gift, I couldn't help but think of my mother and grandmother. I wanted them to experience the material blessings I was experiencing.

## THE LAST WORD IN LONESOME IS ME

Before I came to America, I would often imagine how I would feel being so far from my family and homeland. I was determined I wouldn't be overcome with homesickness. I had a plan to keep myself super busy, but when I arrived, even though Dennis' family extended love and warmth to me, I still felt like an outsider. I didn't understand the language very well, and there were no other Vietnamese people. Not only did I have to become familiar with the language and customs, but American food is not like Vietnamese food. I craved the familiar foods I had grown up on. To add to my heartache, Dennis would have to work, which left Terri and me to entertain ourselves all day. I attempted to fight my homesickness by replacing lonesomeness with busyness. I wrote two or three letters every day. When Dennis had a day off, we would go to the post office and mail them. But no matter how active I was, I was drowning in a sea of despair. When I was young and missed my grandmother or mother, I would quit my job, even if I had only worked for a few months, and go see them. I didn't see any possible way for me to relieve the ache in my heart. I lived too far away and couldn't bear the thought of being away from Dennis.

A year went by, and I was still suffering greatly with lonesomeness for my homeland and my people. To make matters worse, I thought I might be pregnant. It was bittersweet to me. I was happy to be having a baby with the man I loved, but there was something about the pregnancy that made me want to be near my grandmother and mother even more. Dennis was so compassionate and realized what a difficult transition I was having. My homesickness was a frequent topic of conversation around our house. Dennis is also a fixer. He rolls up his sleeves and thinks of ways to solve the problems. He decided to apply for jobs in Vietnam. He wrote over twenty letters to different companies, but everyone was getting ready to pull out of Vietnam and come back to America. In the midst of my pain, I made an appointment to see my doctor. She confirmed my suspicion: I was pregnant. Dennis was so happy. He hugged me and almost danced with delight. There was something in the way Dennis reacted to the pregnancy that settled me down. My homesickness and anxiety lessened. I realized our baby was going to be born in America, and this was my home now. After I became a Christian,

I read in the Old Testament about a woman named Ruth who followed her mother-in-law to a foreign land and made a similar consecration.

*But Ruth replied, "Don't urge me to leave you or to turn back from you. Where you go I will go, and where you stay I will stay. Your people will be my people and your God my God."*

RUTH 1:16

Oh, how thankful I am God brought Dennis into my life. How blessed I am to live in America, where someone shared the gospel with me. I can say with sincerity to my husband, "Your people are my people, and your God is my God."

## TEARS ARE A LANGUAGE GOD UNDERSTANDS

Even though I was more content, from time to time I still experienced waves of homesickness. Fortunately, it was never as severe as those early months and it seemed to reappear whenever Dennis and I had a misunderstanding or when I missed my mother and grandmother. I learned a little secret. If I could find a private place and cry, I would feel better.

There was a secluded place in the desert where I took Terri. I would build a fire and sit and cry. I've heard people say tears are a language God understands. Somehow He saw my pitiful state, and in the best way I knew how, I reached out to Him, even though I didn't personally know Him. He saw my tears. His Word tells us He keeps track of all our sorrows. When He was on the Cross, I was on His mind, but I wouldn't accept His love for me yet. He didn't give up on me though. He kept wooing me and waiting to gain entrance into my heart. How thankful I am for His amazing grace.

*You keep track of all my sorrow. You have collected all my tears in your bottle. You have recorded each one in your book.*

PSALM 56:8 NLT

# BABIES

he doctor had given us June 27, 1972, as an approximate due date for the arrival of our little bundle from Heaven. As my pregnancy was nearing the end, I became more dependent upon Dennis. He and Terri were my world. I can remember watching the hands of the clock on the wall in our living room. I could hardly wait for Dennis to get off work. There were many times Dennis would be the only adult I would talk to all day. Most days he was home right after work, but he is such a social butterfly. God has gifted him with such a love for people. His friendships mean so much to him, and there were a few times he would go visit a buddy or two after work. I don't know if my pregnancy made me more sensitive, but one day after Dennis clocked out of work, he didn't come straight home. I kept watching for him, and I waited and waited. He had visited his friends other times, and my feelings may have been slightly hurt, but this time I was starting to get really upset. It was the early evening of my due date. I had fixed a nice meal and, dreamer that I am, I had some high expectations of enjoying a lovely evening with my husband. Everything would have been wonderful except for one minor detail: Dennis didn't show up. Terri and I kept looking for him. I tried to think how I could reach him, but I couldn't figure out a way. I didn't know it then, but the next day our baby would be born, which could be part of the reason why I was so emotionally dependent on Dennis. I'm sure I was experiencing a hormonal imbalance of some kind. After a couple hours of watching and waiting, Dennis came waltzing through the door. I was so distraught, I just exploded. I informed him I was done, and he needed to purchase a plane ticket pronto. I would return to Vietnam as soon as possible. I will never forget the look on his face. He tried to calm me down and asked why I was so angry. Once again Dennis knew how to diffuse me. He spoke gently to me, but I was too far gone. I couldn't stop crying. He promised me he would be more sensitive to my needs and would come right home after work. Our romantic dinner was ruined. There was no way I could eat, and my outburst ruined any appetite Dennis might have had. I stormed off to the bedroom and cried. I couldn't stop. Dennis tried to comfort me, but no matter what he did or how much he apologized, I still couldn't stop wailing. He kept rubbing my back, trying to comfort me. He realized I was experiencing an emotional meltdown and did his best to calm me. He had never seen me this hysterical before. He knelt by the bed and said, "Honey, I am really sorry. I didn't mean to hurt you. I promise you I will never do this again."

By this time, it was about nine o'clock at night. I could tell he was very sincere, and I began to respond. We stayed awake until the wee hours of the morning, reassuring each other and making a fresh commitment to stay emotionally connected. I felt so blessed to have an understanding husband who was sympathetic to my needs.

After we fell asleep, I was awakened through the night with mild contractions. At times they became quite uncomfortable. I waited for a little bit, but then it became clear our baby was on its way. I woke up Dennis and said, "I think the baby is going to come today."

Dennis got up, took a shower and shaved. I was having labor pains seven minutes apart. Someone advised us when my labor pains were five minutes apart we should head to the hospital. It took about twenty minutes from Apache Junction to Mesa General Hospital. We dropped Terri off at Mrs. Atwood's and hurried to the hospital, where I was admitted. As my labor progressed, Dennis was right by my side. All my dreams and hopes came true as he supported me through the birth of our child. I couldn't help but remember a few years before when I gave birth to Terri and how different my life had been. I was alone and abandoned, but with this baby, the father of my child stayed right beside me, holding my hand and sharing the pain and joy of each moment with me. I realize I didn't yet know Jesus as my personal Savior, but He still heard and answered my prayers by giving me a husband who was committed to me and our children. A few hours after I was admitted, our son Timothy Troy Spencer was born. We were overjoyed as we examined every inch of him. He had dark skin like me, but when I looked into his eyes, I saw his daddy. Dennis' feet hardly touched the ground. He was thrilled to have a son. Something was permanently settled in my heart after Timmy's birth. I knew Dennis' home was my home. Even though I missed my grandmother and mother, my first priority was to my American family. I accepted my place. Amy Carmichael, a missionary to India in the early 1900s, said, "In acceptance lies peace." When I accepted my circumstances, I no longer experienced such tormenting homesickness. The intense "tug-of-war" in my soul subsided. My restlessness was replaced with a deep sense of belonging.

## JEALOUS SIBLING

After a brief hospital stay, Timmy and I went home to a houseful of family and friends. Everyone was so kind and seemed excited to meet our baby boy. Everyone, that is, except Terri. She was jealous of her little brother. When we laid Timmy on the bed next to her, she took a quick look at him and then turned her face to the wall. Dennis was the first to notice Terri's intense struggle. He picked her up in his arms and assured her, "Terri, no matter how many babies we have, there is enough room in our hearts for you."

Dennis' bigheartedness reminds me of a little country saying: When God's love reigns in a home, the walls are made of elastic.

It seemed I learned so much as I watched Dennis interact with our children. I had seven younger siblings, and there wasn't one person who told me there was enough room in their heart for all of us children. I counted my blessings and marveled that God had given me such a special husband and father to my children.

The Lord kept blessing us. As our little family was growing, our financial needs were growing, too. The Lord had it all under control. Dennis received a promotion at A. J. Bayless, a supermarket chain. God was taking good care of us.

## BABY FEVER

Dennis and his high school friend Leroy joined the Army together. Leroy married Kathy, and when Leroy and Dennis finished their military service, we bought a house next to them. Terri was a year younger than their little girl Jennifer. They were such a blessing in our lives. We would picnic together, and our children would have so much fun playing. Leroy and Kathy had a new baby boy, Jason. The first time I saw their tiny son, I was stricken with "baby fever." Timmy was about three years old at this time. I went home and told Dennis of my new malady. He agreed with me. A new baby would be a great addition to our family. I went to the doctor, and to my delight he announced, "Mrs. Spencer, you are pregnant." Dennis and I were so excited. We thought life just couldn't get any better.

## DOUBLE BLESSING

At the time of my pregnancy, I weighed one hundred pounds sopping wet. I am only five-foot-two inches tall. I'm proof that dynamite can come in small packages! As the pregnancy progressed, my belly swelled to enormous proportions. If I sat in a chair, it was very difficult for me to get up. It seemed to me that I was much larger than when I was pregnant with Terri or Timmy. I thought for sure this baby was going to be our biggest.

On the morning of June 18, 1976, I woke up early to help Dennis straighten his wavy hair. While I was standing working on his hair, I felt my first contraction. I winced and said to him, "I think our baby will come today."

Dennis smiled and said, "No, honey, you still have a month to go. Remember what we learned at our prenatal classes. You are probably experiencing the false labor pains that happen in the final weeks. I remember them warning us about that."

A few minutes later, I experienced another contraction. I told him again that it felt like I might be having the baby that day. He could tell by the look on my face I was serious. One of Dennis' job responsibilities was opening the store. We talked it over and felt he had ample time to head to the supermarket and open. If my contractions continued, I would call him. After he left, I started doubting if I was really in labor or if it was just Braxton Hicks contractions. Not wanting to be alone, I decided to call one of my girlfriends to come over until I knew for sure what was going on. By the time she arrived I was pretty miserable. I was lying on the couch writhing in pain. She had been trying for years to have a baby but was unable to conceive. After assessing my condition, she felt I should phone my doctor and explain my condition—plus request an appointment for her to find out why she had been unable to get pregnant. I was in no condition to argue with her. A friendly nurse answered the phone, and I explained my situation and then requested an appointment for my friend. I was shocked when the nurse informed me they were having a slow day at the office. If my girlfriend came in immediately, she could be examined by the doctor. I hung up the phone and told my girlfriend she should head over to the clinic. I also asked her to tell the doctor I was having some pretty intense contractions. She promised she would and flew out the door. I think my friend was so obsessed with her infertility, she didn't realize I was about to give birth. The Lord knew how clueless I was and sent my stepmother-in-law Dorothy. She "just happened" to drop in. (After I gave my heart to Jesus, I stopped believing in coincidences.) I know the Lord was watching over me and sent Dorothy to my door. Just as she entered the house, I had another contraction. I was so uncomfortable and moaned, "I think this baby is going to come today."

Dorothy looked at me with panic in her eyes and said, "Mai, you better get up and get ready. I'll get you to the hospital."

I must have been in complete denial because I told her I needed to fold a basket of laundry first. She looked at me in disbelief. When I stood up, my water broke and the intensity of the contractions increased. I knew this was the real deal. Dorothy took Terri and Timmy and buckled them into the back seat. I hurried to the bedroom to change my clothes. I called Dennis at work and told him I was hurting too much for this to be false labor. I had another contraction. I never even hung up the phone but dropped it and hurried to the car. On the way to the hospital, I knew the baby's birth was imminent. In between contractions, I became keenly aware Dorothy was having trouble finding the right road to the hospital. I pleaded with her to please put the emergency flashers on. She was so nervous and wrapped up trying to find the street, she forgot to do so. I looked out the window and saw a policeman. I thought he could help us get to the hospital faster. I called out, "Dorothy, there's the police. Do you have your flashers on?"

She replied, "Oh no, I forgot to turn on the emergency lights, but I have my headlights on."

I was in too much pain to even respond. About that time, she squealed, "We're on the right road. I see the hospital."

She pulled the car right up in front of the hospital. I hollered, "I think the baby is coming."

A nurse ran out to meet us and said, "Step on out, honey."

I shook my head. I couldn't move. A man came with a stretcher and carried me in through the double doors to the delivery room. Another nurse looked down at me and asked, "Do you want me to call your husband?"

I answered, "Yes."

The nurses kept insisting, "Wait for Dr. Jenkins. He's almost here."

The minute the doctor walked in the door, the baby was born. He rushed over to catch our newborn baby girl, Michelle Ann Spencer. I sighed, thinking everything was over, but Dr. Jenkins tapped on my tummy and held up two fingers and exclaimed, "Two babies!"

Another contraction hit me. Five minutes later, another baby girl, Brenda Kay Spencer, was born. I was thrilled to have twin daughters. In Asian culture, twins represent a type of blessing on the family.

By the time Dennis arrived at the hospital, I had already given birth to Brenda and Michelle. We had it planned that he would be in the delivery room with me, but our baby girls had other ideas. A nurse took him down a hallway, showed him a room, and asked him to wash his hands and put on scrubs over his clothes. After he finished the medical protocol, he walked out into the hallway. A nurse came around the corner holding Brenda. Dennis told her who he was and asked if this was his newborn daughter. The nurse smiled and said, "She is *one* of them."

Dennis was shocked and replied, "What do you mean she is *one* of them?"

The nurse smiled again and told Dennis to go to the delivery room, and the doctor would explain everything. Dennis hurried to find me. I looked up at him and told him we were the parents of twin daughters. We were elated and shocked at the same time. Never once during the pregnancy did the doctor mention the possibility of twins. Michelle weighed less than two pounds, and Brenda weighed around three pounds.

## BAD NEWS

Our celebration came quickly to an end when we were informed that preemies can develop serious complications. Brenda and Michelle were no
exception. They needed to be transferred to the Neonatal Intensive Care
Unit at Saint Joseph's Hospital in Phoenix. There were pediatricians there
who were trained and equipped in saving the lives of preemies. We hurried
to the nursery to say goodbye to Brenda and Michelle. We peeked through
the window and saw our two tiny daughters in incubators. More medical
experts had been called to examine them. We realized they needed the best
care available, and that was in Phoenix. Dennis stayed with me for a little
while, but we both agreed he needed to be with our babies. He kissed me
goodbye and hurried to be with them.

Three days later, I was dismissed from the hospital. Dennis came and
took me to see Brenda and Michelle. Because of their delicate condition, we
were not allowed to hold them for four weeks. The incubators they were in
had openings on the side where we put our hands through and touched
them. They were so tiny and so precious.

Brenda was released from the hospital after a month, but Michelle had
to stay for two months. The doctors and nurses insisted Michelle couldn't
go home until she weighed at least five pounds. At seven weeks, she weighed
four pounds and five ounces. They felt she was making progress and decided
to let us take her home. Dennis and I felt Michelle had some medical issues
and even questioned her pediatrician about her eating habits. It would take
her two hours to drink one ounce of formula. Her doctor calmed our fears
when he told us that this was common preemie behavior. He assured us
Michelle would eventually grow out of it. We felt relieved. We brought her
home and were so thankful to finally have our four children all together
under one roof. It was a very busy time, but Dennis and I enjoyed every
minute.

When Michelle had her six-month birthday, she started crying one
night. No matter how much we tried to comfort her, she would not stop
crying. We knew immediately something was drastically wrong. We took
her to our pediatrician, and he listened to her heart and lungs. We never
dreamed she was terminally ill, but he looked at us and gave a grim diag-

nosis: pulmonary hypertension. Our beautiful baby girl also had a hole in her heart and only a few months to live. We were in shock and couldn't believe what the doctor was telling us. Dennis wrapped his arms around me, and we wept. We were devastated. At that time, we didn't know Jesus, so I didn't pray to Him. Oh, how I wish I had known Him. He would have come and helped us, but instead, I turned to the god of my childhood, Buddha. I purchased a two-foot tall Pha Thich Ca Buddha from a pottery shop and placed it next to my smaller Happy Buddha. In the center of our house, I built an altar in front of these two false gods. I knew the central location had significance. It represented us giving Buddha a place of honor in our home. I went through all the motions and rituals of lighting incense and praying to Buddha, just like my grandmother had taught me. Dennis and I bowed to Buddha and asked him to heal Michelle.

## THE HOLY BIBLE

While we were facing our baby's terminal illness, God brought a Catholic Vietnamese couple, Mr. and Mrs. Nam Nguyen, into our lives. Of course, we were clueless to the fact that God had orchestrated this meeting. He was working behind the scenes to draw our hearts to Himself, but hindsight is always 20/20. When we look back now, we realize this was a pivotal point in our lives. God was going to place into our hands, through this Catholic couple, the Book that would point us to the true God. Mr. and Mrs. Nam had experienced many adversities in their own lives. While living in Vietnam, they had feared for their existence. They became "Boat People" and fled to escape the oppression and poverty of their homeland. Because of their past pain, they were broken and very compassionate. In 1976, there were few Vietnamese in Arizona. I was very thankful the day they came to visit us. Mr. Nam saw how deathly ill Michelle was. He asked if it would be all right if he and his wife became Michelle's godparents. They promised to take their role seriously and faithfully intercede and pray to Mother Mary for her healing. We were desperate and thought if praying to Mother Mary would do any good, then they should pray to her. We agreed to allow them to be her godparents.

I had many conversations with them about their religion. They encouraged me to learn more about the Catholic Church. I teased them and told them I would never leave my Buddha and follow their Jesus. I guess they saw I really wasn't open to their beliefs, so they didn't pursue religious conversations with me again. I think they saw we were hurting, too, because of Michelle's delicate condition. They asked their Catholic priest to come and visit us. I barely remember the visit. I have absolutely no recollection of him praying with us for our terminally ill baby. The one memory that is etched in my mind is the single act of kindness Mr. Nam bestowed upon me. In the years to come, this one generous gift would change my life forever. He gave me a New Testament in Vietnamese. He asked me to read it and told me I would find the stories fascinating.

I was curious about this new Book. It was the first Bible I had ever seen. In 1976, there were very few books written in the Vietnamese language. I was growing older and was far away from my people, my country, my culture, my food and my language. Any books I read in my native tongue were precious to me and gave me a touch of nostalgia. I read through the Bible twice. I didn't grasp much of what I read except these two things: First, Jesus was the Son of God and, second, Jesus was the Savior of the world. When I look back, I think I was earnestly longing for something to believe in. I wanted to find a god who could help me carry my heavy burdens, and I wanted him to heal our baby daughter.

A few weeks later, Mr. Nam came to visit me. He asked if I had read the Bible. I told him I had read it twice. He asked what I thought of it. I told him I didn't understand much of what I read, but I did find it a little bit interesting. He made a prophetic statement that would one day come to pass: Mai, I believe before you leave this world by death, you will come to know the Lord Jesus.

At that time I had no clue what he was talking about, but now I realize he had great confidence in God's Word producing fruit in my life. He knew the scripture in Isaiah that teaches God's Word shall not return empty-handed, but produce a mighty harvest.

*I don't think the way you think. The way you work isn't the way I work.*
*For as the sky soars high above earth, so the way I work surpasses the*

*way you work, and the way I think is beyond the way you think. Just as rain and snow descend from the skies and don't go back until they've watered the earth, Doing their work of making things grow and blossom, producing seed for farmers and food for the hungry. So will the words that come out of my mouth not come back empty-handed. They'll do the work I sent them to do, they'll complete the assignment I gave them.*

ISAIAH 55:8–11 MSG

Even though I didn't comprehend what Mr. Nam was trying to teach me, my ignorance didn't hinder his prophetic word from being fulfilled. Little by little, God peeled away the layers of sin that had blinded me for years. I have learned a valuable lesson from my own personal experience. There are some souls who come to Jesus and are instantly transformed, but there are others, like me, who come to the Lord inch by inch. The prophet Isaiah teaches that precept must be upon precept and line upon line. Jesus never gives up on a soul. He keeps drawing their heart and wooing until the light of His love dawns upon their soul. How thankful I am Jesus was patient with me.

*For precept must be upon precept, precept upon precept; line upon line, line upon line; here a little, and there a little.*

ISAIAH 28:10 KJV

There's a Christian chorus that says it this way:

*Little by little He's changing me,*
*Line upon line He's teaching me,*
*Precept upon precept until all can see,*
*It is Jesus! He's changing me.*

I once was lost, but now I'm found. Hallelujah! I am living proof that God's Word does not return void. He took me from disgrace to His grace. When I think back on Mr. Nam giving me that New Testament, it gives me strength to believe for others who seem disinterested in the ways of the Lord. We must never give up on them, but keep praying and loving them into the Kingdom. We must have faith for others. There are times I meet strangers in the store and I feel a gentle nudge from the Holy Spirit to share Jesus' love with them. They might not know Him, but that doesn't discourage me. I realize I might not be the one to lead them to Christ, but I can be part of the process. God promises to do the rest. I can be part of what the Holy Spirit is building in their soul. They might want to pray to accept Christ that day or it might be five years later, but this one truth I know: Jesus never fails and His Word will not return empty. He may choose to use me to water the seed one time and plant the seed the next, but it is God who makes spiritual truth grow in the hearts of men and women.

*For when one says, "I follow Paul," and another, "I follow Apollos," are you not mere men? What, after all, is Apollos? And what is Paul? Only servants, through whom you came to believe—as the Lord has assigned to each his task. I planted the seed, Apollos watered it, but God made it grow. So neither he who plants nor he who waters is anything, but only God, who makes things grow.*

1 CORINTHIANS 3:4–7

Mr. Nam did not introduce me to a personal relationship with Jesus, but he did introduce me to the Jesus of the Bible. Those fertile seeds had been planted in my heart. They just needed time to produce fruit. We continued to be friends with Mr. and Mrs. Nam, but a few years later they moved to Texas. We lost contact with each other. I am trusting that one day we will meet again and I can share with him that his prophetic word came true. I came to know the Lord Jesus before I left this world by death.

I tucked the New Testament Mr. Nam had given me away in my storage box. We moved numerous times, and every time we moved, I would give away many different items I didn't think we needed anymore, but I never gave away Mr. Nam's New Testament. I might not have read it for several years, but there was something inside me that wouldn't let me part with the precious Book.

## TAKING BUDDHAS DOWN

Looking back, I believe reading Mr. Nam's New Testament brought light to my soul. It was very similar to what happened in creation. God moved upon the darkness and said, "Let there be light."

My soul was in darkness. When I read the sacred Scriptures, the Holy Spirit moved on my darkened soul and said, "Let there be light."

*And the earth was without form, and void; and darkness was upon the face of the deep. And the Spirit of God moved upon the face of the waters. And God said, Let there be light: and there was light.*

GENESIS 1:2, 3 KJV

After I read the New Testament, something changed in my heart. Suddenly I felt uncomfortable having idols in our home. I took down my Buddha statue and threw it in the trash. I placed the garbage bag on the sidewalk to be picked up and taken away. There was a stirring in my soul for truth. I could have given the statue to a friend, but I felt I was to get rid of it once and for all. How I longed to speak to someone about the one true God, but I didn't know how to even initiate a conversation about spiritual matters. Light was pouring into my soul. The Holy Spirit was trying to teach me Buddha was a false god. He was only a good man, not the Savior of the world. He didn't die for my sins. There's a Buddhist Vietnamese saying, "Ta khong phai la nguoi dem chan ly den, ma ta la nguoi di tiem chan ly." Translated, Buddha is saying, "I am not the one who brings the truth, but I go to seek the truth."

As I read from Mr. Nam's New Testament—I didn't realize it then, but I know it now—the Holy Spirit was trying to be my Teacher and bring truth to my hungry heart.

*But the Comforter (Counselor, Helper, Intercessor, Advocate, Strengthener, Standby), the Holy Spirit, Whom the Father will send in My name [in My place, to represent Me and act on My behalf], He will teach you all things.*

JOHN 14:26 AMP

*As for you, the anointing you received from him remains in you, and you do not need anyone to teach you. But as his anointing teaches you about all things and as that anointing is real, not counterfeit—just as it has taught you, remain in him.*

I John 2:27

Throwing a statue of Buddha in the garbage would be considered blasphemy to a Buddhist. Now that I am a believer, I can see this was a pivotal point in my life, but I still didn't know how to take the final step toward salvation. The Holy Spirit continued to call me to the foot of the Cross. Even though I wasn't saved, there was a conviction in my soul to put away any idols in my home. From that day on, I never brought another idol into my home. I would do like Asa in 2 Chronicles and remove all the detestable idols.

*When Asa heard this message from Azariah the prophet, he took courage and removed all the detestable idols from the land of Judah and Benjamin and in the towns he had captured in the hill country of Ephraim. And he repaired the altar of the Lord, which stood in front of the entry room of the Lord's Temple.*

2 Chronicles 15:8 nlt

## Safe in the Arms of Jesus

Timmy was just a little boy in kindergarten when Michelle was dying. He had such a tender heart and was so concerned for his baby sister. The minute he came home from school, he started dropping a trail of stuff behind him. He dropped his sweater, backpack and lunch box as he headed straight to Michelle's bed. He would take her hands, pull her up and talk to her. Michelle loved him and always responded. They had a special bond.

The dreaded day came, just like the doctor had warned us. Michelle grew weaker and died. I was grief-stricken. Even though I had Brenda, my arms and heart ached for Michelle.

I found the best way for me to deal with my grief was busyness. If I filled my schedule with activities, I had less time to be consumed with the loss of our baby girl. I signed up for an English class twice a week and began to absorb as much as I could about the English language.

# THE FALL OF SAIGON

❧

On April 30, 1975, I turned on the television and was appalled to see Saigon had fallen. The North had taken over the South. With American fighter planes flying overhead and Marines standing guard on the ground, Americans fled the city by helicopter. This evacuation took more than nineteen hours. Saigon residents panicked, storming the United States Embassy in search of refuge. I was devastated and called some of my Vietnamese girlfriends who had married American men, and invited them to come to my house and watch the newscast with me. We scanned all the Vietnamese faces on the television, hoping to catch a glimpse of some of our family members. I couldn't help but think of the many times I had prayed for my family to come and live in the U.S. I remembered writing a letter to my mom in 1973. Sharing from my heart, I told her how I wished I had enough money to bring each family member to America. I knew my mom was looking for a way of escape, but we just didn't have the funds. Just a few months later, my girlfriends and I felt there was a good possibility we might not ever see our families again. The Communist rule would not let any news leak out as to the condition of Vietnamese citizens. My dream of bringing them all to the States was crumbling. I felt completely hopeless. We sat and cried as we watched the communistic horror unfold before our eyes. Within one month, Saigon's name was changed to Ho Chi Minh City. The Vietnam War was over at last.

## THE TELEGRAM

In 1978, I received a telegram from my mom. Dennis and I were skeptical of it at first because we had heard of so many scams where people preyed on family members in the United States whose family were still in Vietnam. We decided to send a telegram back to my mom and ask her personal questions about my childhood. I knew if it was really my mom she would answer the questions correctly. In a few days, we received another telegram from her with the correct answers.

The telegram was quite lengthy. I had a difficult time deciphering it because there were no spaces between the words. I was aware how fortunate I was to receive any news from Vietnam; it was almost impossible because of the militant government. The thought crossed my mind that the telegram was possibly written in code. At that time, people were fleeing the country and crying out for help. I hoped my mother wasn't in that number. I found a quiet spot and attempted to read the telegram. My mother started by giving me an update on our family. She said they were doing well, and she was especially lonesome for me. A wave of sadness swept over me as I continued to read her words. She told me she was crying a lot and hoped to see me at least one more time before she died. She spoke of the difficult time the family was going through because there was no food in the South. When I read about the hunger they were experiencing, I thought my heart would break in two. She asked me to send $5,000 to Hong Kong. She pleaded with me to help get them out of the country. After I read of all the pain my family was enduring under communistic control, I couldn't function. I walked around like a zombie. How could I eat when I knew my people were hungry? How could I smile when my people were depressed and hurting? I was heartbroken. When Dennis came home, I shared the news from the telegram. He was very understanding. When he saw I was in deep emotional pain, he hurt for me. We tried to think of a way to help my family financially. We didn't have any extra money at the time because we were in the process of building a new home. It had taken over a year to finish it, and during that time, the price of the house went up $45,000. When we finally moved in, we had enough equity in the house to take out a second mortgage of $10,000 to send to my family in Vietnam. Borrowing the money was only the first hurdle. Now we needed someone we could trust to place the cash in my family's hands. I felt helpless when I laid my head on the pillow to try to get a good night's sleep. I dozed off for a few minutes, but woke up anxious. As was my custom when I couldn't sleep, I walked outside and looked up at the stars in the sky. Placing my hands on a wooden fence, I cried out to the Lord for help. "Lord, I love my family and I know You love them, too. I really want them to come and live in America with us. Over there life is so hard and food is scarce. I feel helpless, Lord, please bring them to America."

Years later, when I gave my heart to Jesus and looked back on this time in my life, I realized I was obeying biblical principles by wanting to honor my mother and help my family in their time of need. Once again God was at work within my heart.

*For God said, "Honor your father and mother."*

MATTHEW 15:14a

*If you see some brother or sister in need and have the means to do something about it but turn a cold shoulder and do nothing, what happens to God's love? It disappears. And you made it disappear.*

1 JOHN 3:17 MSG

After I prayed that night, I felt I must write my stepfather a letter. When I lived in Vietnam, we irritated each other. I realized I must make an attempt to make peace with him. I shared from my heart my desire to bring them all to the United States. I heard from my family later that when they read the letter, their hearts were touched and they all wept openly. It seemed our family would have the possibility of a fresh start. I promised to work very hard to make money and buy their way to America.

God honored my prayer. Many times, because of the corruption in the government, people never received the money sent to them. Dennis and I were thankful when we received the news the $10,000 were safe in my mother's hands. Life seemed to be changing for the better, but then we hit another roadblock. My stepfather changed his mind. He made the decision to send his second son from his first wife to the United States. My heart was broken again. I thought he could have at least sent one of the children from his second family. It probably was a selfish thought, but I could never understand his reasoning. He was always thinking about his first family and not the children he had with my mother. His son came, but he didn't like living in America. He returned to Vietnam.

My family had never had so much money before. Dennis and I were counting on them using the money to come to America, but instead, they spent it all. They bought a bus and built a house. The money was gone and so were my dreams of having my family come and live with us in the States.

Two years later, my grandmother discovered I had sent my mother $10,000. She knew nothing about it. It's a Vietnamese custom not to hide information from your elders. Grandmother was our family's matriarch. It was a blatant show of disrespect to not inform her of the money. Grandmother didn't take the offense quietly. She called a meeting with my mother and stepfather and confronted them. My sister wrote me a letter and told me how angry my stepfather was when Grandmother questioned him. He chased my elderly grandmother around her yard with a knife. I wasn't sad anymore. I was livid. How could he treat my precious grandmother that way? I thought of all the times he had hit my mother and made our family suffer and live like second-rate citizens. Oh, I was fighting angry. When I was a little girl, I was a gentle, sweet child, but after working in the bar, I could hold my own in a fight. My heart was hardened, and I was determined to let my stepfather know he was never to threaten my grandmother or my mother again.

## DEBT

Dennis and I now had a huge debt. I tried to think of some way I could help pay it off. My dear husband had borrowed all that money because of his love for me. I felt so guilty and didn't want to take advantage of my husband's generosity. Dennis has old-fashioned values. He didn't want me to work outside the home. He enjoyed providing for us, but I felt I must help repay the debt I helped incur. I cried out to the Lord again. "God, bless me with a job so I can work and help my husband pay off this large debt."

## SEW BUSY

Even though I didn't know Jesus personally, He heard and answered my prayer. One of my Vietnamese friends worked at a clothing factory and subcontracted sewing jobs from her home. One day while I shared my dilemma with her, she took me to the company she worked for and they hired me, too. My first job was to sew decorative rickrack on the hem of jackets. I sewed about twelve of them and only made a little over two dollars per jacket. I continued to work diligently. God blessed me with a wonderful supervisor. She came from Texas and had a heart as big as Dallas. She took an interest in me and inquired if I knew how to sew according to a pattern. I told her I didn't, but I was willing to learn. She began to teach me. The first two days, I didn't get much sleep. I sewed them over and over again until I thought they were sewn correctly. It took me almost a week to finish one blouse. My supervisor had given me a sample to take home and study. I hung it on the wall. When I finished mine, I would hang my newly-sewn blouse next to the sample. I was such a perfectionist. If it didn't look perfect, I would rip out my stitches and start over again. The first three days, I was so consumed with getting my stitches just right that I only slept two or three hours. Dennis would leave early in the morning and when he came home at night, I would still be sitting there, trying to perfect my craft. One day he came home and saw me slumped over my sewing machine sound asleep. He woke me up and could tell I was frustrated. He tried to comfort me. "Honey, you don't have to do this. Why don't you quit?"

There was no way I was going to quit. I had already invested in a new sewing machine. Once again I prayed and asked God to help me understand how to piece together the jackets. He heard my prayer, and I finished my jackets. I knew two of them were nearly perfect. I took them to my supervisor to have her inspect them. She pointed out the two that were correct and then offered to give me some "hands-on" training. She took my "mistakes" home, ripped them out, and pinned them together correctly. The next day, she handed them back to me. As I examined her work, I started to understand how the jackets were to be sewn together. For the next six months, I poured my life into making jackets. I strived for excellence. My supervisor saw the improvement and began to give me more work. I was unable to keep up. I had more work than I could handle. I decided to hire some other Vietnamese people to help. God blessed my business, and within two years, we paid off our debt. We even had money left over and decided to purchase another new house in 1981.

## PROMOTION

It was around this same time that Dennis was promoted to Division Labor Scheduling Coordinator at A.J. Bayless. The vice president of the company called and requested an interview with Dennis for an executive position that would be opening up in the near future. It was the talk of the company. All the management team had great hopes of climbing the corporate ladder. After the interview, Dennis came home and I asked him how he felt the interview went. He shared from his heart that he felt one of two other hard-working men would be promoted to Coordinating Scheduler. He was sure he wasn't in the running. He has always been so humble and esteems others better than himself. I knew deep down he hoped he could have the coveted position. After he went to bed, I walked out into our backyard, sat down and looked up into the sky. I was discovering the power of prayer. Even though I didn't know Him as my Savior, I cried out to Him again. "God, I know people say You can do miracles. They tell me You know all things. You know how much I love my husband. He has been so good to me. He always sacrifices himself for others. He always gives me good things. He loves my family. He loves everyone around him. I want my husband to be happy. I'm not asking you for this promotion for my sake, but I want to see my husband happy. Please give him this job. Please answer this prayer for my dear husband."

## DRESSED FOR SUCCESS

Every time I prayed to the Lord, He answered. This time was no different. One week later, the owner of the company called Dennis and set up an appointment. We knew when the big boss called employees into his office, they were either promoted or fired. That night after supper, I announced, "Dennis, you are going to get that promotion! You need a new suit when you go into that meeting tomorrow. I want you to be dressed for success."

Dennis wasn't positive he would be offered the position, but I knew in my heart the job was his, and I wanted him to dress the part. We headed to town and bought some new clothes. After we arrived home, I gave him a fresh haircut. He looked like a true professional.

The next morning he went to see his boss. He took one look at Dennis and exclaimed, "Dennis, you look prepared for the next level. If I give you this job, do you think you can handle it?"

Dennis replied, "I haven't had any experience with this type of job before, but if you give it to me, I promise I will do my very best for you."

He was offered the job on the spot. The following Monday, they gave him a company car, his own office and a personal secretary.

Of course I was at home anxiously waiting to hear if he was given the position. When I heard him drive up to our house, I ran to meet him. He closed the car door and looked up at me.

I squealed. "Did you get the job?"

He picked me up and twirled me in the air and answered, "I got it! Thank you, Mai, for praying for me."

I pointed my thumb toward the sky and said, "He did that. I didn't."

When I look back, I am humbled by the mercy of God. We didn't deserve His goodness to us, yet He took the time to answer my prayers. It's proof to me of the love our heavenly Father has for people.

## BLESSINGS

The more money came in, the more money went out. In 1981, we bought an even bigger house. I continued to work and send money and gifts to Vietnam for my family. Even though I had lived in America a number of years by this time, I knew I still had to honor the culture of my homeland. So, whatever gifts I sent to my family, I would have to send the same presents to my stepfather's first family. I felt it was the right thing to do since his family needed help, too.

Year after year, until 1995, we continued to send gifts home. It took large amounts of money. To send one pound of merchandise to Vietnam cost over two dollars. Each box weighed seventy pounds. Most of the money I made was sent to Vietnam to help meet the needs of my family, but it seemed the more we gave, even though we didn't know the Lord personally, the more He showered financial blessings upon us.

*Give, and it shall be given unto you; good measure, pressed down, and shaken together, and running over, shall men give into your bosom. For with the same measure that ye mete withal it shall be measured to you again.*

LUKE 6:38 KJV

## FAREWELL TO GRANDMOTHER

In 1983, I received a letter from my family informing us of my grandmother's failing health. I sent money to them and asked them to take Grandmother to a good doctor. It was so sad because all the qualified doctors had fled from Vietnam. The physicians who were left were inferior, and many of them practiced witchcraft. After Grandmother had been examined by a few doctors, she wrote me a letter. I was appalled by the primitive practices she had to endure at their hands. They practiced voodoo and took razorblades across her stomach. They even tried to convince her someone had cast a spell on her. They insisted there was only one way to break the spell. Grandmother must undergo some type of surgery. Supposedly their hands were to go through her skin and pull out nails. I had never heard anything like this before, but one day I was watching television and saw a charlatan trying to do this strange type of bizarre surgery. I immediately discerned these doctors were con artists. They were like vultures preying on the sick and weak for money. I felt helpless and grieved over my grandmother's failing health and desperate situation. Depression seized me, and I didn't leave my bedroom for a few days.

For two years, Grandmother's health continued to decline, and I received word she passed away at home in 1985.

## DISTRICT MANAGER

Dennis and I continued to prosper. His company was pleased with his work ethic, and the sewing company I worked for asked if I would consider purchasing a set of sewing machines that were programmed to make buttonholes. I started seeing dollar signs. If I made more money, it meant more help for my family in Vietnam. I put a business plan in motion. We bought two machines, and I trained Terri to operate them. She learned quickly, and we made forty cents for each buttonhole. In one year, we paid off the machines. After the machines were paid for, I was so excited. I realized we would be making clear profit for each buttonhole. However, in the meantime, my supervisor met a young woman who saw the money that could be made by buttonhole work. This lady started to bring nice gifts to my supervisor in an attempt to get on her good side. The next thing I knew, the supervisor had given this girl half my buttonhole jobs. I couldn't believe it, but didn't feel I was to say anything. One day I showed up to pick up my job assignment for the week, and this girl was there just minutes before me. I saw my supervisor, and she informed me there was no work for me that week. I was devastated. That evening I went to bed, but I couldn't sleep. I got up and went out to our backyard and began to pray. I thanked Him for the job He had given me. I told Him I was hurt by what my supervisor had done. Then I felt compelled to ask Him to give me a company with my own name and my own line of clothes, so I did. I poured out my heart to Him.

In the midst of my loss of work, God blessed Dennis with another big promotion. A new vice president had observed Dennis' job performance. He was impressed and went to some of the other executives and insisted, "A talented man like Dennis Spencer deserves to be promoted. I want him to be our new District Manager if he is willing to move to Tucson."

Dennis told him we were willing to relocate. Before we moved, we enjoyed a trip to Hawaii Dennis had won. When we returned from our trip, Dennis commuted from his office in Tucson to our house in Mesa weekly until our children finished school that year.

## GOOD INTENTIONS

During this time, I felt a stirring in my heart to find a church. One evening as Dennis and I were visiting, I expressed how I felt such a need for our children to be in church. Dennis agreed, but we never followed through. It reminds me of a line in a sermon by an elderly country preacher. He hit the pulpit and thundered, "The road to hell is paved with good intentions."

Dennis and I meant well. I'm so thankful Jesus didn't give up on us. We were spiritually deaf. We didn't have ears to hear what the Spirit was saying to us at this time in our lives.

Terri was sixteen. She was quite rebellious and started hanging out with a troubled young man. We tried to end the relationship, but Terri wouldn't listen to us. To make matters worse, she ran off with him. Dennis and I were just sick. We went over to her boyfriend's house and found her there. Terri had convinced this young man's mother that Dennis and I were horrible parents. For some reason, this mother believed Terri's lies and felt she needed to protect her. We didn't know what to do.

One day Terri's boyfriend beat her, and she ended up in the hospital. She called us, and we hurried to her side. Her heart was tender toward us. We hoped she had learned her lesson and took her home. After she recovered, we took her to a counselor, but it didn't seem to help. She continued to go back to her abuser. Dennis and I felt the only way to save her from herself was to move. Our house wasn't completely finished, but we felt it was a necessity for Terri's mental and physical health.

## BANKRUPTCY

Just when our family was starting to get back to normal, Dennis received devastating news. His company was filing bankruptcy. He never saw it coming. Some of the company executives knew it all along, but never bothered to share the situation with their employees. Here we were in our brand-new home with bills coming in. The future looked bleak. We decided to sell our home and rent an apartment for a while until we knew where Dennis was going to work.

To make matters worse, the executives kept telling Dennis and the other employees they were trying to save the company. In hindsight, we feel this was a lie to keep employees from leaving the company before it completely collapsed. There were attempts to get Dennis to deceive some of the other employees. Dennis and I felt this was unethical, and he gave his two-week notice.

## DEATH IN THE FAMILY

In the midst of these troubled days, Dennis' stepmother died. Thirty days later, his father died and left Dennis in charge of his entire estate. Dennis' dad had two sons and two daughters, who were stepsiblings to Dennis.

Large-hearted Dennis told them he didn't want anything inside the house. They could divide all the contents between themselves. After his stepsiblings cleaned out the house, Dennis contacted a realtor and put the house up for sale. The day Dennis came to pick up the key, his family asked him if he was sure there wasn't something of his father's he wanted. After a few moments, Dennis decided he would appreciate some family pictures. As he was leaving, his stepbrother approached him carrying two of his father's guns: a shotgun and a pistol. He asked, "Dennis, are you sure you don't want Father's guns?"

Dennis held the guns and examined them. I could tell the guns took him on a sentimental journey. He answered, "My father and I used to do target practice in the desert with these guns. I think I would like to have them." He tucked them in his trunk and then forgot about them.

A few weeks later, Dennis was driving one of his supervisors somewhere. They had to stop and get something out of the trunk. When Dennis opened the trunk, his supervisor spotted the guns. He asked him why he was carrying around guns in his car. Dennis told him he forgotten to take them into the house. As soon as Dennis returned home that night, he put the guns in a locked file cabinet in Timmy's bedroom.

## HEADED BACK TO VIETNAM

Just before my father-in-law's death, Dennis had agreed to watch the children so I could take a trip to Vietnam for three months. I was lonesome for my family and wanted to spend some extra time with them. I wanted to check on each of my siblings and make sure they were OK. I had applied for a visa, but the Vietnamese government was very strict and only allowed a small percentage of people into the country. It took six months for the government of Hanoi to write to me and tell me my visa was ready. I started packing for my trip. I was only allowed two seventy-pound suitcases and one carry-on bag. I had so many things I wanted to take to my family, but I knew I had to prioritize and only take necessities. I knew I would need to take at least $20,000 in cash to share with my family when I arrived in Vietnam. The day for my departure arrived.

My plane landed in Malaysia and I was forced to spend the night there.

I had such anxiety and was unable to sleep. The next day when we flew into the Saigon airport, my knees started shaking. I was so excited. My eyes were wet with tears of joy. The first change I noticed was the government was different than it was when I left in 1971. There were around three hundred people on the plane. I was almost the last person to exit the aircraft. The government officials inspected every piece of luggage thoroughly. They examined me to make sure I wasn't smuggling anything into the country. They insisted every item must be registered. I was honest and listed the $20,000 cash and fifteen ounces of gold I had with me. I had been warned by some of my friends who had been to Vietnam to bring only new money and staple the cash together because there were those who would steal the loose bills. I had seen a lot of corruption in my life and was street smart. I stapled my bills together and counted them. I knew the exact amount I had. I took inventory of everything I brought with me and recorded it on a piece of paper. I informed them exactly how many pieces of luggage I had. In the midst of my interrogation, I glanced up and saw my mom standing with my siblings and a few of my cousins. I couldn't believe how old they all looked. I don't think I would have recognized some of them because they looked so different. Their skin looked like a dry grocery sack. It looked like they had no oil on their skin to keep it soft and supple. Everyone looked depressed. I couldn't wait to visit with them, but I had to wait until the officials finished checking me in. I looked down and counted my gold rings. I noticed two were missing. I didn't know how the thief stole them off the chain. About that time, my sister pushed through the door, threw her arms around my neck and kissed me. She whispered in my ear, "Mai, give them something so we can go."

I thought I knew the ropes, but bribing them never crossed my mind. I gave them one of the gold rings that was worth around $200. It worked. The officials told me I was free to go as long as I promised to stay in Saigon. I argued with them and insisted I be allowed to go to Binh Chau or I would turn around and go immediately back to America. They finally agreed to let me go to Binh Chau.

We got on a bus and traveled into the night to my mother's home. It was ten o'clock by the time we arrived. When I walked into the house, I tripped and fell over a deep hole right in the middle of the living room floor. It had been eighteen years since I had been in Vietnam. I felt so far removed from the poverty and primitive lifestyle. I looked around the house and felt so sad for my family. There was only one bed. Everyone else slept on the floor. During mealtimes I was unable to eat anything except fruit. I was sensitive to the offensive odors coming from the food. My mom noticed I wasn't eating much and worried her cookware wasn't clean enough for me. I didn't want to hurt her feelings; it was just so different from my American way of life.

## FINDING NGA

After settling in for four days, I noticed I hadn't seen my younger sister Nga. She was next to me in birth order, and it was no secret in my family that we shared a special sisterly bond. I asked my mom where Nga was. She said she didn't know. I thought of every time I sent packages from America to my family. I always included something special for Nga and her children. Mom explained some of the hardships Nga had been through. From 1975 to1988, they had severe financial setbacks. Mom also told me some of the packages I had sent were vandalized before they arrived. Many of the gifts were stolen, and only a few of my presents were received. I continued to ask other family members if they knew where I could find Nga. Someone mentioned they had seen her in Vung Tau, which was an hour drive from Binh Chau. They had heard a rumor that Nga was literally begging for food in the marketplace because her husband had lost a leg during the war. My heart broke for my sister. I insisted we make an attempt to locate her. We looked all over, but had no success. I wasn't about to give up. We met an old acquaintance of Nga's. She told us Nga now lived in the cemetery. In the Vietnamese cemeteries, there is a house on the grounds where people place all kinds of idols. It looks like a temple, but it's a dark place where evil spirits dwell. We went to check out the cemetery and see if we could find Nga. Sure enough, I looked up, and there she stood with her grandmother, the mother of her father. She had one small bed and one pot to cook in. I started crying when I saw her dire circumstances. I was angry because I had sent my family $10,000 and not one of them had compassion and shared the wealth with her. I couldn't understand such cruelty. I embraced my sister and asked her to please come back to Binh Chau and stay with me during the remainder of my visit. She agreed to come.

That night my mind raced, trying to figure out a creative way for Nga to make a living. I was haunted by the hopelessness in the eyes of the Vietnamese people. They looked hollow and empty. The next morning, I came up with a plan. I asked my mother to give Nga her house, and I would build Mom a new house. This way Nga and her family wouldn't have to live in the cemetery.

My mother was open to the idea, but Nga would need a place to live while we were building the new house. Mom suggested we find a house close to the market to rent and buy two pool tables. At that time, this was the only entertainment the Vietnamese had. Very few of them had radios or television sets. For recreation, they enjoyed playing a game of pool. I thought it was a feasible plan and agreed to financially back it.

Time was of the essence. I realized I needed to get things rolling. I made the arrangements and started building a house for my mother. Thanksgiving was just around the corner, and I became homesick for Dennis and the children. I wanted to go home, but I had so much I wanted to accomplish. In order for Nga's family to survive, I knew I had to stay in Vietnam and finish what I had started.

## GENERATOR

Nineteen eighty-eight was the first year the Vietnamese government allowed the Catholic Church to celebrate the holidays. It was exciting, watching people in the streets headed to church to worship. My mom's friend Mrs. Hoa came over and asked if she could borrow the generator I had bought for my mother. She went on to tell us how thankful she was for the opportunity to celebrate Christmas with her church family that year. They didn't own a building, but rented one near the ocean. We felt it would be in the spirit of Christmas to share the generator with her church. She was thrilled and took the generator to the church service on top of a sandy hilltop. We lit the oil lamps and missed the coveted generator and the luxuries it seemed to provide.

## THE PROMISE

During the two months I was visiting in Vietnam, I didn't see very many people who had a joyful heart. My family did occasionally laugh when we reminisced about old times together, but for the most part, the people seemed depressed and heavyhearted. Mrs. Hoa was different. She had a warm, loving heart. After she left, I kept reflecting on her visit. When she returned the generator, she shared how wonderful it was to sing and worship the Lord in the Christmas service. She had an expression of joy on her face. This was something I had never seen before, but when I became a Christian, I recognized it as the Lord's presence. Mrs. Hoa continued sharing how inspirational the worship service was. After she left, I went outside and stretched out in my mother's hammock in her backyard. It was tied between a coconut and a cashew tree. Everyone else was resting, too. I had time to reflect on all that Mrs. Hoa had shared. I remembered how soft her facial features were. She didn't have a harsh, hard look. There was no evidence of hopelessness or depression. I kept pondering over and over in my heart, "What was so different about Mrs. Hoa? Why was she so happy?"

In the midst of my contemplation, I heard my mother's neighbor arguing with her daughter. It was a "light bulb moment" for me. I began to think about the Bible Mr. Nam had given me. I began to pray, "God, I am going home in just a few weeks. If you bless me financially, I will come back here and build you a prayer house where people can come and worship and praise You."

Years later, after I gave my heart to Jesus, I read the story of Jacob in the Old Testament. After Jacob had stolen his brother's birthright, Esau was very angry with him and planned to kill Jacob. Rebekah counseled Jacob to flee to her homeland until Esau was over being so angry.

*Esau held a grudge against Jacob because of the blessing his father had given him. He said to himself, "The days of mourning for my father are near; then I will kill my brother Jacob." When Rebekah was told what her older son Esau had said, she sent for her younger son Jacob and said to him, "Your brother Esau is consoling himself with the thought of killing you. Now then, my son, do what I say: Flee at once to my brother Laban in Haran. Stay with him for a while until your brother's fury subsides. When your brother is no longer angry with you and forgets what you did to him, I'll send word for you to come back from there. Why should I lose both of you in one day?"*

GENESIS 27:41–45

Jacob does what his mother, Rebekah, suggests. He flees to Haran, but on his journey he stops to rest for the night. As he is sleeping, he has a dream. The heavens are opened, and he sees angels ascending and descending on a ladder. God made a promise to him that night. Jacob in return built an altar and promised God that as He blessed him, he would give a tenth in return.

*Jacob left Beersheba and set out for Haran. When he reached a certain place, he stopped for the night because the sun had set. Taking one of the stones there, he put it under his head and lay down to sleep. He had a dream in which he saw a stairway resting on the earth, with its top reaching to heaven, and the angels of God were ascending and descending on it. There above it stood the Lord, and he said: "I am the Lord, the God of your father Abraham and the God of Isaac. I will give you and your descendants the land on which you are lying. Your descendants will be like the dust of the earth, and you will spread out to the west and to the east, to the north and to the south. All peoples on earth will be blessed through you and your offspring. I am with you and will watch over you wherever you go, and I will bring you back to this land. I will not leave you until I have done what I have promised you."*

*When Jacob awoke from his sleep, he thought, "Surely the Lord is in this place, and I was not aware of it." He was afraid and said, "How awesome is this place! This is none other than the house of God; this is the gate of heaven."*

*Early the next morning Jacob took the stone he had placed under his head and set it up as a pillar and poured oil on top of it. He called that place Bethel, though the city used to be called Luz.*

*Then Jacob made a vow, saying, "If God will be with me and will watch over me on this journey I am taking and will give me food to*

*eat and clothes to wear so that I return safely to my father's house, then
the Lord will be my God and] this stone that I have set up as a pillar
will be God's house, and of all that you give me I will give you a tenth."*

GENESIS 28:10–22

And God kept his word and blessed Jacob with lots of cattle, children
and material possessions.

*But Esau ran to meet Jacob and embraced him; he threw his arms
around his neck and kissed him. And they wept. Then Esau looked up
and saw the women and children. "Who are these with you?" he asked.
Jacob answered, "They are the children God has graciously given your
servant."*

GENESIS 33:4–5

When I read those verses after I gave my heart to Jesus, I felt God had
made that same promise to me. The God of Jacob was my God, and if He
blessed me, I made this promise to Him in return, "I will come back to my
homeland and build you a house of prayer."

It was settled in my heart. I felt an assurance God would help me honor
my vow. After all, this prayer house would be for His glory, not mine.

*When you make a vow to God, do not delay in fulfilling it. He has no
pleasure in fools; fulfill your vow. It is better not to vow than to make
a vow and not fulfill it.*

ECCLESIASTES 5:4, 5

## HEADED HOME

My visit was almost over. My mother's house wasn't quite completed, but I
was so lonesome for Dennis and our children I thought my heart would
burst. I called Dennis, and we agreed it was time for me to come home even
if the house wasn't finished. I promised my mother I would come back in
about a month and help her furnish and decorate her new home. I even
offered to bring back some American décor. My mother understood, and we
said our goodbyes.

When I arrived in Tucson, I saw Timmy, Brenda and Dennis waiting for me. They were so excited to see me. The children told me, "Mommy, Daddy had a big calendar hung up on the wall, and every day you were gone, he crossed off each day to show us you were one day closer to coming home."

It was a visual for their little eyes to understand how much longer I would be gone. They made me feel so loved. I was thrilled to be back with them again. We hurried home, and I heard one story after another of what life was like without Mommy in the house. I couldn't help but giggle when they told me about the rotating menu Daddy had made for them: hot dogs, macaroni and cheese, hamburgers and chicken. Then Dennis shared his traumatic experiences attempting to do the laundry. It felt so good to be missed and needed. I realized I was blessed beyond measure to have such a loving family. I never wanted to take them for granted. Little did I know I would be tested greatly in the weeks ahead. I had faced storms before, but I was about to face the fiercest storm of my life.

Chapter Fourteen

# Dark Night of the Soul

After I returned from Vietnam, life quickly returned to normal. The big news was Timmy had a girlfriend. Her name was Debbie, and she was a very nice, young lady. Timmy was excited because her family was kind to him and seemed to sincerely like him. It was hard for me to believe our son was 16 and smitten. It seemed only yesterday Dennis and I were holding him in our arms. We were so proud of the young man he had become. He had a tremendous work ethic and was hired by a local restaurant as a dishwasher. He enjoyed making extra cash so he could buy little extras.

I've heard from other mothers about the special relationship fathers and daughters seem to enjoy, and I've also heard them speak of the bond between a mother and her sons. I'm sure the fact Timmy was our only son intensified the bond we had. Timmy and I shared something very special. In his temperament he mirrored his father. He was very gentle and respectful. Terri, on the other hand, was our squeaky wheel. She was constantly "squeaking" out of one problem after another and getting into big trouble. In some ways, I guess I was exhausted from all the drama Terri had put us through. It truly had become too much drama for this mama. My Asian culture was steeped in children honoring and obeying their parents. Terri was one person in our home and became entirely someone else the minute she walked out the door with her friends. We finally decided to let her go, and hopefully one day she would come to her senses. Timmy's relationship with us was different. We never saw any "red flags" or "flashing lights" to tell us our son was in trouble. He never caused us any grief. He was placid and loved to please us.

When I was in Vietnam, it was difficult for my mother to let me return to the United States. She wanted me to stay for another month so we could finish her house. If I had stayed, I wouldn't have been with Timmy in his final weeks of life. Once again God showed mercy upon me. He knew what was ahead, and He put it in Dennis' and my hearts that I should come home earlier than I had planned. I'm so thankful I did.

After a few weeks with Dennis and our children, I made plans to return to Vietnam to oversee the completion of my mother's house. I purchased my plane ticket and was ready to leave Monday morning for Vietnam.

## TIMMY

The Friday before I was to leave, Timmy came back from work around 11 o'clock. He had a flat tire on his car, but worse than that, Debbie had broken up with him because he worked such long hours and they rarely were able to spend time together. He was upset. He hurried straight to his bedroom and turned on his stereo.

Around one o'clock he came to the living room, where Brenda was half asleep on the sofa. She looked up and saw he had a jacket on. She asked him where he was going, and he told her he was headed over to Debbie's house. It was about two miles away. He insisted she wasn't to tell us she knew where he was. Dennis and I had no idea he had left the house that evening.

The next morning I woke up and walked past Timmy's bedroom. He wasn't there. I asked Brenda if she knew where he was, and she said she didn't. While I continued looking for Timmy, I discovered the strangest note. I immediately called Dennis, informing him of the fact Timmy wasn't home most of the night. Then I read the note to him. "Dennis, he says he's sorry he has disappointed us. He wants us to be sure to tell Terri and Brenda how much he loves them. What does this note mean?"

Dennis thought it had to do with the breakup. Timmy was taking it very hard. Dennis wondered if he was at Debbie's house trying to patch up the relationship. He suggested I head over there.

The thought of suicide never entered my mind. I wondered if he ran away like Terri had done so often, but the pieces of this puzzle just didn't fit. Timmy was never rebellious. He had always been our docile child who loved to please. He had such a giving heart.

An example of Timmy's generous spirit is from 1985, when we had two young people in our home. We met a young Vietnamese woman and her brother. They had relatives in Mesa and came for a lengthy visit. There was some personality clash between the kinfolks and this sister and brother. When I heard their story and how they fled Vietnam by boat, my heart went out to them. Dennis and I talked it over and decided to open our home to them. We wanted to help them get established. I hired them every weekend. They were such hard workers and had two other jobs. Timmy would get up early every morning before he went to school and fix a nice breakfast for everyone. He would fry bacon and eggs and make toast. He just loved to cook. The first morning our new friends came into the kitchen, Timmy asked them if they wanted something to eat. They said they did. Timmy worked his magic and made a breakfast fit for a king. That particular morning, there weren't enough eggs to feed everyone. When I came into the kitchen, I watched as Timmy fed them, but he went away hungry. He never told anyone. It was just how he was—such a sensitive, caring soul.

## Shocked

I jumped out of the shower, threw on some comfy clothes, called Brenda to join me, and we hopped into the car. As we approached Debbie's house, I noticed three or four police cars with their lights spinning. Once again, suicide never crossed my mind. The first thought I had was Timmy and Debbie must have run away together and Debbie's parents called the police. After I was got out of the car, an officer approached me and asked if I was Mrs. Dennis Spencer, the mother of Timothy Spencer. I told him I was. I don't know if he was a rookie policeman or what, but he bluntly stated, "Your son, Timmy Spencer, has committed suicide."

It sent me reeling. I collapsed and couldn't get up. I almost lost consciousness. I kept trying to discern whether it was reality or a frightening nightmare. I thought to myself, "If this is a dream, the only way to wake up is to run. If it's really happening, I will feel pain when my feet run on the rocks, but if it's just a dream, I won't feel anything."

The policeman helped me up, and I started to run. I'm not sure what happened to my shoes because, for some reason, I was barefoot. I ran down the gravel road. A policeman started chasing me. My feet started to hurt and even bled. I fell to the ground and realized this was no dream. Our beloved son, our only son, bone of our bone and flesh of our flesh was dead. I started to scream and wail. The policeman picked me up, placed me in the police car, and drove me to the front of Debbie's house. When I look back on this dark day in our lives, I still grieve. I hurt because I was oblivious to Brenda's pain. I can't even remember who was taking care of her. I was lost in my own grief. It didn't even cross my mind to empathize with what Brenda must be going through. She must have been so frightened. She was only a child, but I was in complete shock and mentally I shut down. The police called my medical doctor, and she came to the scene and examined me. Another police car pulled up behind us with Dennis inside. He hurried to be with me. I'll never forget the hopelessness I saw in his eyes. He looked at me and choked, "Honey, I killed our son."

At first I didn't make the connection, but then I realized he felt responsible because he had brought his father's pistol into our home. His comments constantly replayed in my mind. One day I woke up and I agreed with his statement. If he hadn't brought that gun home, Timmy would still be alive. I started to blame Dennis, and bitterness welled up in my heart.

As I look back, I feel I must have been in such deep grief that I had an emotional breakdown. I was not thinking rationally. Instead of realizing how heartbroken Dennis must have been because he lost his son, too, I only felt my own pain. At one point, they even brought a straightjacket for me. How I wished I had known Jesus at this dark time in my life. I would have called upon His name to help me, but I didn't know Him. Instead I fell to pieces, and I felt I could never function again.

As we sat there suffocating in our grief, the gruesome details of Timmy's suicide unfolded. He had taken the pistol and tucked it inside his jacket. In his right hand he held a picture of Debbie, and with his left hand, he shot himself in the forehead around three o'clock in the morning. His body fell next to his girlfriend's bedroom window. It was more than I could bear.

More policemen showed up to investigate the crime scene. Debbie's mother talked to the officers and invited us inside their home. Dennis and I talked it over and decided we would accept their invitation. Debbie and her mother were visibly shaken, too. Both were crying uncontrollably.

As I sat there thinking of the traumatic events, I realized I hadn't seen Timmy's body. I told the policeman I wanted to see it. He shook his head and informed me I wasn't allowed to see him. Anger welled up inside me. I lost it. Looking the officer squarely in the eye, I said, "Timmy came from my womb. If he's dead or alive, he belongs to me. I have every right to see him. Don't you dare tell me I can't see my own son."

As the years passed by, I realized this officer was only trying to protect me from seeing my son lying in his own blood. But I couldn't be reasoned with. My grief was mixed with intense sadness and deep anger. I couldn't help but spout off. The officer looked at me and saw nothing could change my mind. He walked with me to see Timmy's body. He was slumped on the ground with a hole in his forehead. I knelt by him, picked him up, and laid him against my shoulder. When I kissed him, I could smell the oil on his hair. As I held him, I sensed how sorry he was for the agony he was putting us through. I held him for approximately one hour. Then the police told me it was time to take his body away.

Dennis took me home. The phone started ringing, and friends, neighbors and coworkers started pouring into our home. It was too much for my fragile state. Dennis called the doctor, and he prescribed sleeping pills so I could rest. The next morning, I woke up and was so sick. Some friends came over, made a pot of coffee, and helped me get ready for the day. I was unable to function. I was completely helpless. Everywhere I looked there was darkness.

As I look back on this tragic event, I wonder who was taking care of Dennis and Brenda. I don't even know who contacted Terri to tell her about Timmy's death. My life was a complete blur, and the fog of grief had swallowed me whole. It would be years before I found my way out.

## CHRISTMAS MEMORY

So many precious memories flood my soul when I reflect on Timmy's short life. One Christmas, when he was four, we had our Christmas tree up in the corner between our kitchen and family room. We had so many presents piled around the tree. On Christmas Eve, we had a nice dinner with family and close friends. After the meal, we went to bed. Timmy woke up around one o'clock in the morning and opened every single gift. He then carefully separated them. There was a pile of girl toys for Terri, a pile of socks and masculine presents for Dennis, a pile of boy toys for Timmy, and a pile of kitchen supplies for me. Dennis woke up and heard something. He went to see where the noise was coming from. There was little Timmy with all the opened Christmas presents in stacks. Dennis laughed to himself and carried Timmy back to bed. Dennis stayed up and rewrapped the presents so Terri would enjoy opening her gifts in the morning.

As Timmy grew, the children loved taking a walk down Memory Lane and hearing about the Christmas Timmy opened and sorted all the presents. Timmy enjoyed hearing the familiar story and especially loved hearing us laugh.

If only we had known we only had a few more Christmases left with Timmy. We would have sold everything we owned to buy the best Christmas present ever for him. We'd even let him open his gifts early and stack all our presents in piles. I've learned it is best to shower love on those we love while they are still with us and not wait until we can afford it.

An elderly grandmother was constantly telling her family, "If you're going to give me flowers, be sure to give them while I'm alive so I can enjoy them. Don't waste your money later setting them on my graveside. I won't enjoy them once I'm gone."

## I DON'T LIKE SPIDERS AND SNAKES

Another "Timmy story" that still makes us smile was the time we were in the middle of moving into our new house in Tucson. I was constantly telling Timmy I would always stand behind him no matter what. I assured him, if I ever saw him fall, I would be there to catch him. I had communicated this so often he knew my speech by heart.

We built a new house in the middle of the desert. Timmy had walked up to the front door and rang the door bell. There was a rattlesnake curled right at the front door. He spotted it and ran around to the back door. He was afraid I was going to answer the front door and be bitten by the snake. He didn't catch me in time and as I was opening the front door, he screamed, "Mom, don't open the door! There's a rattlesnake!"

I slammed the door, started screaming, and ran to the garage. After the crisis had somewhat passed, Timmy couldn't stop laughing. He teased me. "Mom, do you remember how you were always going to stand behind me no matter what? You said you would catch me when I fall. Well, the rattlesnake was right in the front yard, and you slammed the door in my face and locked me out of the house. I was stuck in the front yard with the venomous snake."

We were laughing so hard we could hardly breathe. Timmy had a great sense of humor. We called the fire department, and they came and took care of our unwanted guest.

Oh, when I remember Timmy's life, I can't help but smile. He was the heartbeat of our home. We all loved him so much and enjoy reminiscing about the silly things he did. These memories have helped keep him alive in our hearts.

## BUDDY SYSTEM

Timmy loved his big sister Terri. He knew she was always pushing the limits. She seemed to always be grounded or in trouble of some kind. Timmy would go and buy a bouquet of flowers and bring them back to Terri. He enjoyed lifting her spirits.

When Terri turned 17, she thought she had to go somewhere every single night. Dennis and I would allow her to go out a few nights a week, but we didn't feel it was necessary for her to go out every night. Dennis and I didn't know it, but some nights when we would go to bed, Timmy would come and help Terri push the car out of the garage without starting the engine. Terri would go on her merry way, and Timmy would close the garage door and go back into the house and fall asleep. Terri would sneak back in around five o'clock the next morning. They had a "buddy system" of their own.

## THE FINAL FAREWELL

After Timmy died, I walked into his room. I was hoping to examine every piece of clothing, pictures, writings or anything I could find that was his. It was my feeble attempt to find comfort in the room where I had seen my son so many times before. I was hoping to keep his memory alive and fresh in my heart. I didn't want anything in his room changed. When I opened his bedroom door, I was appalled to discover someone had gone into his room and cleaned it up spic-and-span. I felt like someone had kicked me in the stomach. Why would anyone clean his room without first discussing it with me? His room was never dirty, just messy. I thought of how many times I had scolded him for his messy room. Now I ached to see it that way again. I fell apart. The doctor was summoned and ordered more sedatives to calm me down so I could rest. When I woke up, I begged to go to the morgue. I was met with great resistance, but I completely fell apart. Dennis agreed to take me to see Timmy's body again.

The funeral is a blur, but when we arrived at the graveside, I remember demanding the casket be opened one last time. The funeral home staff insisted they couldn't honor my request. Once again I lost it. I couldn't be reasoned with and gave them an ultimatum. Reluctantly they opened the casket so I could see my son for the last time in this life. I was so overcome with grief I passed out.

When Michelle passed away, we buried her in Mesa. When Timmy died, we were living in Tucson, but we decided to have him buried beside the baby sister he loved so much.

## UNABLE TO COPE

I was drowning in grief. Looking back, I believe this was the blackest night of my soul. If only I had known Jesus, I would have called upon Him, and He would have comforted me, but Dennis and I didn't know the Lord. We really didn't even have each other to lean on during this time because I was caught in my own tangled web of pain, blame and agony. Many of our friends attempted to console us, but I was in such intense anguish I was unable to accept their sympathy. It felt like I didn't have room to breathe without people hovering over us. Instead of appreciating their love and concern, I would tell them to leave us alone. One night I went ballistic and the paramedics were called. They brought a straightjacket. I glared at Dennis and said, "If you let them put that straightjacket on me, I will never forgive you, Dennis."

He looked in my eyes and saw the distress I was in. He motioned for them to take the jacket off. Then he sent the paramedics out the door, wrapped his arms around me, and held me as I wept. I rested on his shoulders and cried until I fell asleep.

The loss of a child is the greatest heartbreak a parent can experience. You not only bury your child, but you bury all the dreams, hopes and plans you had for that child. Unless you have lost a child, you can never understand the depth of pain, but God never wastes our trials. How thankful I am for this light from Heaven. God gave us the Comforter. Now when I am holding the hand of another mother who has just lost her child, I can understand her pain. Oh, God is so good to us. In whatever storm you are facing, it may look like Satan is winning, but if you come to Jesus, He will make the stumbling blocks in your life stepping-stones to help others find their way. His Word declares that He comforts us, and then we comfort others with the same comfort we have been comforted with.

*Praise be to the God and Father of our Lord Jesus Christ, the Father of compassion and the God of all comfort, who comforts us in all our troubles, so that we can comfort those in any trouble with the comfort we ourselves have received from God.*

2 CORINTHIANS 1:3,4

There were days I attempted to run away from the pain, but when I came to Jesus I discovered this valuable secret: Find your mess and you'll find your ministry. When I found the painful messes in my life, I found the areas of ministry where God has used me the most.

I was a poor child in Vietnam, and now I help poor children in Vietnam. I know what it was like to be hungry, and so I do my best to feed the hungry. I lived for many years feeling unloved, and now every day I pray my life will reflect Jesus' love to those who are hurting. Oh, isn't the love of Jesus something wonderful? It changes you from the inside out.

## GOD'S MERCY EXTENDS BEYOND THE GRAVE

There is a story about a missionary couple's son who was born and raised in China. As a young child he had a heart for the Lord, and when he grew up, he decided to preach and became a pastor for many years of small churches in New York. In his early retirement years, he taught at a small Bible college in Arizona. He and his wife had two gifted children, a son and a daughter. The son is presently a successful lawyer in Chicago, and the daughter pursued a career as a flight attendant. One day while teaching, a note was delivered to this professor in his classroom. He excused himself and headed for the school office where he received the horrifying news his beloved daughter had committed suicide. His mentor was notified and came to visit the grieving couple. Their pain was crippling. They couldn't stop sobbing.

The seasoned saint said these comforting words to the hurting couple, "God's mercy extends beyond the grave. He understands mental anguish, and He will judge fairly."

## I WILL GO TO HIM

The problem with broken hearts is they still have to beat. God's Word is full of comfort for bleeding hearts. When Timmy died, I felt I could say, like King David when his son died, "I cannot bring my boy back, but I will one day go to him."

*David pleaded with God for the child. He fasted and went into his house and spent the nights lying on the ground. The elders of his household stood beside him to get him up from the ground, but he refused, and he would not eat any food with them.*

*On the seventh day the child died. David's servants were afraid to tell him that the child was dead, for they thought, "While the child was still living, we spoke to David but he would not listen to us. How can we tell him the child is dead? He may do something desperate."*

*David noticed that his servants were whispering among themselves and he realized the child was dead. "Is the child dead?" he asked.*

*"Yes," they replied, "he is dead."*

*Then David got up from the ground. After he had washed, put on lotions and changed his clothes, he went into the house of the Lord and worshiped. Then he went to his own house, and at his request they served him food, and he ate.*

*His servants asked him, "Why are you acting this way? While the child was alive, you fasted and wept, but now that the child is dead, you get up and eat!"*

*He answered, "While the child was still alive, I fasted and wept. I thought, 'Who knows? The Lord may be gracious to me and let the child live.' But now that he is dead, why should I fast? Can I bring him back again? I will go to him, but he will not return to me."*

2 SAMUEL 12:16–23

## RESOURCE

It is my prayer that this book will be a ministry resource to other parents. I wish someone would have shared bits of wisdom with us, and even Timmy, to possibly prevent his suicide. After I came to know Jesus, it was as if the scales fell off my eyes. I've read in the Book of Acts, when Ananias prayed for Saul, scales fell from his eyes. Saul was blinded by his own ambition. He persecuted the Church, but Jesus passed by and sent His servant to pray for Saul. He received spiritual sight and became one of the greatest apostles who ever lived.

*Then Ananias went to the house and entered it. Placing his hands on Saul, he said, "Brother Saul, the Lord—Jesus, who appeared to you on the road as you were coming here—has sent me so that you may see again and be filled with the Holy Spirit." Immediately, something like scales fell from Saul's eyes...*

ACTS 9:17, 18a

Before I came to Jesus, I walked in spiritual blindness. There were situations right under my nose, but I wasn't able to see them because I thought that's how everyone lived. When Jesus gave me spiritual sight, I retraced my steps and could see places where Timmy was hurting and crying out for help.

I want to take this time to share with you what I have learned through our family's ordeal. Maybe you have a child suffering with depression. Here are some of the warning signs Dennis and I discovered after Timmy's death. May the Lord grant you the discernment and wisdom you need.

## BE CAREFUL LITTLE EARS

When Dennis and I went into Timmy's bedroom, we noticed a cassette was in his stereo. Timmy listened to heavy metal music. As I have said before, I was in darkness and had no clue what poison was being spewed into our son's soul. We didn't let our children listen to music that repeatedly used profanity, but there were some songs that slipped through the cracks. We just missed it. When Dennis and I looked at the cassette, we recognized the rock group – The Doors. One of the last songs Timmy was listening to before he died was a song entitled "The End." It's a very depressing song and repeats this line over and over: This is the end.

I would warn every mother and father to take the time to really know what your children are listening to. Satan comes to kill, steal and destroy, but Jesus comes to give us life more abundantly. Satan is after our children and takes delight in attacking them. So, parents, I plead with you to know what your children are listening to.

Timmy was very artistic. Before I knew the Lord, I thought he had a tremendous gift of drawing. After I gave my heart to Jesus I went through some of Timmy's artwork. The scales were off my eyes. It was evident to me, as I saw his drawings of skulls and demonic figures that Satan was attacking him. Once again, I would counsel every parent to know your children inside out. Know who their friends are and what is influencing them. Read some of their writings. Examine their artwork. How I wish someone had given us this counsel.

It isn't enough to know what our children are doing and who they are hanging out with, but we need Jesus to help us train them in the ways of the Lord. They won't make it in this dark world without the Light of the World showing them the way. They need to have a steady diet of solid biblical teaching. His Word can show them the way.

*Thy word is a lamp unto my feet, and a light unto my path.*

PSALM 119:105 KJV

## LIGHT

A minister shared the story of a mother taking her two little girls to a mountain where there were no lights. The three of them stumbled around in the darkness, trying to find the narrow path for their feet. Finally, the young mother pulled out a flashlight from her pocket. She took the time to explain to her daughters the lesson she was trying to teach. "This world is very dark. There will be days you can't even see where to take the next step, but God has given you His Word as a light unto your path. If you obey the teachings in the Bible, you will not have to stumble through life."

My prayer for all who read my story is that each one would come to know how much Jesus loves you. I pray you will taste and see how good the Lord is. When you get a drink of the Living Water, it will change your life forever.

*O taste and see that the Lord is good: blessed is the man that trusteth in him*

PSALM 34:8

## BLAME GAME

Something snapped inside of me when Timmy died. I was unable to function. I began to play the blame game. I couldn't let go of the fact that it was Dennis who brought the gun into our home. I was self-absorbed and self-destructive. I don't know why I was unable to see the pain my precious husband was in.

I also neglected our daughter Brenda. I was drowning in a sea of grief. I was so busy mourning my dead child, I forgot about the needs of my living child. Years later, I held Brenda in my arms and we wept together. I said, "Brenda, do you forgive me for neglecting you?"

She so sweetly answered me, "Mom, I already have."

We decided to move from the apartment where we were living at the time of Timmy's death because directly across the street from us was a funeral home. Every time we looked at it, our hearts were reminded of our loss, and we would mourn again. We found a three-bedroom house just a few miles down the road.

## City Lights

After Timmy's death, Terri moved back in with us. I was unable to perform any of my motherly duties. Terri and Brenda were left to fend for themselves. I couldn't cook meals. We ate out almost every meal.

In the midst of playing the blame game, I decided I deserved time away from Dennis and the kids. I called one of my girlfriends, and we headed to Las Vegas. I spent days gambling, smoking and drinking. I was looking for something to dull the pain, but nothing helped.

Over this two-year period, I gambled away thousands of dollars in an attempt to hurt Dennis. I entertained thoughts of divorce, and my top priority was to make his life miserable. It got so bad that one day I looked him square in the eyes and said, "You killed Timmy."

He just held me. He knew I was hurting, and he never retaliated. One night I came home and told him I needed to talk with him. He sat down and listened as my story unfolded. I had gambled away all the money he had given me. I wanted him to scream at me and tell me he wanted a divorce, but he didn't. He looked at me and said, "Honey, it's only money. We've made money before; we can make it again. The only thing that is important to me is that our family stays together." He continued, "Did it bring you any relief from your pain by being in Las Vegas?"

I told him I thought it did.

He lovingly whispered, "It's worth it all if it gives you only five minutes of relief."

His loving words were just what Dr. Jesus ordered. I buried my face in his chest and cried. He started to talk to me about our family's future and buying a new house. Dennis seemed to understand why I said hurtful words. He looked beyond my ugly comments and saw I was a broken-hearted mother who had lost her son. I can never repay him for his patience with me through the most traumatic event of our lives.

The next morning, I made breakfast. It was the first time I had cooked in several months. Then Dennis and I went house shopping, and we found a home for the new beginning for the remaining members of the Dennis Spencer family.

When I became a Christian, I was comforted by the kindness of the Lord. He knew Timmy would take his own life, and the Lord brought me home from Vietnam so I could spend the final weeks of Timmy's life with him. If I had stayed as I had planned, I might have been in Vietnam when Timmy died. Oh, God is so good to me. Even when I didn't know Him personally, He was watching over me and trying to prepare me for what was ahead.

## Back to Vietnam

I decided I needed to go back to Vietnam to see my mother and check on my family. It had been over two years since I had been there. When Timmy died, one of my girlfriends had sent a telegram to my family informing them. When I arrived in Saigon, they expressed their heartfelt sympathy over Timmy's death. Being in Vietnam was a distraction and seemed to comfort me. I really enjoyed the first two weeks of my visit. The second two weeks, I contracted malaria and was horribly sick. I realized I needed to get back to the States and get medical attention. I promised my mother I would return to Vietnam in one year.

Little did I realize, when our family was just starting to heal from Timmy's death, we would receive another devastating blow that would change our lives forever.

# BURN VICTIM

enjoyed my trips to Vietnam to see my family. I can remember when I returned to see my mother's new two-bedroom house. It was very nice, and I was so happy to help her build it. I stood in the living room and was surprised to see she had made a shrine with numerous altars and Buddha statues in the dining room. At this time in my life, I was beginning to grasp God as a higher power with my head, but I had not given my heart to Jesus. I went to my mother and asked her why she had to have all those idols and altars in her new house. I suggested she take them down and use the room for a dining area. I remember she looked at me and said, "I want to carry on the traditions of my mother."

During this trip, I bought my sister Nga two pool tables so she could charge a fee to the people who might want to shoot a game. Four weeks into my trip, I contracted malaria and needed to return home to America. After I was home for two weeks, I received a telegram from Nga. Her son Ty had been in a terrible accident. Some people came to their house one night after it was dark to play pool, but there were no lights. Ty lit a propane lantern, and it exploded, burning his entire body except his hands and face.

We found out just how corrupt businesses can be. Gasoline was cheaper than propane. Some companies would buy gasoline, mix it with the propane, and sell it to customers so they could make more money. This made the flammable liquid even more dangerous.

My sister begged me to come back to Vietnam and try to save her son's life. She pleaded, "Mai, in his condition, there are only two people who can save him: you and God!"

A wave of confusion swept over me. I had just given my mother $3,000 while I was in Vietnam two weeks before. I had also given my sisters and brothers a thousand dollars each. I assumed they had not shared any of the money with my sister and her family in their time of need. I was greatly troubled and wondered how my family could be so heartless. I immediately called Dennis and asked him if there was anything we could do to help Ty. Dennis' large heart once again beat steadily. He gave me $10,000 and bought me a plane ticket to Vietnam. He wanted me to go there and assess the situation to see if there was anything I could do to help.

When I was getting ready for my trip, I called one of my friends. She told me aloe vera would soothe and aid in healing burn wounds. I had her cut me seventy pounds of the plant. The next day, I boarded the plane and flew to Vietnam. My plane stopped, and we spent the night in Thailand. The next morning, I was having breakfast next to a group of eight Vietnamese tourists. Some of them looked quite wealthy. They had a tour guide with them. As they visited with each other, I heard them share that they didn't have a visa to go in Vietnam. I told them I didn't have a visa either. They thought if I joined them, we would have a larger group and it might speed up the process. I felt a check in my spirit. I wasn't to join their group. I declined their offer.

When we arrived in Saigon, the tourist group attempted another time to get me to join them, but I once again declined. We arrived at customs, and the authorities questioned me. I explained to them I was in the country because of my nephew's medical emergency. They checked my luggage and saw I brought seventy pounds of aloe vera. I explained to them that the sap from the plant had healing properties. After they stopped laughing at me, they informed me I would be detained by the government for one night because I didn't have a visa. I was shocked and questioned them about spending the night in jail. They explained it just meant those of us who didn't have visas were going to be spending the evening in a motel. I was relieved. When we arrived at the motel, we couldn't help but notice the guards standing outside. My heart skipped a beat, but inside it looked like a typical motel.

That evening I ordered a sandwich and sat on the balcony to eat. A little later, I saw the tourist group again. They once again pressured me to join them. I still felt I wasn't to be part of their group. I thanked them for their kind invitation, but declined. That evening I asked one of the officials for a ride to the hospital. When we arrived, I asked the taxi driver to deliver a note to my sister. In the note, I asked the doctor to please give my nephew the best medical treatments possible. I promised to reward him with prompt payment. The custom's official told me it would take three days for me to get my visa. I felt helpless and pleaded with him. I told him my nephew might be dead in three days. He had compassion on me and placed orders to permit me to have a visa and leave the motel jail. I had my visa in my hands at 10 o'clock, but the tourists were stranded there for three days. I knew it was the favor of the Lord.

I hurried to downtown Saigon and checked into a motel. After a quick shower, I headed to the hospital. When I walked into the burn unit, the stench was overwhelming. It smelled like rotten meat. I have a weak stomach and started to get nauseated. The conditions were heartbreaking. I saw two burn victims in one bed. Both were severely burned. I wanted to ease their pain, but realized there was very little I could do.

When I entered my nephew's room, he turned his neck slowly and looked at me. Tears streamed down his face. Even though a sense of helplessness seemed to grip my soul as I watched him wince in pain, I knew my presence brought comfort to him.

I introduced myself to Ty's nurses and doctor. I realized they didn't make much money, so I gave them $200 and asked them to buy the best medicine and whatever they needed to help Ty. It's sad to say, but the more money you have, the better care you receive in Vietnam. I knew my gifts helped because, when I came back a few hours later, Ty's room smelled fresh and he had crisp, clean sheets.

## FAVORITISM

Nga and I wept as we held each other. She kept telling me how thankful she was that I came. I gave her some cash for the needs of her family. I visited with my sister for about two hours. I asked her if any of our family had given her any money or come to see her. She said, "No."

I was angry at my family. How could they neglect their own flesh and blood? I just didn't understand their lack of compassion. I stayed in Saigon three or four more days. In my heart, I hoped some of our family members would walk through Ty's hospital room door to show their love and support, but they didn't come. Only his brothers and sisters stopped by to see him. I was so disappointed in my family.

I took a taxi to Binh Chau. My mother seemed thrilled to see me. A few minutes after I arrived, all my other sisters showed up. I knew I had to tell them how sad I was they didn't try to help our sister and her family during one of the most difficult times in their lives. They didn't say a word. After they went home, I asked my mom, "Where is the money I gave you? Why didn't you take a couple hundred dollars and help your grandson?"

Mom looked at me and told me she gave all the money to somebody and couldn't get it back.

I sat stunned. I asked, "Who did you loan the money to who won't pay you back?"

She refused to tell me until the next day. "I gave the money to your brother."

I should have known. This was the firstborn son she favored and paid attention to more than any of the rest of us. She seemed to inherit Grandmother's gift of picking favorites. They adored the males and neglected the females in the family.

I was angry and scolded her. "Mom, you gave all the money to Hoa?"

She nodded her head and whispered, "Yes."

"Does he know Ty has had a serious accident and is burned?"

"Yes," she replied.

I continued, "And he won't help him?"

She made some excuse about him needing the money for his business.

God opened my eyes that day to the depravity of human nature. We are born selfish and obsessed with ourselves. We are greedy and self-absorbed. When left to ourselves, we only take and never give. My eyes were opened, and it wasn't a pretty sight to behold. I was reminded of what the Bible teaches about the love of money and how it is the cause for all types of wrongdoing.

*For the love of money is a root of all kinds of evil.*

1 TIMOTHY 6:10

I didn't know the Lord at that time, but in reflecting back, the Holy Spirit calmed my heart. Without His touch of mercy, I would live in the flesh and not care for the needs of others. I was humbled by God's grace in my life. I decided to let it go and let God deal with my family. I couldn't scold them into doing God's will. The Lord had to build the spiritual house in their hearts or it wouldn't last.

*Unless the Lord builds the house, its builders labor in vain. Unless the Lord watches over the city, the watchmen stand guard in vain.*

PSALM 127:1

I thank the Lord He has changed my family and they are generous and compassionate. He changed them. They are not the same people they were.

There was an old country preacher who used to begin his Sunday sermon with these words: I'm not what I want to be for Jesus, but thank God, I'm not what I used to be.

As each of my family members walked through those hospital doors to visit my nephew, I couldn't help but thank God they were not what they used to be. God had taught them a valuable lesson.

My three-week visit to Vietnam was nearing an end. I left money for Nga and her family. I paid the entire bill before I left to return to the United States.

## APRONS

When I got back from Vietnam, a neighbor dropped over to visit me. As she walked through our garage, she was shocked to see two, large industrial machines. I explained to her about my sewing business. She started to tell me about the needs of her friends, Paul and Jan Eastlack. They purchased lead aprons from a manufacturer and then sold them to X-ray technicians and other medical professionals. These aprons protected the techs from dangerous levels of radiation. The Eastlacks had a customer who was very large.

They had not been able to find a manufacturer who supplied aprons for obese individuals. My neighbor told them about my industrial sewing machines and my sewing business. Paul called and asked if I might be interested in trying to design this apron for him. I agreed to try. They brought the material to my house and gave me the dimensions for the apron. I was having difficulty figuring out how to work with the material. It was twenty-five inches wide and could not be cut because any break in the vinyl-covered lead material would cause radiation exposure. I told the Eastlacks I would do my best to come up with something, so they left the material with me.

The next morning, I poured a cup of coffee and headed to my cutting table in our garage. As I was looking over the material, I realized I had no idea how to make this apron. I knelt down and began to pray for wisdom. I specifically asked the Lord to help me complete this design because I knew I couldn't figure it out without His guidance. My prayers were answered. As I began to work, the Lord gave me creativity to come up with a solution and a design that overlapped pieces in the front and allowed the apron to be expanded to fit a larger person. I then adjusted the arm holes to make the apron fit right. I looked it over and felt it just might work and let the Eastlacks know.

When the Eastlacks' customer tried on the apron, he said it fit perfectly. As I reflect on this story, I marvel at God's love for me. Even though I did not truly understand who God was because I had not accepted Jesus as my Lord and Savior, He had mercy on me and answered my prayer.

As I became acquainted with the Eastlacks, I discovered they had five children and were missionaries. They attempted to make extra money by selling the aprons. They received a commission. I told Paul he could make more money if he sewed them himself. He told me they just couldn't afford the thousand dollars it would take to get started.

I talked to Dennis, and we decided to help Paul. We loaned them $1,000. We know the reason God has prospered and blessed us is because we give to others. We can never out give the Lord. The biblical principle of casting your bread upon the waters and it coming back to you has proven true in our lives. God has always blessed us above and beyond what we expected. I honestly believe the Lord blessed Spencer Creations because of our generosity to the poor.

*Cast your bread upon the waters, for after many days you will find it again.*

ECCLESIASTES 11:1

I worked with the Eastlacks for about a year. During that time, Paul constantly witnessed to me. He was bold in his testimony and shared with me about who Jesus is. Seeds were planted in my soul even though I didn't get saved at that time. Still, God was placing Christians in my path to share the Good News with me. This should be a great encouragement to those who are praying for lost loved ones. God hears your prayers and is working behind the scenes, sending someone to share the love of Jesus with your loved ones. Paul and Jan had shared the English version of the Bible on cassette with me. Every day I would listen to the Word of God in my car and in our home. God orchestrated every detail of our lives. I would even play it while my Vietnamese employees worked for me. Most of them couldn't understand English, but I realize now the Lord was drawing my heart. As I listened to the tapes, I would dream of one day taking back the Bible on cassette in the Vietnamese language. I began praying about it and as you have already read, God answered my prayer. His Word is so true. If we take delight in His ways, He will give us the desires of our hearts.

*Delight yourself in the Lord and he will give you the desires of your heart.*

PSALM 37:4

# THE VALLEY OF THE SHADOW OF DEATH

A few months after Timmy's death, Terri announced she was pregnant. I was upset because I felt she wasn't ready to face the responsibility of being a mother. She didn't even have employment.

Terri dropped out of high school her senior year. She was just two credits shy of graduating. Pursuing her dream of becoming a beautician, she was accepted and graduated from a local cosmetology school.

When Terri went into labor, Dennis stood on one side of the bed and I stood on the other side. We asked the doctor for an epidural. It gave her instant relief. After that, Terri looked up at Dennis and said, "It's a piece of cake, Daddy."

## FRESH START

A few hours later, our granddaughter Cherée was born. She wasn't your typical fussy newborn. Little Cherée wasn't even crying. The nurse placed her in Dennis' arms. She just looked around with her big chocolate eyes. An inner healing began to take place in our family. God sent this precious baby girl to give our family a fresh start. We fell in love with Cherée. As we held her in our arms, it was as if God was holding us in His, without us even knowing it, and healing our broken hearts. I still have a memory of Dennis placing Cherée on his chest. She would fall fast asleep. As she snuggled close to his chest, she became Papa's girl. Dennis and I would look at her, and then we would look at each other and smile. Something was different. This baby girl was giving us a new lease on life. I babysat our new granddaughter while Terri worked as a cosmetologist at J.C. Penney's salon.

I made a definite decision to keep myself busy. I didn't want to fall back into the deep depression I had been in since Timmy's death. I inquired about my old sewing job. Without hesitation they rehired me. I purchased two new machines. Once a week, I picked up my orders. After five months, I sat down and figured out my profit. I was making a mere pittance. I tried to think of a way I could generate more income. As I looked around our beautiful home, I decided to make custom drapes.

## BAD NEWS

Terri fell in love and married a young soldier. One day as I was busy sewing drapes for our bathroom window, Terri dropped by to see me. She complained about the heavy hemorrhaging she was experiencing. I insisted she call the doctor immediately. She told me she had already been to one of the Army physicians, and he couldn't find what was causing her problem. Her condition deteriorated, and six months later, she returned to her doctor. After her appointment, she came to see me. I was standing on a stepladder hanging a new shower curtain when she blurted out, "Mommy, the doctor said I have ovarian cancer. I am going to die. He said I only have six months to live."

I felt an electric shock flow through my body as my heart raced wildly. I was short of breath and felt like I could have a heart attack. I climbed down the stepladder and began to whimper. "Why, God? Why do these tragedies happen to our family?"

Terri and I embraced. We decided she needed to get a second opinion. She seemed restless and troubled when she announced, "I've got to get out of the house. I cannot stay here or I will go crazy."

After Terri hurried out the door, I found a pen and paper and began writing a letter to God. I wasn't angry, just hurting. I didn't know who I could talk to and felt powerless to change our desperate situation. In my letter, I poured out my heart to Him and asked why all these bad things were happening to our children. I didn't understand. I reminded God I had been a loving daughter to my mother. I began to sob as I penned my feelings. My emotions began to race out of control. Painful memories of Timmy's premature death swept over me. As was my habit during times of intense stress, I decided to lock myself in my bedroom and stay there for several days. I decided to take a bottle of liquor and my favorite cigarettes and isolate myself from everyone. As I stumbled from the kitchen to my bedroom, I had to cross our hallway. There was an entry to the living room with a row of windows. I had passed that way many times before, but this time was different. The light shining through the windows captured my attention. It mesmerized me. In the corner was a favorite wing chair. I hurried to that chair, collapsed on my knees, continued sobbing and cried out to Jesus in sheer desperation. Suddenly I remembered what I had read in the New Testament Mr. Nam had given me. This Book declared Jesus was the Son of God and the Savior of the world. I whimpered, "Jesus, if You are the Son of God and the true Savior of the world, will You help me?"

I knew I wasn't going to function without divine intervention. For fifteen minutes, I stayed on my knees. When I stood up, both my feet had fallen asleep, but a peace had permeated my being. I had never experienced a peace of that magnitude before. It was just as the Bible describes: a peace that passes all understanding.

*And the peace of God, which passeth all understanding, shall keep your hearts and minds through Christ Jesus.*

PHILIPPIANS 4:7 KJV

I didn't know exactly what I was experiencing, but I knew in all the years I had prayed to Buddha, I never sensed anything like it. A revelation from Heaven came to my soul. This Jesus was indeed the Son of God and the Savior of the world. I could trust the One who died for me. He paid a great price for my redemption, and I was forever changed.

## THE PHONE CALL

I walked around the house and pondered what I had just experienced. About an hour later, my girlfriend Noomie Pieth called me. She was the same friend who was with me when I had a major meltdown after Timmy died. She and her husband were the ones who called the paramedics. After that humiliating experience, I told Dennis I wanted all our friends to leave. I refused to have company over or even answer phone calls. They honored my requests. We didn't see or hear from them for approximately three years. God must have spoken to her heart to call me. She said she had been thinking about me and wondered how we were doing. I don't remember if I shared with her about Terri's terminal diagnosis, but she sensed I was hurting. She called her Lutheran pastor and asked him to pay me a visit. He was the same minister who officiated at Timmy's funeral. He immediately came over, but he never mentioned Jesus, and he never prayed before he left.

## GRANDMA MARGE

Later that day, we all sat down as a family and listened as Terri shared with us the details of her diagnosis. We were heartbroken, but we felt Terri shouldn't give up. We made the necessary phone calls to another doctor for a second opinion. Once again our hopes were dashed when the second doctor gave the same grim prognosis.

Terri wanted to keep working for as long as she could, which was about one month. Surgery was scheduled by her gynecologist. It was during this difficult time that I walked over to my neighbor's house looking for Brenda. Denise and her family lived a few houses down from us. They had a girl around Brenda's age. I sat and visited with Denise. She told me she was expecting her mother to come for a visit and how she wanted her mom to meet our family. I told her I would be happy to meet her.

Just before Terri's surgery, my phone rang. It was Denise. "Mai, my mom is here. Can you come over and meet her?"

I assured her I would come right over.

The first time I saw Denise's mother, who we affectionately call Grandma Marge, she was standing over the stove in Denise's kitchen cooking. I asked what she was doing in Arizona.

She smiled sweetly and replied, "I don't know, child. All I know is the Lord spoke to me to come. He showed me He has some work He wants me to do. I'm waiting for my instructions from Him. I know He's going to show me."

I had never heard anyone speak that way before.

A few days after meeting Grandma Marge, Terri came to see me again. She was sobbing and ran into my arms.

"Mom, I don't believe I am going to die. I don't feel sick. Usually people who have cancer are bedridden and in a lot of pain."

I remembered how Grandma Marge heard from the Lord. So I suggested we walk over to Denise's house and ask her to pray for Terri. After we arrived, we sat down with Grandma Marge and explained the doctor's report and all our fears. She listened intently, and I knew immediately she had the gift of discernment. She spoke frankly to Terri about her years of rebellion. She looked Terri right in the eye and said, "The doctors say you are going to die in six months, but they are not God. If you repent and turn your life around and receive Him as your Lord and Savior, He will bless your life."

Terri looked at me with tears streaming down her face and asked me to forgive her for all the heartache she had put us through. I assured her of my forgiveness. I also asked Terri to forgive me where I had failed her. It began the healing process in our relationship.

Grandma Marge led us both in a prayer to receive Jesus into our hearts. As we were praying, I realized I was born again when I cried out to Jesus kneeling by the wingback chair in my living room. Her prayer time with us was a confirmation to my soul that God was at work in my life. I appreciated the prayers of this seasoned saint.

After we finished praying, I knew I had to call Dennis and share the good news with him. When he answered the phone, I asked him to come to Denise's house. There was something very important I wanted to share with him. He arrived and Grandma Marge explained the way of salvation to him. Dennis prayed the sinner's prayer, but I think he was just trying to support Terri and I in our decision. He really didn't grasp what it all meant.

## OUR ANGEL

After Terri's operation, she came home with us so we could take care of her. We set up a hospital bed in our bedroom. Grandma Marge informed me that God had shown her why He had brought her to Arizona. She knew the assignment He had given her. She was to care for Terri in her final months of life. I marveled at the goodness of the Lord. He was watching over us and sent us one of His finest servants to help us in our time of need.

When Jesus was facing death in the Garden of Gethsemane, God sent an angel to minister strength to Him. Grandma Marge was our angel. We were facing death and difficult days, and she ministered strength to our hurting family.

*Jesus went out as usual to the Mount of Olives, and his disciples followed him. On reaching the place, he said to them, "Pray that you will not fall into temptation." He withdrew about a stone's throw beyond them, knelt down and prayed, "Father, if you are willing, take this cup from me; yet not my will, but yours be done." An angel from heaven appeared to him and strengthened him.*

LUKE 22:39–43

The poem "Footprints in the Sand" tells us it is in our darkest hours when God carries us. I believe He also uses his saints, like Grandma Marge, to lead us through those dark valleys. Not only did she shower us with her love, faith and compassion during Terri's sickness, but she has continued to comfort, encourage and strengthen us in our walk with Jesus. She is truly a forever friend and we see the Son in her eyes. I consider her my mentor and spiritual godmother. While Grandma Marge went back to her home in Los Angeles, her daughter and son-in-law, Denise and Anthony Barnett, have remained a blessing to us over the years. They have shown tremendous patience with us, as they willingly give of their time to train us in the ways of the Lord. Dennis and I thank the Lord for arranging for our lives to be intertwined with those of like precious faith.

*…to them that have obtained like precious faith with us through the righteousness of God and our Saviour Jesus Christ.*

2 PETER 1:1b KJV

## VISITS

In the first few weeks, Terri slept on the hospital bed, but then she begged to sleep in our bed. She knew she was dying and fear would grip her heart, and she would cry, "Mom, I just want to be your little girl again."

I did my best to listen to her and comfort her. We would laugh and cry together. When she started chemotherapy, she became violently ill and was unable to eat much. In the final weeks, she was fed through a tube in her stomach.

We prayed a lot during this time. Terri asked God to give her a chance to raise her little girl. Cherée was too young to realize the seriousness of the situation. She was so precious and wanted to help make her mommy better. Towards the end, Terri was so weak that she could barely sip juice through a straw. Cherée would cheer on her mommy. "Come on, Mommy, suck it hard."

One thing Dennis and I had a hard time understanding was why Terri's husband would agree to a short-term tour in Korea when his wife was dying. We tried to not speak of it very much because it upset Terri. We attempted to keep life as calm and as peaceful as we could for her and our darling Cherée.

## No Secrets Between Us

About two weeks before Terri went home to be with the Lord, she had a request. "Mommy, I am craving your sour soup."

I went into the kitchen and cooked her favorite soup. She ate about three spoonfuls and made an unexpected request.

"That soup made me feel so good. I would like to walk around the block."

Terri leaned against me. We took small steps and attempted to walk around the block. We visited as we walked. Since I had become a Christian, the Lord convicted me about the secret I had kept from Terri. I felt I was supposed to be honest with her about her birth-father. I dreaded the talk, but knew in my heart the time had come for me to tell her. Hot tears stung my eyes as I choked out, "Terri, you know your daddy and I love you very much. You have seen with your own eyes the special love your daddy and I have for each other. I have something I want to tell you because now we are children of God, and we should always be truthful and honest. I don't want you to go to Heaven and not know the truth from my own lips." Our eyes met. Terri didn't say anything, but waited for me to continue. "When we first got married, you were just two. We made a decision at that time to tell you that Dennis was your father. We wanted to raise you equally with the children we would have in the future. We didn't want to introduce you as 'Mai's daughter.' We made a choice to keep this secret from you. Will you forgive us? Dennis is not your biological father. Your real father is in Vietnam, and he is still alive, and he is a good man. I have not seen him since I left the country years ago. Dennis loves you and has been a wonderful father to you. Do you ever have any complaints?"

"No," she whimpered. "I am not disappointed because you hid the truth from me, but I am disappointed that I am not Daddy's blood daughter."

After a few moments of silence she weakly replied, "I am getting tired, Mom. Can we take a shortcut home?"

When we got back, I tucked Terri in. When Dennis came home from work, he could tell we had been crying and asked what was going on. I pointed to Terri and said, "You need to ask Terri."

Dennis sat by the side of the bed and asked, "Terri, can you tell me why you and Mommy have been crying?"

Terri looked up at Dennis and answered, "Mommy told me today that you are not my biological father. That's why we are crying."

Dennis gently took her hand and said, "Terri, when you were growing up, did I ever not treat you like a real daughter?"

Terri shook her head and replied, "No."

"That's because I feel you are my daughter. I love you so much, and that's all that matters. You are my daughter and I am your father, and nothing can change that."

Terri reached for Dennis and sobbed. "Daddy, if I had a second chance, there are some things I would ask God to change, but there is one thing I would never change: I would keep you as my father."

Dennis held Terri in his arms, and we all wept and expressed our love for each other. After this emotional visit, coupled with seeing Terri deteriorate before our eyes, Dennis slipped into deep grief. Grandma Marge began to minister to him. She told him of the Lord's love for him and how Jesus wanted to carry his heavy burdens. He broke down and started to cry. This time he understood with his heart, as well as his head, when he prayed to receive Jesus.

While they were praying, I sat in the bedroom with Terri. How my heart ached for my firstborn child. I wished there was a way I could take her place. She placed her head on my chest. From time to time I would whisper to her, but she didn't respond. Later, as her body was shutting down, she whispered, "I want Grandma Marge."

I called for Grandma Marge. As she stood by the bed, Terri said, "Grandma Marge, I saw Jesus."

We knelt beside her bed and began to pray. We thanked God for allowing us to have Terri and for what she had meant to us.

We knew the end was drawing near. Around six o'clock in the morning on New Year's Day, I stood by her bed and watched her respirations. I knew she was about to leave us. I went out into the kitchen and called for Grandma Marge, Dennis and another dear friend, Betty, to come. We all knelt around Terri's bed. Dennis kissed her on the cheek and whispered the Lord's Prayer into her ear. We all realized Terri was about to cross over Jordan, but there seemed to be a slight resistance on her part. To help her let go, Dennis lovingly said, "Terri, it's OK. You go home and be with the Lord. You don't have to fight anymore. Just go." God's peace filled the room, and a few minutes later, we watched as she took her final breath.

"She's gone!" I sobbed as I crawled onto the bed and laid her head on my chest. Brenda brought Cherée over and sat her down by her mommy. She didn't know her mommy had left us. She squeezed her mommy's nose and asked, "Do you want a drink, Mom?"

After we said our final farewells, Dennis called the funeral home. They came and picked up her body around eight o'clock. Dennis was very sensitive to Cherée's tender spirit and wanted to protect her. He took her into another room while the mortician took Terri's body away.

The Army allowed Terri's husband to come home for the funeral. When we saw him, he told us how sorry he was for leaving her. We didn't understand why he left her alone to face her terminal illness, but we forgave him. He has since remarried, is the father of twins, and teaches in a military school in England.

I was stunned that my beautiful daughter who was only 23 was gone, but God had given us wisdom and direction for Cherée's future. When we realized Terri was dying, we went to a lawyer and began adoption proceedings so we could have full custody of Cherée.

## MOMMY AND DADDY

When we stood before the judge, she said, "Mrs. Spencer, you are now not only Cherée's grandmother, but also her mother."

Then she looked at Dennis and replied, "Mr. Spencer, you are not only Cherée's grandfather, but also her father."

Cherée's tiny ears must have understood every word because after the adoption was finalized, and we were in the car leaving the parking lot, Cherée piped up and asked, "Can I call you Mommy and Daddy now?"

Dennis said, "It's up to you, honey, if you want to call us Nana and Papa or Mommy and Daddy; whatever you decide is OK with us."

You could see the wheels in her mind turning. She thought a little bit and said, "I want to call you Mommy and Daddy."

From that day to this, she has always called us Mommy and Daddy.

God is so amazing. He gave us the right bandage for our broken hearts when He blessed us with Cherée. She was the perfect medicine for the sickness of grief that plagued our souls. There are days I look at her and see Terri, but her nature is like Dennis. She has brought so much joy to us. When she was just five, she came home one day and announced, "I want to be a doctor when I grow up."

That dream is still alive in her. She is a straight-A student, volunteers at the hospital and will graduate from high school this summer. I marvel at the Christian friends God has given her and the hunger she has for the Word of God. She is proof to me that God keeps His Word and watches over the orphans.

*The Lord protects the foreigners among us. He cares for the orphans and widows…*

PSALMS 146:9a NLT

The promises of God are true. He has never left us comfortless, but in the midst of great pain, has restored the years the enemy tried to steal from us.

*And I will restore to you the years that the locust hath eaten, the canker-worm, and the caterpillar, and the palmerworm, my great army which I sent among you.*

JOEL 2:25 KJV

Satan meant it for evil, but God brought good out of it. He gave us, as His Word declares, beauty for ashes and the oil of joy for mourning.

*And provide for those who grieve in Zion—*
*to bestow on them a crown of beauty*
*instead of ashes,*
*the oil of gladness*
*instead of mourning,*
*and a garment of praise*
*instead of a spirit of despair.*
*They will be called oaks of righteousness,*
*a planting of the Lord*
*for the display of his splendor.*

ISAIAH 61:3

I began to see more clearly how Satan wanted to destroy our family, but God had other plans. As we allowed His supernatural touch upon our hearts and lives, He was taking our tragedies and making them triumphs. With the Holy Spirit working behind the scenes, our heartaches would bring healing to the brokenhearted.

*You intended to harm me, but God intended it for good to accomplish what is now being done, the saving of many lives.*

GENESIS 50:20

# Chapter Seventeen

# DREAM COMES TRUE

uring those six long months that Terri was sick, I began sewing jackets, slacks, skirts and blouses while she rested. Our house looked like a boutique with many of my creations draped all over the furniture in every room. My creative juices got the best of me one day after I had purchased several new patterns. As I looked them over, I was inspired to make little changes here and there. Just the tad bit of tweaking seemed to give the article of clothing an entirely different style. People would rave about the new designs I created. It seemed to give me a little reprieve from the stress of Terri's terminal illness. In fact, it was therapeutic for me to stitch away on the nights I couldn't sleep. Rather than lie in bed and be consumed with tormenting thoughts, I would get up and sew. The Lord knew I needed this creative outlet in my life. It relaxed me and helped me cope.

## SEW AND SEW

One day our doorbell rang. I was surprised to see two ladies standing at my front door. The first words out of my mouth were, "Did God send you here?"

They nodded their heads. I invited them into our living room, where they sat in our two wingback chairs. I didn't recognize either of them, but they knew an acquaintance of mine, Marti, a local doctor's wife. Marti owned her own clothing business. She specialized in fancy southwestern-style vests and jackets. She had seen some of my work and invited me to contract with her and sew the jackets and vests. Before Terri's devastating illness, I filled a few orders for her, but I was forced to stop when Terri was diagnosed with ovarian cancer.

Patti introduced her friend to me. "Mai, this is Betty Olsen. She was in town on business."

Betty was so sweet. She looked at me and said, "I heard your young daughter has cancer and wondered if it would be all right if I prayed with her?"

I assured her we appreciated all the prayers we could get. After Betty prayed, she was enthralled with my sewing creations strewn throughout the house. She turned to me and asked, "Are you in the garment business?"

I told her my dream of creating my own clothing line. She marveled at how stylish my clothes were and wondered if I would be willing to allow her to display some of my latest designs at her upcoming fashion shows in New York, Dallas and Denver.

I thanked her for her kind offer, but let her know Terri's care was my top priority. She understood, but wanted my phone number so we could keep in touch for business opportunities down the road.

Three weeks later, my phone rang. I couldn't believe my ears. It was Betty. She gushed, "Mai, I am headed to New York for a show. I would be honored to take some of your samples with me."

I was very flattered Betty was so impressed with my work, but I knew it wasn't feasible for me to even consider such an opportunity.

"Thanks, Betty, but I'm afraid I have to decline your kind offer." I continued, "I'm not quite ready yet. I don't have a label, and if you sold a lot of orders I wouldn't be able to fill them. Let's keep in contact over the next few months, and I will let you know when I'm ready."

When she returned from her trip, she called and was so excited because of record sales. As she was sharing, I was reminded again of how God had answered my prayers. I had specifically asked Him to bless me with my own clothing line, and now it was becoming a reality.

## GOOD GRIEF

In the midst of my dreams coming true, I was drowning in waves of grief. I wasn't crying uncontrollably or losing my temper, but I was filled with deep sadness. I learned there are no shortcuts in the grieving process. We have the Lord's promise in the twenty-third psalm that, when we walk through the valley of the shadow of death, He is with us. The Great I Am will never leave us in want. All we need He will always be. He shall supply all our needs, even walking with us through the most difficult valleys we face in this life.

*The Lord is my shepherd, I shall not be in want.*
*He makes me lie down in green pastures,*
*he leads me beside quiet waters,*
*he restores my soul.*
*He guides me in paths of righteousness*
*for his name's sake.*
*Even though I walk*
*through the valley of the shadow of death,*
*I will fear no evil,*
*for you are with me;*
*your rod and your staff,*
*they comfort me.*
*You prepare a table before me*
*in the presence of my enemies.*
*You anoint my head with oil;*
*my cup overflows.*
*Surely goodness and love will follow me*
*all the days of my life,*
*and I will dwell in the house of the Lord*
*forever.*

One evening I couldn't sleep and I could feel myself sinking in despair. I tried to give my pain to the Lord. He seemed to show me there are healthy and unhealthy ways of grieving. I realized the enemy was trying to destroy me through intense sadness and a feeling of hopelessness. The Lord seemed to reveal to me that I needed to stay busy. This would keep me from smothering in the suffocating pain. I tried to think of what gifts I had, and without hesitation I knew God had blessed me with a creative mind and the gift of sewing. I prayed again about developing my own clothing line. I felt the

Holy Spirit speak into the depths of my soul these words: Take your work out the door, and I will bless you.

For three days in a row, I heard the Lord speak this same phrase into my heart. Hope rose in my heart, and I knew God was going to bless the work of my hands.

*The Lord will open the heavens, the storehouse of his bounty, to send rain on your land in season and to bless all the work of your hands. You will lend to many nations but will borrow from none.*

DEUTERONOMY 28:12

*You will again obey the Lord and follow all his commands I am giving you today. Then the Lord your God will make you most prosperous in all the work of your hands, and in the fruit of your womb, the young of your livestock and the crops of your land. The Lord will again delight in you and make you prosperous, just as he delighted in your fathers.*

DEUTERONOMY 30:8–9

## DISNEYLAND

After Terri's funeral, we took Brenda and Cherée to Disneyland. We were trying to have a fresh start and give our girls some happy memories after all the heartache they'd been through. I sat on a park bench and watched Dennis and the girls squealing with delight as they rode different rides. I smiled to myself and thanked the Lord for helping our shattered family have new beginnings. I looked up and saw a gift shop. My curiosity was aroused when I saw broom-skirts. The colors were brilliant. I walked over and picked one up and was shocked to see a price tag of over $400. I went back and sat on the bench, and the numbers started clicking in my head. When Dennis and the girls finished their ride, I told Dennis about the expensive skirts. I asked him to guess how much they cost. He thought around $200. I laughed and told him the outrageous price. I was convinced I could make them. When I returned home, I went to Hancock Fabrics and bought four yards of the same material the broom-skirts were made of. I went home and cut out the skirt, but I was having trouble figuring out the crinkle technique. Then, inspiration struck. I took my broomstick, starched the fabric, wrapped it around the broom handle and placed it outside to dry. The next day, I carefully unwrapped it, and it looked like an exact replica of the skirt in the Disneyland gift shop. I was on a roll and decided I could make them and sell them for a lot less, and I would still be making a substantial profit.

## My Own Label

I found some colorful Alexander Prints and started making more broomskirts. A month later, Betty Olsen came to visit and saw the Alexander Print with a rodeo theme. She said she knew this would be a hot seller and asked if I was willing to have my own label and make some for a show she was going to.

I considered Betty's offer and felt the timing was right. I contacted my dear friends, Anthony and Denise Barnett, and asked them to help me design a label for my new sewing business. Anthony looked out the window of our house and, inspired by the view, he said, "Let's have a mountain and a cactus on your label."

It seemed perfect. Now we just needed a name for my new business. One night I prayed and asked God to give me a name. I felt Him whisper into my heart that it should be called Spencer Creations. We sent out all the information, and in just a few days, the labels came back with our logo and name on them. We started production. I stopped purchasing my fabric from Hancock Fabrics because it was too costly. Someone had shared with me about a garment district in Los Angeles, so I drove there and paid cash for $10,000 worth of prints and fabrics. I used all our savings at that time, but Dennis was willing for me to step out in my new business venture.

I made close to 200 skirts, shirts and vests. I sent them with Betty and she sold between six and eight thousand dollars worth of orders. I had four to eight weeks to finish each order and ship it out. I was busy, but I was able to sew them all myself.

## BOOMING BUSINESS

Betty was positive more of her clients would want to purchase my clothing line. She sold them from store to store and kept placing more orders. The wheels in my head started turning, and I thought if I spent my whole time sewing and in production, I wouldn't be able to create new designs. Dennis and I talked it over and decided to purchase a couple more sewing machines and hire a few people who were willing to work from home. This really worked out well for me. My business was booming.

In the middle of my growing success, Betty's marriage began to unravel. She wasn't able to go out and promote my clothing line, so sales began to drop. I began to pray about my business and felt I should sign up for classes at a trade school. As I became more knowledgeable about the business side of my company, the Lord opened another door of opportunity for my booming business. Betty called and said she knew of two men who would be an asset to my company. They were both excellent salesmen and had showrooms in Texas, Wyoming, Colorado and Iowa. After visiting with them, they agreed to represent my clothing line. They took some of my samples and sold $20,000 worth of merchandise. I took another road trip to California and bought more fabric and materials. I hired eight new employees to sew samples, press, pleat, cut, box and ship orders. We were swamped and enjoying every minute of our success. Our entire house, except for two of our three bedrooms, had been invaded by Spencer Creations.

My employees were all Vietnamese and practicing Buddhists. Some worked in our house; others subcontracted from their own homes. I delegated many of the jobs I used to do. Now my main responsibilities were to take orders and make a possible chaotic situation run as smoothly as possible.

## REVIVAL FIRES

My heart was burdened for all my employees. I wanted them to know Jesus. When they came to work at my house, I had the Bible on cassette playing in the background. The only problem was it was in English. I wanted to find the Bible on cassette in the Vietnamese language. I thought of all the older people in Vietnam who did not read or write who I could give these tapes to, but I couldn't find the recordings anywhere.

It was around this time I took a trip to Vietnam. When I got into the vehicle, my brother popped a cassette into his player. It was the Bible on cassette in the Vietnamese language. I couldn't believe my ears. This was exactly what I had been praying for. My brother told me some tourist had given it to him. He ejected the tape from the player and let me read the label. It was from some ministry in California. I wrote down the contact numbers. When I returned to the States, I called and ordered a set. They only had the New Testament, but I was so thankful just to have that. I played the tapes every day for my employees. In fact, we used the tapes so much we wore out two sets.

I decided to begin our day with a staff prayer meeting. Every morning we would pray together and then listen to the Bible on cassette while we worked. Anthony and Denise, our neighbors, started hinting to us that we needed to find a church. I listened to what they said, but didn't take any action. I told them I was so busy working seven days a week, I didn't have time to stop and go to church. I was a workaholic. I was just a baby Christian and didn't know about the commandment of the Lord in Exodus.

*Remember the Sabbath day by keeping it holy.*

EXODUS 20:8

## CHURCH HOME

Two years later, God sent a young man named Ho to my door. He really needed a job, but because of his troubled past, people were hesitant to hire him. When he told me about his life, my heart was filled with compassion for him. He was an Amerasian. His father was an African American, and his mother was Vietnamese. The biracial children of Vietnam were so often tormented by their peers that many did not attend school. The more Caucasian or African American they looked, the more severely they were harassed. Faced with these pressures, many Vietnamese mothers abandoned their Amerasian children. Some were placed in orphanages, while others became street kids involved in criminal activities to survive. Biracial children were called "Con lai," which means half-breed or "Bui doi," which means the dust of life.

Ho had come to America through the American Homecoming Act that Congress passed in 1987. Approximately 25,000 Amerasians arrived in the United States, accompanied by 60,000 family members. You can imagine the difficult adjustment to American society most of these young adults had. Many returned to Vietnam.

If the child was fortunate enough to have adequate information on their father's identity, the Red Cross would attempt to locate him. The father had the option of whether or not he wished to be a part of his child's life. It was very sad because approximately only two percent of the fathers contacted their children.

Ho asked if I would give him a chance. Mercy strummed on my heartstrings as I looked into his eyes. I decided to hire him even though he was illiterate and had been in trouble with the law. It seemed as if God was asking me to give this young man a chance. I began to teach him how to sew accessories on the garments. He worked hard to please me. During the time I was training him, we had some good talks. My heart went out to him, and I said, "You need to find a church."

Looking back, I have to laugh because I didn't belong to any church, but I wanted him to go to church. I thought maybe he could find someone who'd pray with him and discuss his problems.

I knew a Vietnamese family who went to a Vietnamese Baptist Church in our area. Someone had told me this church had a van and would pick up people who didn't have a ride to church. Ho and I parked my car in front of this Vietnamese family's house. Sure enough the church van pulled up and people piled in. We followed the van. When we arrived at the church, we got out of my car and I introduced myself and Ho to the two pastors. One was an American pastor and the other a Vietnamese pastor. We went inside and stayed for the service. Afterwards Ho and I returned to my house to work.

When we met the two ministers, I invited them to come out to the house to visit with Ho. I wanted him to receive all the help he needed. A few days later, Pastor Hoang was at my door. We had a nice visit, and then he left.

The next Sunday, Ho called me and asked, "Auntie Mai, are you taking me to church today?"

I told him he could just borrow my car. He said he didn't want to go without me. I felt I had to go for Ho's sake. This became the routine several weeks in a row. We had another visit from Pastor Hoang Lee. He started talking to all my employees. The next Sunday, my entire crew attended the Vietnamese Baptist Church. We had invited Dennis, but he didn't go with us.

For two years, my employees and I attended the Sunday services when we could. Many times they got ready for church at our house. For several months, I began to have an ache in my heart for Dennis to go with us. One night I asked him to pray with me. Little Cherée walked in and said, "I'll pray with you, Mommy."

Dennis prayed with me, but it seemed he only did so to appease me. I felt so sad. I wanted us to be one for Jesus and our hearts to be united for His kingdom and purpose for our lives. I felt I was carrying a heavy burden on my shoulders. One night I was so troubled about it I was unable to sleep. Around two o'clock in the morning, I got up and knelt by the side of my bed and began to pray for my husband to go to church. I knew Dennis loved me, and I dearly loved him, but I felt it would please the Lord for us to attend church as a family. I asked the Lord to deal with Dennis and convince him to attend the Lord's house with me.

Three months later, God answered my prayer. One of girls who worked for me and I were getting ready to go to church one Sunday morning. Dennis asked me, "Honey, do you care if I come to church with you today?"

I tried not to show how excited I was, but calmly replied, "No, I don't mind. You can come to church with me."

I went out to the girl and exclaimed, "Dennis is coming to church today. When he comes, try to act normally. Don't make a big deal of it."

The entire church was Vietnamese except for Dennis. The Vietnamese pastor preached in Vietnamese, but if an English speaking person attended, the American pastor would interpret. Dennis seemed to enjoy it. Once again God had answered my prayers. We have attended church as a family ever since.

We were faithful members of that church for about five years. Cherée was nine and spoke English. I could speak and understand both languages, but Dennis and I felt it made more sense if we went to an English-speaking congregation, one that would minister to all our family's needs. We began to pray about where we should go. Pastor Hoang invited Dennis to Catalina Foothills Church to take Evangelism Explosion Training Classes. When we started looking for a new church home in Tucson, we remembered all we had learned in those soul-winning classes and the kindred spirit we felt with the senior minister, Pastor Mark. Dennis said he felt God was leading our family to the Catalina Foothills Church. I could see how God had orchestrated every step, but little did I know, it was just the beginning of His divine plan. He was preparing the groundwork for a ministry in Binh Chau, Vietnam.

## DELIVERED

*So if the Son sets you free, you will be free indeed.*

### JOHN 8:36

As I began to grow in the Lord, I felt Him lovingly ask me to lay down my cigarettes. He never condemned me, but He lovingly charmed my heart. I wanted to be all I could be for Him and His vineyard.

Cigarettes were a giant in my life. God was calling me to be a giant slayer. I had smoked since I was nine. Many times I attempted to quit, but it never lasted for more than a few months. I tried several remedies—even the patch—but nothing worked.

One day I knelt and prayed, "Lord, would you please help me quit smoking?" I didn't want anything in my life to be a stumbling block to others. Every time I lit up a cigarette, I felt I wasn't a good testimony for Jesus. I continued to pray, "How can I go out and witness to other people and tell them how You set people free when I am bound by these cigarettes? I want to be free for You. In my own strength, I can't do it, but You can do it through me."

Several weeks passed. One morning I woke up and poured myself a fresh cup of coffee. I pulled the kitchen drawer open, expecting to pull out a pack of cigarettes, but the package was empty. Dennis looked up and asked if he should stop by the store and buy more.

"No, I quit," I blurted out.

I was serious. I believed Jesus would help me conquer my addiction to nicotine. His Word declares that, through Him, we are more than conquerors.

*No, in all these things we are more than conquerors*
*through him who loved us.*

Romans 8:37

I prayed, "Lord, I need You to help me quit smoking."

I was so excited when I made it through the morning without much trouble, but around lunch time I was starting to sink. The Holy Spirit prompted me to go pray. As I prayed, the strong desire to smoke lessened. I made it through the afternoon, but after I ate supper, I was tempted to smoke again. I knew I couldn't beat this addiction on my own, but I also believed, as weak as I was, that Jesus would prove Himself strong on my behalf. I began to pray harder, and the Lord came and helped me.

*For when I am weak, then I am strong.*

2 Corinthians 12:10b nlt

For two weeks I went through this same routine, and every day that passed, I felt Jesus was giving me victory. One day after not smoking for four months, I was driving past a gas station and Satan whispered in my ear, "Stop and fill the car with gas. Buy a pack of cigarettes and a lighter. Then you'll know if you've really quit."

I glanced down at the gas gauge. It was three-quarters full, but I was weak and pulled into the gas station. I bought a pack of cigarettes and a lighter. I pulled out a cigarette and lit it up. I took one puff and started to feel queasy. I couldn't even finish the cigarette. I cried out to the Lord and thanked Him for delivering me from this addiction that had held me captive for 35 years.

*In my distress I cried unto the Lord, and he heard me.*

Psalm 120:1 kjv

## HEART CHANGE

Even though the Lord had given me an outward victory over cigarettes, I discovered I had inward enemies in the crevices of my soul. My nature was my worst enemy. God blessed Dennis with a sweet disposition and even when He wasn't a Christian, he had the gift of affirmation. He has always been able to encourage people and knows just what to say in delicate situations. I was born with spunk and a feisty temper. I hold grudges, have a tendency to exaggerate, and am chief among sinners. I experienced what Paul described in the Book of Romans.

*I have discovered this principle of life—that when I want to do what is right, I inevitably do what is wrong. I love God's law with all my heart. But there is another power within me that is at war with my mind. This power makes me a slave to the sin that is still within me. Oh, what a miserable person I am! Who will free me from this life that is dominated by sin and death? Thank God! The answer is in Jesus Christ our Lord. So you see how it is: In my mind I really want to obey God's law, but because of my sinful nature I am a slave to sin.*

ROMANS 7:21–25 NLT

I learned a valuable secret through my victories and defeats: Only time in His presence can expel the weaknesses in the flesh. I cannot change myself. As I began to read His Word and pray, He brought the fruit of the Spirit into my life. I cried out to the Lord and pleaded with Him to take away my harsh temperament. At times the words in my mouth were so sharp they caused people much pain. I realized the Lord had to set up His kingdom in my soul, and any efforts I made were fruitless.

*Unless the Lord builds the house, its builders labor in vain. Unless the Lord watches over the city, the watchmen stand guard in vain.*

PSALM 127:1

As I spent time getting to know Jesus and devouring His Word, He began to stamp His image on my heart. He was being permanently formed inside of me.

*My little children, for whom I am again suffering birth pangs until Christ is completely and permanently formed (molded) within you.*

Galatians 4:19 amp

## The Prophesy

Betty Olsen called me one day and invited me to go and hear a minister from England who would be speaking at revival services for two weeks in Tucson. I agreed. The praise and worship ushered me into the presence of God. After the evangelist spoke, there was a time of ministry. He came up to me and laid his hand on my shoulder and began to prophesy.

"The Lord has shown me you are not to worry about your family because within two years all your family will come to know Christ."

At that time, all my family was worshipping Buddha. They had numerous idols in their homes. I was just young in the Lord and couldn't imagine how they were going to come to Jesus, but it still thrilled my heart.

When I came home and told Dennis what the minister had prophesied, he just looked at me. He didn't say a word, but he told me later what he was thinking: Good luck, God, on that one! Mai's family have been Buddhists for generations.

I was like Mary. I pondered this word from the Lord in my heart.

*But Mary treasured up all these things and pondered them in her heart.*

Luke 2:19

# Chapter Eighteen

# KEEPING A PROMISE

was thrilled with the way God was moving in our lives. Dennis and I could sense the winds of revival in the depths of our souls. We were so hungry to grow in our newfound faith. One day as I began to thank God for the many times He had answered my prayers, I had a strange revelation. I realized there was one prayer God didn't answer. I had asked Him to bring my family to the States, but He never provided a way for them to come. As I sat there analyzing all the "whys" and "why nots," suddenly it hit me: It wasn't God's will for my family to move to America because He wanted them to stay in Vietnam and use them to bring souls to Jesus. I sat dumbfounded and marveled at the awesomeness of God. His ways are far above my ways, and He never makes a mistake. The scales had fallen off my eyes. I decided I needed to take a trip to Vietnam and see my family and share with them what the Lord had revealed to me.

*For as the heavens are higher than the earth, so are My ways higher than your ways and My thoughts than your thoughts.*

ISAIAH 55:9 AMP

When I arrived in my homeland, my sister-in-law invited me to see a new church in Long Hai. As I stared at the dilapidated building, I couldn't believe my eyes. The little church looked like a shack or some type of storage shed. My sister-in-law hoped I would be able to financially help them. Tears pooled in my eyes as I looked at the pitiful structure. I was deeply moved by the sincerity of the people who desired to have a building to worship the Lord in. Suddenly, in the depths of my soul, I remembered the promise I had made. I had vowed, if He would bless me financially, I would return to my homeland and build a prayer house for Him. This promise burned in my heart, and I knew it was the Spirit of the Lord. He was calling me to fulfill my promise.

*It is better not to vow than to make a vow and not fulfill it.*

Ecclesiastes 5:5

The small congregation invited me to share my testimony, and I accepted their gracious invitation. At the end of my talk, an altar call was given. Five precious souls came forward to receive Christ.

## Divine Destiny

When I returned to America, I kept thinking about the promise I had made to the Lord. I shared my heart with Dennis. I showed him the pictures of the little church. It was an emotional time for me. I wanted to sell everything I owned and build a prayer house for the Lord. I knew God was calling me. This was my spiritual destiny. As my eternal vision increased, my temporal vision diminished. I was losing my materialistic appetite. My heart was now consumed with helping the people of Vietnam. One night as Dennis and I were visiting, I thought my heart would burst.

"Dennis, is it all right with you if I completely shut down Spencer Creations?"

Without hesitation Dennis assured me I could dissolve my sewing business.

I explained to him I felt I was to be about my Father's business. He fully supported my decision to follow my heart.

*And He said to them, How is it that you had to look for Me? Did you not see and know that it is necessary [as a duty] for Me to be in My Father's house and [occupied] about My Father's business?*

Luke 2:49 amp

After I helped each of my employees find other employment, I was able to devote the majority of my time to the Lord. My priorities had changed.

At the time, Cherée was nine, and we enjoyed spending quality time together. Joy bells continually rang in my heart. I had learned a valuable lesson, a little secret that makes the joy of the Lord bubble up in your soul.

*Jesus first!*
*Others second!*
*Yourself last!*

Implementing this biblical principle in my life made the joy of the Lord well up in my soul and spill over onto all those I came in contact with.

As I spent time in His presence, the Lord began to show me I had spent most of my life obsessed with my own agenda and consumed with the ways of the world. I began to devour God's Word. When I read the parable of the sower, it was as if I was looking in a mirror. I saw how, for years, spiritual seeds had been planted in my heart, but the cares of this world and the deceitfulness of riches had snuffed out any possible spiritual crop in my life.

## PARABLE OF THE SOWER

*That same day Jesus went out of the house and sat by the lake. Such large crowds gathered around him that he got into a boat and sat in it, while all the people stood on the shore. Then he told them many things in parables, saying: "A farmer went out to sow his seed. As he was scattering the seed, some fell along the path, and the birds came and ate it up. Some fell on rocky places, where it did not have much soil. It sprang up quickly, because the soil was shallow. But when the sun came up, the plants were scorched, and they withered because they had no root. Other seed fell among thorns, which grew up and choked the plants. Still other seed fell on good soil, where it produced a crop—a hundred, sixty or thirty times what was sown. He who has ears, let him hear."*

*The disciples came to him and asked, "Why do you speak to the people in parables?"*

*He replied, "The knowledge of the secrets of the kingdom of heaven has been given to you, but not to them. Whoever has will be given*

*more, and he will have an abundance. Whoever does not have, even*
*what he has will be taken from him. This is why I speak to them in*
*parables: "Though seeing, they do not see; though hearing, they do not*
*hear or understand. In them is fulfilled the prophecy of Isaiah: 'You*
*will be ever hearing but never understanding; you will be ever seeing*
*but never perceiving. For this people's heart has become calloused; they*
*hardly hear with their ears, and they have closed their eyes. Otherwise*
*they might see with their eyes, hear with their ears, understand with*
*their hearts and turn, and I would heal them.' But blessed are your eyes*
*because they see, and your ears because they hear. For I tell you the*
*truth, many prophets and righteous men longed to see what you see*
*but did not see it, and to hear what you hear but did not hear it.*

*"Listen then to what the parable of the sower means: When any-*
*one hears the message about the kingdom and does not understand it,*
*the evil one comes and snatches away what was sown in his heart. This*
*is the seed sown along the path. The one who received the seed that fell*
*on rocky places is the man who hears the word and at once receives it*
*with joy. But since he has no root, he lasts only a short time. When*
*trouble or persecution comes because of the word, he quickly falls away.*
*The one who received the seed that fell among the thorns is the man*
*who hears the word, but the worries of this life and the deceitfulness of*
*wealth choke it, making it unfruitful. But the one who received the*
*seed that fell on good soil is the man who hears the word and under-*
*stands it. He produces a crop, yielding a hundred, sixty or thirty times*
*what was sown."*

MATTHEW 13:1–23

## THE PARABLE OF THE WEEDS

*Jesus told them another parable: "The kingdom of heaven is like a man*
*who sowed good seed in his field. But while everyone was sleeping, his*
*enemy came and sowed weeds among the wheat, and went away. When*
*the wheat sprouted and formed heads, then the weeds also appeared.*

*"The owner's servants came to him and said, 'Sir, didn't you sow*
*good seed in your field? Where then did the weeds come from?'*

"'An enemy did this,' he replied. "The servants asked him, 'Do you want us to go and pull them up?'

"'No,' he answered, 'because while you are pulling the weeds, you may root up the wheat with them. Let both grow together until the harvest. At that time I will tell the harvesters: First collect the weeds and tie them in bundles to be burned; then gather the wheat and bring it into my barn.'"

MATTHEW 13:24–30

## THE PARABLE OF THE WEEDS EXPLAINED

Then he left the crowd and went into the house. His disciples came to him and said, "Explain to us the parable of the weeds in the field." He answered, "The one who sowed the good seed is the Son of Man. The field is the world, and the good seed stands for the sons of the kingdom. The weeds are the sons of the evil one, and the enemy who sows them is the devil. The harvest is the end of the age, and the harvesters are angels.

"As the weeds are pulled up and burned in the fire, so it will be at the end of the age. The Son of Man will send out his angels, and they will weed out of his kingdom everything that causes sin and all who do evil. They will throw them into the fiery furnace, where there will be weeping and gnashing of teeth. Then the righteous will shine like the sun in the kingdom of their Father. He who has ears, let him hear."

MATTHEW 13:36–43

Something was settled in my heart. I couldn't afford any more wasted years. I wanted to be fruitful for Jesus and His kingdom. I surrendered what time I had left to the work of the Lord. I was determined my life would produce a bountiful harvest of souls for my King. I was now Christ's ambassador.

We are therefore Christ's ambassadors, as though God were making his appeal through us. We implore you on Christ's behalf: Be reconciled to God.

2 CORINTHIANS 5:20

## SITTING AT THE FEET OF JESUS

The more I became acquainted with Jesus and His ways, the more I realized how little I understood about spiritual matters. Yes, I was saved and belonged to Him, but Jesus was asking more from me. As I studied the Scriptures, I realized He had paid a great price for me. He gave His all for me. Surely in return I should and would willingly give my all to Him.

*You were bought with a price [purchased with a preciousness and paid for, made His own]. So then, honor God and bring glory to Him in your body.*

1 CORINTHIANS 6:20 AMP

I became keenly aware that, even though I had given up my Buddha gods, I still put other things ahead of Jesus in my life.

*"You shall have no other gods before me."*

EXODUS 20:3

In deep repentance, I wept before the Lord. The Holy Spirit breathed on me and gave me a fresh infilling. Jesus became more real than ever before. It became clear that, just as I had gotten rid of all the Buddha idols in my home, I must now destroy the god of busyness in my life or I would never experience deep intimacy with Christ. As I continued in prayer, the Holy Spirit shone His light in all the nooks and crannies of my soul. Busyness of life was stunting my spiritual growth. Jesus was calling me to spend time in His presence, praying and studying His Word. I was to be like Mary of Bethany and sit at His feet and listen to His voice.

*As Jesus and his disciples were on their way, he came to a village where a woman named Martha opened her home to him. She had a sister called Mary, who sat at the Lord's feet listening to what he said.*

LUKE 10:38, 39

I remembered when I had read Mr. Nam's Bible and never grasped what the Spirit was trying to say to me, but now I was a believer, and Jesus was precious to me. As I fed upon His Word, I knew life as I had known it would never be the same.

*Unto you therefore which believe he is precious.*

1 Peter 2:7 KJV

## Damascus Road Experience

The conversion of Saul of Tarsus has always been such an encouragement to me. Before he became a believer, he persecuted the church. Then he had a "Damascus Road" experience that changed him forever. Instead of being an enemy of the Church, he became one of the greatest apostles and wrote almost half the New Testament. Can you imagine God choosing a persecutor of His people to become such a useful vessel of the Lord? He was so transformed that God gave him a new name: Paul. Toward the end of his life, Paul writes:

*Here is a trustworthy saying that deserves full acceptance: Christ Jesus came into the world to save sinners—of whom I am the worst.*

1 Timothy 1:15

## Stoning of Stephen

I am sure Paul grieved over his past persecutions of the Church and Satan attempted to condemn him after Paul became a Christian. He must have relived the stoning of Stephen over and over in his mind.

*But Stephen, full of the Holy Spirit, looked up to heaven and saw the glory of God, and Jesus standing at the right hand of God. "Look," he said, "I see heaven open and the Son of Man standing at the right hand of God."*
*At this they covered their ears and, yelling at the top of their voices, they all rushed at him, dragged him out of the city and began to stone him. Meanwhile, the witnesses laid their clothes at the feet of a young man named Saul.*

*While they were stoning him, Stephen prayed, "Lord Jesus, receive
my spirit."*

*Then he fell on his knees and cried out, "Lord, do not hold this sin
against them." When he had said this, he fell asleep.*

ACTS 7:55–60

This story should be an inspiration to each one of us. Jesus' blood can
make the vilest sinner clean. There is hope for everyone. If God can change
Saul of Tarsus and make him a saint for His purposes, He can transform you.
If the Lord can take a little Buddhist girl from the jungles of Vietnam and
bring her to America where she would hear and respond to the goodness of
the Lord, God can transform you. Nothing is impossible with Jesus.

*Jesus looked at them intently and said, "Humanly speaking, it is impos-
sible. But not with God. Everything is possible with God."*

MARK 10:27 NLT

## NOT I, BUT CHRIST

When I was just starting Spencer Creations, God began waking me up at
night to pray. I decided to have a room dedicated to prayer and counseling.
One day while I was sitting in my prayer room all alone, I opened my Bible
and read the following verses in the Old Testament.

*When the Lord your God brings you into the land you are entering to pos-
sess and drives out before you many nations—the Hittites, Girgashites,
Amorites, Canaanites, Perizzites, Hivites and Jebusites, seven nations
larger and stronger than you—and when the LORD your God has delivered them over to you and you have defeated them, then you must destroy
them totally. Make no treaty with them, and show them no mercy.*

DEUTERONOMY 7:1, 2

The Lord put in my heart that these seven nations were the bad habits
in my life that I must conquer. He confirmed in me that these were the
seven things that were detestable to Him.

*There are six things the Lord hates, seven that are detestable to him:*
*haughty eyes, a lying tongue, hands that shed innocent blood, a heart*
*that devises wicked schemes, feet that are quick to rush into evil, a false*
*witness who pours out lies and a man who stirs up dissension among*
*brothers.*

PROVERBS 6:16–19

I saw myself in these scriptures. I asked the Lord to deliver me from the strongholds in my life. Slowly He began to soften my heart and give me the Spirit of Christ. His peace in my heart began to overflow from my mouth. God has taken a tongue that used to curse and criticize and has given me a new tongue that blesses and encourages others. Old friends see me and ask me what has happened to change me. They say my face looks radiant and peaceful. I don't hesitate to share the love of Jesus with them.

During this spiritual "growing season" in my life, I was so excited about the way God was moving in our family. I continued to reflect back to that church service where the minister prophesied my family would come to know Jesus. God was about to open the floodgates of Heaven on my family. I sat back in amazement as I watched this prophecy come to pass.

*Chapter Nineteen*

# HIS PROMISES
# ONE BY ONE

❧

y mother was especially fond of her oldest son, Hoa. Anytime Dennis and I sent money to her, she gave him a portion of it. When Hoa and his wife, Hang, got married, my mother gave them a large chunk of her assets. Hoa had a taxi business and owned a bus, but hard times hit, and he lost everything. He and Hang moved and worked in Kieng Giang, a very small island several hours south of Saigon. They had a business loaning money to squid fishermen. When the fishermen returned from the ocean, they sold their catch to them. Hoa and Hang dried the squid for export. One day a horrific storm hit the small island and destroyed all the boats. The fishermen had nothing left, and most went back to their hometowns. The people who did business with Hoa and Hang had moved away. They had no other choice but to go bankrupt. It was during this difficult time, they wrote Dennis and I a letter and asked for financial assistance. After we read the letter, we wrote them back instructing them to cry out to the Lord for help. We also sent money to help them with their immediate needs.

## TWICE RELATED

During this time, my sister went to see my brother and invited him to church. He made excuses and insisted his clothes weren't nice enough. Two of my sisters put their money together and bought him a nice outfit. We were so excited because now he couldn't refuse to go to the Lord's house. The next Sunday, he attended church and shared with us how the sermon touched his heart. During this time, my sister-in-law wrote me frequently, keeping me updated on Hoa's and Hang's spiritual journey.

After Hoa attended the church service, he sent a letter to Hang pleading with her to come to Saigon and accept the Lord. She immediately packed a few belongings and made plans to check on what was happening in her husband's life. Before she left, she looked around the house and tried to find a book she could read during the long bus drive. She couldn't find one anywhere. In Vietnam, books are rare because the country is so poor. She happened to glance up at their ancestral altar and noticed a book, stuffed it in her handbag, and headed out the door.

She decided she would first stop by a certain village and collect money from some people who were past due on their debts to them. After she got on the bus, she pulled out the book and discovered it was the Bible—the same Bible Mr. Nam had given me. She read the entire New Testament on her way. When she got to the village, she couldn't find any of the people who owed them money. She hurried on to meet her husband. She seemed to forget about all the money people owed them, because the first words out of her mouth when she saw her husband were, "I want to accept this Jesus into my heart, too."

This was a real miracle, because my sister-in-law was in a religion called Dao Hoa Hao, a mixed religion of Buddha, Jesus and Mary. They sometimes put Jesus' picture on the same altar with their Buddha statues. It reminds me of a scripture found in the Old Testament that should be a warning to all of us.

*They worshiped the Lord, but they also served their own gods in accordance with the customs of the nations from which they had been brought.*

2 KINGS 17:33

My sister-in-law made a decision to move to Saigon with my brother and begin again. They began to wholly follow the Lord. In their home was an altar with a large incense pot. After she gave her heart to Jesus, my sister-in-law took the altar down. She felt she couldn't throw it away, but she gave it to the neighbor. Later on, after we fed on the Word of God and grew in the Lord, we saw we were to break down the altars, burn them and throw them away.

*Hezekiah son of Ahaz began to rule over Judah in the third year of*
*King Hoshea's reign in Israel. He was twenty-five years old when he*
*became king, and he reigned in Jerusalem twenty-nine years. His*
*mother was Abijah, the daughter of Zechariah. He did what was pleas-*
*ing in the Lord's sight, just as his ancestor David had done. He*
*removed the pagan shrines, smashed the sacred pillars, and cut down*
*the Asherah poles.*

2 KINGS 18:1–4a NLT

When Hoa and Hang came to know Jesus, I thought my heart would
burst for joy. We were twice related. We were born into the same earthly
family, and now we both had been born again into the family of God.

## DIVINE INTERVENTION

My younger brother is a hard worker. A few years after he was married, he
started his own taxi business. Even though we sent thousands of dollars to
my family, they still suffered from severe poverty. My brother was using a
motorcycle to take people from one town to another. My mom had
accepted the Lord and wanted her son to know what Jesus had done for her.
He wouldn't accept anything she said. He was a workaholic. Even though
he worked from morning until night, he made only enough each day to
buy food and other basic necessities. He was always trying to think of ways
to make more money so he could get ahead. My mother tried to get him
to go to church, but he wouldn't go. He would say to her, "You guys go
ahead and do what you want, but I am going to stay here and worship my
ancestors."

A few weeks passed. One day he worked all day, but came home with
nothing. He was so discouraged. He saw my sister who had become a Christian. God had blessed her life. She seemed to always have enough for her
family's needs and even some to share with others. He decided to test out
our Jesus. Most Vietnamese were used to praying and making deals with
idols. They would pray a bargain prayer such as, "if you do this for me, I will
do this for you."

My brother prayed, "Lord Jesus, if You want me to follow You and become a Christian, when I go out to work today, send one person to bless me with money by noon."

That morning he left for work at seven o'clock. His first client was a Vietnamese American who had come to Vietnam for a visit. When they arrived at their destination, the man gave him a very large amount of money as a tip. My brother remembered his prayer and knew Jesus had answered his request. He came home at ten o'clock and removed all the altars and incense pots. He went to church on Sunday and accepted Christ.

Two weeks later, he went to work and met a customer who came from Hanoi. At that time, there were many gang members from Hanoi who robbed people. This man asked my brother to take him outside the city to a plantation in the countryside. It would take over two hours to get there by motorcycle. About an hour into the trip, the man asked my brother if they could stop and buy a soda pop. My brother pulled in at a little store. His customer asked him to leave the keys for the motorcycle with him.

My brother gave the keys to him, and when he came out, the man and his motorcycle were gone. He went to the police station and reported his Honda and 20 dollars in cash were stolen. The police loaned him a phone, and he called my sister's house. (I had installed a business phone in her house. People came and paid to use the phone.) My brother told her what had happened. My sister called me in the United States and told me about the stolen Honda. Dennis and I had bought that motorcycle for my brother the year before. We felt so bad for him and his family. My brother asked us to buy another motorcycle. He knew he had no other way to put bread on the table for his family.

I told him we should wait a few days. I felt we should pray and give God time to work. My brother was upset and didn't want to go home to his pregnant wife and tell her what had happened.

I felt this was an attack from Satan. A holy boldness came over me. The word of the Lord rose up in my soul. I told my family in two weeks the motorcycle would be returned. I knew God wasn't going to allow Satan to win. I counseled my brother to keep praying and not stop.

The mystery was solved just a few days before the two-week deadline. The man who stole the Honda sold the stolen motorcycle to a man in

Saigon. The thief had instructed the new owner to go to my sister's address and ask her to sign the title. My sister's house is just down the road from my brother's. My sister heard a knock at her door and was surprised to see a stranger who said, "Your brother sold me his Honda. I need you to sign over the title to me."

My sister was dumbfounded. When she looked outside and saw the stolen bike, she was shocked to see the once red motorcycle had been painted beige. The Lord gave her wisdom.

"Can you excuse me for one minute? My husband is next door, and I will get him."

She appeared at my brother's house and barked an order. "Call the police!"

In just a few minutes, the police arrived and questioned the stranger. It came to pass just as the Lord had shown me it would. The Honda was returned within two weeks. We couldn't help but smile because the motorcycle was actually in better shape when it was returned than when my brother had it. The bike's engine had been tuned up, and it looked sharp with its new paint job.

## Domino Effect

After I accepted the Lord, it had a domino effect on my family. One by one, almost all my relatives came to know the Him. There is only one of my relatives who still worships idols, and we continue to pray for this family member to have a revelation of Jesus Christ.

I think often of how God used the Bible Mr. Nam had given me. One of the most inspirational stories about this precious Book happened a few years ago when I was visiting Vietnam. I have a second cousin who heard I was home. She came to see me. Her family was very poor, and she came to see if there would be a way I could financially assist them. I shared the Gospel with her, and she prayed to receive Christ. Then I gave her Mr. Nam's Bible and encouraged her to find a Bible-believing church. I told her to surround herself with other believers. She took the Bible home, but her village was home to no other Christians or a church. God knew the end from the beginning. He knew she was going to die six months later. He sent her to me so I could share the Gospel with her. I believe God placed those Holy Scriptures in her hands. Since that time, I don't know where Mr. Nam's Bible went, but I believe with all my heart that God continues to use it to draw souls to Himself.

I cannot stop praising God for all He has done. I realized He had begun a work in me and my family. He had kept all His promises to me, but I had made a promise to Him, and I needed to fulfill it. I had to build a prayer house for Jesus. I had to finish what I said I would do.

*...being confident of this, that he who began a good work in you will carry it on to completion until the day of Christ Jesus.*

PHILIPPIANS 1:6

# FROM DISGRACE TO HIS GRACE

❧

Once I realized God had kept my family in Vietnam for a plan and purpose, I started to connect all the dots, and a beautiful picture was emerging. God's will became quite clear. The same God who had prospered Joseph in Egypt had prospered me. When Joseph's family needed food because of a famine, they came to Egypt and Joseph blessed them with grain. My family was experiencing their own famine in Vietnam, and they needed Dennis and me to help them whenever we could. We shared all our spiritual and financial blessings with them. I realized the main reason God didn't allow my family to come to America was because He wanted two Americans named Dennis and Mai Spencer to go to Vietnam and build a church and minister to the Vietnamese.

## SEND ME

After the Lord anointed my eyes with spiritual eye salve, I began to see with a new eternal perspective. I took a trip to Vietnam and returned to America, changed forever. My heart was burdened for the people of my native land. Everything else seemed like empty husks. I felt the call of God churning in the depths of my soul. I attempted to share my heart with different people, but nobody really understood the fervent compassion I felt for Vietnam. My heart was with my people. I began to spend time in prayer and the study of God's Word. It was almost unbelievable, but I knew I was hearing His voice. God was calling me, a former Buddhist girl, to be a laborer in his vineyard.

*And then I heard the voice of the Master:*
*"Whom shall I send? Who will go for us?"*
*I spoke up, "I'll go. Send me!"*

ISAIAH 6:8 MSG

There was no mistaking the voice I was hearing in my soul. I had spent years adhering to the world's philosophy, but those days were over. I was not the same person. I had enrolled in His university and began devouring the Word of God. I found a Christian bookstore and purchased some study materials. I saturated myself in sound Bible teaching.

One day as I read the Sermon on the Mount, my heart burned within me. I read where the people sat down on the green grass and listened as Jesus spoke. This is what I felt Jesus was asking of me. He wanted me to shut down my secular endeavors and open the windows of my soul to Him as I sat at His feet. My faith began to grow by leaps and bounds as I studied His Word.

*So then faith cometh by hearing, and hearing by the word of God.*

ROMANS 10:17 KJV

I remember being specific in my prayers. I asked the Lord to help me plant a church in my hometown of Binh Chau.

## NEW CHURCH – NEW MINISTRY

After Dennis and I changed churches, I extended an offer of service in any capacity to a precious woman named Ann. I told her if there was anything I could do to let me know. Little did I know that as I walked through the door to serving, God was going to open a ministry to Vietnam.

I have always enjoyed cooking for small or large groups. While I was attending the Vietnamese Church, I cooked every Sunday for over five years for our little group. God rewarded my faithfulness. Ann had let Kathryn Farris, a missionary to Mexico and our church's missions director, know about my willingness to serve, and Kathryn asked me to prepare an Asian meal for about 35 people who would be watching a video: Jesus in China. After the guests enjoyed the meal, we watched the video. As I sat enthralled with what God was doing in China, my heart couldn't help but be burdened for Vietnam. I wanted God to move in my homeland the way He was moving in China. After lunch, Kathryn approached me and asked me for the receipts from the luncheon expenses so I could be reimbursed. I told her I would like to send the money to the missionaries in China, and then I began to weep. It was so emotional for me. I poured out my heart to Kathryn. I even told her about the promise I had made to the Lord to build a prayer house in Vietnam for Him. I explained every detail of the way God had been leading me. I even told her that, for three years, the call seemed to be stronger and stronger in my soul. I told Kathryn of the vow I made to the Lord about building a prayer house in Binh Chau. I wanted this to be a place where people could come to know Jesus and their lives could be changed forever.

God's fingerprints were all over our encounter. Kathryn is a visionary and has a heart for all countries. She had served as a missionary for over 30 years to the poor in Mexico. She understood my heart's cry. It was as if we were kindred spirits for Jesus and what He wanted to do in Vietnam. Kathryn understood the burden I had. As I continued to share with her my heart's cry for Vietnam, it was as if God was cementing our hearts together.

I explained to Kathryn what I had seen in the Vietnamese people. Their lives were controlled by fear, jealousy, lies and other works of the flesh. I knew if the Holy Spirit could convict and save them, He would be able to guide them. The works of the flesh could be destroyed.

*So I say, let the Holy Spirit guide your lives. Then you won't be doing what your sinful nature craves. The sinful nature wants to do evil, which is just the opposite of what the Spirit wants. And the Spirit gives us desires that are the opposite of what the sinful nature desires. These two forces are constantly fighting each other, so you are not free to carry out your good intentions. But when you are directed by the Spirit, you are not under obligation to the law of Moses.*

*When you follow the desires of your sinful nature, the results are very clear: sexual immorality, impurity, lustful pleasures, idolatry, sorcery, hostility, quarreling, jealousy, outbursts of anger, selfish ambition, dissension, division, envy, drunkenness, wild parties, and other sins like these. Let me tell you again, as I have before, that anyone living that sort of life will not inherit the Kingdom of God.*

*The Holy Spirit produces this kind of fruit in our lives: love, joy, peace, patience, kindness, goodness, faithfulness, gentleness, and self-control. There is no law against these things!*

*Those who belong to Christ Jesus have nailed the passions and desires of their sinful nature to his cross and crucified them there. Since we are living by the Spirit, let us follow the Spirit's leading in every part of our lives. Let us not become conceited, or provoke one another, or be jealous of one another.*

GALATIANS 5:16-26 NLT

I knew I was once controlled by the flesh, but Jesus came to my darkened heart and brought me into His light. Every day He helps me walk in the Spirit. I didn't feel like I was somebody special. I believed Jesus wanted to come to the Vietnamese people and take them from "disgrace to His grace." He was simply calling Dennis and me to be part of what He wanted to do in Binh Chau.

*For God sent not his Son into the world to condemn the world; but that the world through him might be saved.*

JOHN 3:17 KJV

## LET THE LITTLE CHILDREN COME

My heart was especially breaking for the children. I felt the older generation was set in their ways because of the culture and the manmade traditions, but the children's hearts were still tender. If we could reach them, we could change the next generation for Jesus Christ.

*Jesus said, "Let the little children come to me, and do not hinder them, for the kingdom of heaven belongs to such as these."*

MATTHEW 19:14

Kathryn continued to listen intently as I shared how Dennis and I had owned a home when I was running Spencer Creations, but after we closed our business we decided to sell the house. We planned to take the money from the sale and buy some land in Vietnam on which to one day build a prayer house. She could see how earnest I was and decided to present my vision for Binh Chau to Pastor Mark and the Catalina Foothills' Missions' Board.

The evening after our God-appointed visit, the phone rang. It was Kathryn. She had just met with Pastor Mark and the missions board and told them about our burden for Vietnam.

"Mai, I wish you were here so you could see how joyful and excited the staff was when I shared with them what you had told me about Vietnam!" Kathryn gushed.

I could barely believe what she was saying. God had been calling me, but now it was coming to pass. He led me to Kathryn and the Catalina Foothills Church, and now He was leading us to go forward in building a prayer house for Him in Binh Chau.

## Forward March

The church began to pray for Dennis and I as we began to plan a trip to Vietnam. The first step was to sell our house. We hired a realtor and signed a three month contract. After the time elapsed, our home had still not sold. I was getting a little sharper at recognizing "God's fingerprints." In the midst of this, I ran into a woman who used to work with Dennis, and she told me she had just sold her house. I told her we had a house for sale and had even listed it with a realtor. She told me to put an ad in the paper and have an open house on the weekend and we wouldn't have to pay the realtor fee.

I could hardly wait to tell Dennis about her suggestion. That evening, as we were sitting on our sofa watching Trinity Broadcasting Network, a plea went over the airwaves for financial support. Dennis and I looked at each other. We both agreed God was asking us to send an offering to TBN. We joined hands and asked God to bless us as we obeyed Him and supported Christian television. We promised the Lord if He would bless us and help us sell our house within seven days, we would know for sure He wanted us to go to Vietnam and buy land for the new church building.

The next day, we went ahead with the plan and put the ad in the paper for the open house. Our phone rang and another realtor told us he had seen our sign: *For Sale by Owner.* He asked if we would pay him a commission if he found a buyer to purchase our home. Dennis and I agreed to give him a three percent commission if he was successful in selling our home. The second couple he brought to look at the house purchased it. The contract was written up and we signed it Sunday afternoon. It was clear to us God had opened a door of ministry for us. Little did we know when we walked through this door our lives would never be the same again.

*... for a wide door for effective service has opened to me.*

1 CORINTHIANS 16:9a

## VIETNAM—HERE WE COME

We headed to Vietnam and decided to rent a house in Saigon for one month. One of our friends was a missionary in Malaysia. She heard we were looking for land to build a church and put us in contact with two pastors who came to visit us. One of the pastors was very wise and helped us understand the way the government and churches were run in Vietnam. His knowledge helped us see the difficulties that lay ahead. We began to bathe Vietnam in fervent prayer. We knew that through prayer tremendous power was available to us and we needed supernatural power to break the strongholds of the enemy.

*The earnest (heartfelt, continued) prayer of a righteous man makes tremendous power available [dynamic in its working]*

JAMES 5:16b AMP

## FIRST ADAM—SECOND ADAM

I am careful with the first open door that comes my way. I remember the Bible teaches about the first Adam and the second Adam. We asked the Lord to make it very clear to us which pastor we should trust with our vision for Binh Chau.

*So it is written: "The first man Adam became a living being"; the last Adam, a life-giving spirit. The spiritual did not come first, but the natural, and after that the spiritual. The first man was of the dust of the earth, the second man from heaven. As was the earthly man, so are those who are of the earth; and as is the man from heaven, so also are those who are of heaven. And just as we have borne the likeness of the earthly man, so shall we bear the likeness of the man from heaven.*

1 Corinthians 15:45–49

## Pastor Quy

While we were in Vietnam, we heard my nephew was very sick. Dennis and I hurried to the hospital to check on him. When we arrived, we discovered they did not have a room for him. He was lying on a cot outside one of the hospital rooms. We gathered around and began to bombard Heaven on his behalf. A woman heard us praying and said her husband was a pastor and very sick. She asked if we could pray for him. We knew God had ordered our steps and this was a divine appointment. We followed her to her husband's room and prayed for him. It was apparent this precious couple needed financial help, but we had not carried any money with us that night. I went back to the hospital the next day and blessed them with some money and talked with his wife again. This time another pastor and some of his elders were visiting them. I shared with them that we felt God wanted us to build a church in Binh Chau. They told me I should get in touch with Pastor Quy because he oversaw several Christian Missionary Alliance Churches in that region. We had heard Pastor Quy's name previously from my family. His name seemed to keep surfacing. I began to sense Pastor Quy was the second Adam, the man God had appointed to labor with us for the Lord. Later we traveled to Ba To and met with him.

*For we are labourers together with God: ye are God's husbandry, ye are God's building.*

1 Corinthians 3:9 kjv

When we met Pastor Quy, he shared how he was burdened for Binh Chau, too, and in previous years had attempted to plant a church there, but it never worked out. He never gave up completely on his vision for Binh Chau because he continued to send one of his elders every weekend to a gathering at one of the believer's homes. Our hearts were united in God's purpose and plans for Binh Chau. We felt confident God was in our friendship and He would guide our steps to bring to fruition the vision He had given us, and nothing could stop God's Church from marching on.

*...upon this rock I will build my church; and the gates of hell shall not prevail against it.*

MATTHEW 16:18B KJV

## LAND

My sister and her husband owned a large piece of land across from the ocean. The view was so picturesque. Dennis and I felt it was the perfect spot to build a church, but we didn't immediately make an offer because we wanted some time to pray and discern the mind of the Spirit. We went back to Saigon and once again joined hands and asked God to make it clear to us if this was to be the land for the church. Two days later, we went back to look at the land. We prayed again and felt God had blessed us with this land and we were confident there was plenty of room for a church building. Land at that time was very expensive, selling for $200 a meter, but my brother-in-law sold the property to us for $13,000. Places in downtown Saigon were being sold for much higher prices. We felt God was blessing us with a real bargain.

## LEADERSHIP

After we returned to America, we visited with the Catalina Foothills Missions Committee about the needs in Vietnam. We were elated when they agreed to financially support the Binh Chau work. We contacted Pastor Quy and told him the good news. He began sending a missionary to Binh Chau three times a week. Dennis and I were so thankful God's Church was being built even though no walls had gone up. His Church was being constructed without the sound of hammers, and we proclaimed again and again that the gates of Hell could not prevail against what God had planned for Binh Chau.

> *...so there was no sound of hammer, ax, or any other iron tool at the building site.*
>
> 1 KINGS 6:7b NLT

# Chapter Twenty-one

# POLICE RAID

N̲o̲ ̲s̲o̲o̲n̲e̲r̲ had we returned from our visit in Vietnam when we began receiving letters and e-mails from Pastor Quy requesting we return as soon as possible to help with the church plant in Binh Chau. He stated that God had granted us favor with those we had the opportunity to meet and talk with during our previous trip. He felt the time was right to reach out to believers and nonbelievers with the Word of God. I realized immediately Dennis wouldn't be able to return because of his obligations at work, but we began to pray and ask the Lord to make it very clear if it was His will for me to return alone. We knew God would have to open the doors for me to take another "missionary journey" to Vietnam. After submitting the invitation to Kathryn, we were given the funds to support my return trip.

I began collecting ministry resources to take to Lam and Mai. They had requested a felt board set so they could bring the Word of God to life to their students. Sylvia, a dear lady from Catalina Foothills Church, sent us information about a website and phone number where this material could be ordered. When we contacted the company, we were hoping to purchase two sets, one for the children's Bible study in Binh Chau and one for the mother church in Ba To. We discovered the sets were quite expensive, so we decided to buy only one. Then God put it in Dennis' heart to explain why we were purchasing the ministry resources. The company offered to give us a 50 percent discount so we could buy two sets.

Later, I went to buy some more teaching materials from Gospel Supplies in Tucson. I went to the register to pay for my items and met a young man named Andy. I shared with him about our ministry in Binh Chau, and he offered to pay for almost half the materials.

I headed to Vietnam with my suitcases full of Bibles, felt board figures, and other teaching materials. Dennis and I had requested special prayer support for my safe travel and favor when I reached customs. We specifically prayed my suitcases would not be subject to inspection and the Bibles and teaching resources would not be confiscated. God answered those prayers above and beyond what I ever dreamed or imagined possible. I breezed through customs without a hitch.

*Now to him who is able to do immeasurably more than all we ask or imagine, according to his power that is at work within us, to him be glory in the church and in Christ Jesus throughout all generations, for ever and ever! Amen*

EPHESIANS 3:20–21

After I got settled in Binh Chau, I called Pastor Quy to let him know I had arrived safely and was at my sister's house. My heart was encouraged when Pastor Quy and a few of his elders came to see me. We discussed what we felt God needed us to do for furtherance of His kingdom in Binh Chau and Ba To. That evening, after they left, I curled up on the floor like a baby, trembling and thanking God for the opportunity to serve Him. I wept as I looked back over my life and saw how He had taken a little Buddhist girl and changed her into a disciple of Jesus Christ. He was changing me from glory to glory just as His Word declares. I realized again the miracle of salvation, and I was determined more than ever before to spend the rest of my life sharing the Good News with anyone who would listen.

*But we all, with open face beholding as in a glass the glory of the Lord, are changed into the same image from glory to glory, even as by the Spirit of the Lord.*

2 CORINTHIANS 3:18 KJV

## SUNDAY

On Sunday morning, I traveled to Ba To and attended the morning worship service at Pastor Quy's church. Sunday night, Pastor Quy held a revival for his church, the three other churches he oversees, and the Binh Chau church. We rented a van and transported people from Binh Chau to Ba To for the revival services. We all had such a joyous time singing, praising and worshipping God. After his sermon, Pastor Quy gave an altar call, and 10 people came forward to receive Christ, including three young people from Binh Chau. God was continuing to add to His Church just like in the Book of Acts.

*...praising God and enjoying the favor of all the people. And the Lord added to their number daily those who were being saved.*

ACTS 2:47

## MONDAY

On Monday, Lam and Mai came to Binh Chau to visit me. Lam had taken a week off from work so the three of us could visit Christian families in the village. We spent the first week ministering to families who were Christians but had not been attending the home meetings or the Bible study classes. We fellowshipped with them and encouraged them not to neglect Christian fellowship.

*Let us not give up meeting together, as some are in the habit of doing, but let us encourage one another—and all the more as you see the Day approaching.*

HEBREWS 10:25

Lam was scheduled to return to work the next week, but God put it in his heart to take another week off so we could visit nonbelievers. We met with several families and invited them to come to the Friday night Bible study. I was overjoyed when 42 hungry souls showed up. After feasting on the Word of God, three more prayed to receive Christ.

*Wherefore laying aside all malice, and all guile, and hypocrisies, and envies, and all evil speakings, As newborn babes, desire the sincere milk*

*of the word, that ye may grow thereby: If so be ye have tasted that the
Lord is gracious.*

(1 PETER 2:1-3 KJV).

## FOOD THE BODY AND THE SOUL

After our Bible study, we enjoyed a big pot of soup and began fellowshipping. Normally, after we looked into God's Word, we had Bibles lying all around the house, but that night we had tucked all our Bibles away. The only Christian literature that was out in the open was an Evangelism Explosion tract. Someone had left it lying on the sofa. We were busy sharing when suddenly seven policemen jumped over the fence, ran through the backyard, and bolted through the back door. We stood there stunned and watched as they searched every room. I watched as they took note ("taking inventory" usually refers to inanimate objects) of each person in attendance. They began to interrogate my sister and questioned why it was necessary to have such a large number of people in one house. My sister stayed calm and explained I was visiting from the United States and all our family and friends had come to greet me.

One policeman didn't seem impressed by my sister's explanation. He asked if we had opened our Bibles. My sister looked at me, and I told him we were believers in Jesus Christ and whenever Christians gather, we always have a time of fellowship and open the Bible to learn more of the Word of God. He glared at me as I asked him if it hurt anyone when we read the Bible.

He was slightly agitated and repeated, "Did you open the Book?"

I told him, if you are a Christian, you always take time to open God's Book.

He informed me it was a violation of the law in Vietnam.

A holy boldness came over me, and I felt it was very important I not back down. I looked him right in the eye and told him I belonged to God, the Maker of Heaven and Earth. Then I quoted from the Book of Joshua.

*Do not let this Book of the Law depart from your mouth; meditate on it day and night, so that you may be careful to do everything written in it. Then you will be prosperous and successful.*

JOSHUA 1:8

The Holy Spirit seemed to guide my words. I told him he was an officer and everywhere he went, he had to carry a weapon for his protection. I told him, as Christians, the Bible is our weapon, a two-edged sword, and we had to carry it with us wherever we went.

*For the word of God is quick, and powerful, and sharper than any two-edged sword, piercing even to the dividing asunder of soul and spirit, and of the joints and marrow, and is a discerner of the thoughts and intents of the heart.*

HEBREWS 4:12 KJV

He insisted on seeing my passport. When I gave it to him, he glanced at it and then quickly handed it to a younger officer. After looking it over, they reluctantly gave it back to me. The older policeman said I needed to register at the police station and rambled on about how he had the power to keep my passport. Suddenly, without warning, he insisted I give my passport back to him. The Lord gave me the words to say. I told him I would call the American Embassy and explain the situation. If I had broken the law, I promised to surrender my passport to him.

I had been instructed by the Vietnamese people that I must stand firm and prove to the government I knew the laws and rules. If I backed down or acted like I was intimidated, they had the power to make life pretty miserable.

"If I have to go to jail I will go to jail, but I am not giving you my passport," I boldly proclaimed.

My family stared in disbelief when the police threatened to haul me to the police station. My sister whispered something to me about giving them a bribe. I told her I would rather go to jail.

I watched as a policeman stuffed the Evangelism Explosion tract into his pocket. I whispered a prayer that he would come to know Jesus.

The older officer insisted I report to the police station immediately. My sisters followed me as they whisked me off on a motorcycle to the police headquarters.

When we arrived, I was taken to the Chief of Police and questioned thoroughly about my faith. He threatened to fine me $1,000 because I did not report to the government my intentions for being in town. God intervened on my behalf, and the Police Chief decided, since he knew my brother-in-law, he would only fine my sister $10 for allowing an unauthorized meeting at her house. He informed me he had a strong dislike for Christians because they tried to force people to believe what they did. I explained we never force our beliefs upon others, but we are called to tell people God loves us so much He sent His only Son that through Him we might have the gift of eternal life and escape the torments of hell.

He looked at me and asked, "How did you become a Christian?"

He didn't have to ask that question twice. He opened the door, and I walked right through it and shared for 45 minutes about my conversion.

After it was all over, I remembered how frequently Dennis and I would pray for the government officials in Binh Chau. God was giving me the opportunity to share the Gospel with the Chief of Police. I thanked the Lord for the tremendous opportunity to plant the seed in this man's heart. I prayed God would send someone else to water this seed and one day I would hear of this Chief of Police coming to know Jesus as his Lord and Savior.

*I have planted, Apollos watered; but God gave the increase.*

1 CORINTHIANS 3:6 KJV

I was told I could go, but was not allowed to hold any more gatherings except in government-approved homes. I was advised by Pastor Quy, Lam and Mai to stop visiting different families since the government might be watching my activities.

## GOD'S LOVE IS CONTAGIOUS

After the police threats, I went to my sister Kim's house to pray for direction. I needed the Lord to reveal to me if I should return to the United

States early because the government was watching me. I was upstairs with Pastor Quy and some of his elders when Kim sent a lady named Thuy upstairs to talk to me about the Christian church. Pastor Quy shared the Gospel with Thuy, but she did not pray to receive Christ at that time. However, the next day, she returned, and using the blackboard, I took her all the way back to Adam's sin in the garden and explained more in detail who God really is. I then shared the Gospel with her, using the Evangelism Explosion techniques. She prayed to receive Christ. The next day, Thuy brought her daughter Kieu to Kim's house, and I was able to share with her everything I had told her mother the previous day. Kieu then prayed to receive Christ, also. Thuy and Kieu went home and told their husband/father, Tien, about their decision to become Christians. A few days later, they brought him to me, and I also shared the Gospel with him. He, too, prayed to receive Christ.

About a week later, they came back and asked me to come to their house to pray and tear down their idol altars. Lam, Mai, and I went to their house and helped them destroy the altars. During that time, I realized they were a very poor family and Tien could only find work for one or two days per week. I saw their house was made of straw and full of holes. Most of the time, they had very little or no food. I prayed about helping them, and three weeks later, Dennis sent me $700 . I gave them $600 to start a motorcycle taxi business. A year later, Tien had to go to Saigon to find work. The Lord gave him a job with a man who was an elder in his church in Saigon. Tien began studying the Bible more and really matured in his walk with the Lord. His wife, Thuy, now teaches one of the children's Bible studies in the Binh Chau church.

Kieu, too, was very vocal about her faith. She went to school and told her friends about Jesus. Thuy brought one of her neighbors, Lien, to speak with me about Jesus. After I shared with her, she prayed to receive Christ. Lien went home and brought her husband, Binh, back to hear the Gospel. I was able to share with Binh, but he did not pray to receive Christ at that time. Over the next three months, Binh began to see many good changes in his wife and started going to church. Lam and Mai were then able to lead him to Christ. Binh and Lien also had a very hard time finding work in

Binh Chau to support their family, so they moved to Saigon to look for work.

## LIVING WATER

The government said I couldn't visit people, so God sent them to me. Every day more and more people came to Kim's house and inquired about the Christian church. At times there were three or four hungry souls waiting downstairs. They wanted an opportunity to come upstairs and hear about Jesus.

Kim was very sensitive to the needs of each one the Lord sent through her doors. Her first priority was to find out if they belonged to Jesus. If they didn't, she would send them upstairs to talk to me. Sometimes I was there by myself, and other times Pastor Quy, Lam, and Mai would be there as well. Many of them prayed to receive Jesus. Satan attempted to disrupt our ability to reach out to people through home visits, but we soon discovered the God within us is greater than the enemy.

*You, dear children, are from God and have overcome them, because the one who is in you is greater than the one who is in the world.*

1 JOHN 4:4

## TAKE MY SILVER AND MY GOLD

I didn't go to Binh Chau with the intention of building a church on this particular trip, but I hoped to encourage and strengthen my brothers and sisters in the Lord. I also had a great desire to share the Gospel of Jesus Christ with the lost. I knew God was in all of this, but He was also giving me favor with those He brought across my path and opening doors of opportunity for His work in Binh Chau. I recognized His voice and felt I must explore the possibility.

*And when he putteth forth his own sheep, he goeth before them, and the sheep follow him: for they know his voice. My sheep hear my voice, and I know them, and they follow me.*

JOHN 10:4, 27 KJV

I didn't want to jump ahead of God, but I didn't want to lag behind Him either. I began to earnestly pray God would make His will very plain. Some obstacles had surfaced with the home where we held our home meetings. The woman of this home was a Christian, but her husband wasn't. The home meetings were putting a strain on their relationship because her husband felt their house was too small to accommodate the group of 40 Christians that showed up three or four times a week. I felt the Lord was revealing we needed a place that could be dedicated solely to the work of the Lord.

Building a church on the picturesque land Dennis and I had purchased failed to become a reality because of the change in rigid tax laws that made it impossible to build in that area. Dennis and I agreed we must find property that was already residentially zoned. Just like God led Moses and the Israelites, He led me to some property that seemed perfectly tailored to meet the needs of the Binh Chau congregation. As Dennis and I prayed, we sensed the Lord asking us to personally purchase the property. We felt it was a step of faith, but as we obeyed the Lord, He would touch the hearts of His children, and they would give financial support for His church in Binh Chau.

## UNDER CONSTRUCTION

Once Dennis and I felt we knew the mind of the Spirit, we never hesitated. The land was purchased, a contractor hired and construction started. The prayer house I had promised to build for the Lord was becoming a reality before my eyes.

Satan wasn't happy with the mighty move of God in Binh Chau. He got busy and started causing trouble. Neighbors were concerned about rumors a church was going to be built in their neighborhood. Government officials reappeared and began to interrogate me. The cost of building materials escalated and was much higher than we first anticipated, but at each roadblock God gave us favor and another door opened. After much opposition, the government finally agreed that we had met all the requirements to build a house there. We couldn't call it a "church" at that point, although it would serve that purpose, because the government would not allow us to build a church. It didn't matter what we called it. We knew it was God's will for us to build a meeting place for His children in Binh Chau. I could relate to the words of Mordecai when he spoke to his niece Esther. It was made very clear to Dennis and I that God had brought us into His Kingdom for such a time as this. Binh Chau would never be the same, and neither would Dennis and I. We were eternally changed.

*For if you keep silent at this time, relief and deliverance shall arise for the Jews from elsewhere, but you and your father's house will perish. And who knows but that you have come to the kingdom for such a time as this and for this very occasion?*

ESTHER 4:14 AMP

## GOD OF DETAILS

*So Solomon broke ground, launched construction of the house of God in Jerusalem on Mount Moriah, the place where God had appeared to his father David. The precise site, the threshing floor of Araunah the Jebusite, had been designated by David. He broke ground on the second day in the second month of the fourth year of his rule. These are the dimensions that Solomon set for the construction of the house of God: ninety feet long and thirty feet wide. The porch in front stretched the width of the building, that is, thirty feet; and it was thirty feet high.*

2 CHRONICLES 3:1–4 MSG

Just as God directed Solomon in every detail of building the temple in Jerusalem, He was guiding our steps, as well. We marveled at the goodness of the Lord and how He even hand-picked our contractor. The Lord sent us a strong Catholic man. We told him we were building a church, but because of government restrictions we must be discreet about our plans. This man was a God-fearing soul and seemed to understand our situation. He agreed to build the church and honor our request to keep it quiet. A few hours before the contractor called his crew to come and break ground, Pastor Quy, his elders, a few others and I met on the property and prayed God would bless us as we began to build for His glory and honor.

Excitement filled the air as the building began, but we also hit some bumps in the road. One of the neighbors was intoxicated, and he started causing trouble and making a lot of noise. I didn't exactly know what to do, but because of the ruckus, a government official showed up on his motorcycle.

"Are you Mrs. Mai Spencer?" he asked.

I nodded as he continued. "We have been informed that you are building a church."

I attempted to divert his attention by answering him. "If I wanted to build a church, I would have to apply for a permit to build a church, but I'm sure the government wouldn't let us build a church. Right?"

"That's right," he replied.

I smiled and I said, "That's why I decided to build a house."

He didn't smile back. He looked at me very sternly and announced. "Mrs. Spencer, if I were to discover that this building was a church, I would have to revoke your visa, and you would never be allowed in the country again."

I looked him squarely in the eye and declared, "Right now I am building a house, but in the future it may be a church; I cannot say."

"Let me see your passport," he barked.

"If you want to see my passport, you must come to my sister's house. I left it there," I said.

Hopping on his motorcycle, he growled, "You haven't seen the last of me, Mrs. Spencer."

When I went back to Kim's house, I looked to see if any government officials were waiting for me, but they never showed up. That night before I fell asleep, I thanked the Lord for His protection and committed my life and the building project to Him.

## Witty Contractor

After the building was up, more rumors flew around the community that we were constructing a church. One day someone showed up and looked around and noticed a big hole where the baptismal tank was to be placed.

"Why is that hole there?" they asked.

Our contractor grinned and quickly quipped, "Maybe they are going to raise fish."

The building went up. Two weeks later, I went back to the United States. The church was born.

Dennis and I had to chuckle at the miraculous way God covered the eyes and hands of our enemies. They had the power to shut our doors and halt our operations, but God was working behind the scenes. God's Word and will prevailed over the forces of evil.

*But no weapon that is formed against you shall prosper, and every tongue that shall rise against you in judgment you shall show to be in the wrong. This [peace, righteousness, security, triumph over opposition] is the heritage of the servants of the Lord [those in whom the ideal Servant of the Lord is reproduced]; this is the righteousness or the vindication which they obtain from Me [this is that which I impart to them as their justification], says the Lord.*

ISAIAH 54:17 AMP

## PETITION

Pastor Quy petitioned the government, requesting our small congregation be allowed to relocate from the home church to our new building.

At first the government declined his petition, but once again God blazed a trail before us, and there were shouts of joy when a signed petition arrived in Pastor Quy's hands. The government approved the move.

I can't help but think of the story in Ezra when letters were being written to high officials for permission to restore the walls and build a house of the Lord. The same God who made a way for Nehemiah was providing for His children in Binh Chau.

*This is a copy of the letter that Tattenai, governor on this side of the River, and Shethar-bozenai and his associates, the Apharsachites who were on this [west] side of the River, sent to Darius [I] the king.*
*They wrote: To Darius the king: All peace.*

*Be it known to the king that we went to the province of Judah, to
the house of the great God. It is being built with huge stones, with tim-
ber laid in the walls; this work goes on with diligence and care and
prospers in their hands.*

*Then we asked those elders, Who authorized you to build this
house and restore these walls?*

*We asked their names also, that we might record the names of the
men at their head and notify you.*

*They replied, We are servants of the God of heaven and earth,
rebuilding the house which was erected and finished many years ago
by a great king of Israel.*

*But after our fathers had provoked the God of heaven to wrath,
He gave them into the hand of Nebuchadnezzar king of Babylon, the
Chaldean, who destroyed this house and carried the people away into
Babylon.*

*But in the first year of Cyrus king of Babylon, the same King Cyrus
made a decree to rebuild this house of God.*

*And the vessels also of gold and silver of the house of God, which
Nebuchadnezzar took from the temple in Jerusalem and brought into
the temple of Babylon, King Cyrus took from the temple of Babylon
and delivered to a man named Sheshbazzar, whom he had made governor.*

*And King Cyrus said to him, Go, take these vessels to Jerusalem
and carry them into the temple, and let the house of God be built upon
its site.*

EZRA 5:6–15 AMP

I returned to the United States and received frequent updates on how
the building project was progressing. Dennis and I rejoiced over every blood-
bought victory.

# Chapter Twenty-two

# THE DEDICATION

❦

n March 2006, Pastor Quy wrote us a letter asking us to come to Binh Chau to dedicate the new building. Dennis and I checked our schedules and everything seemed to fall into place. We boarded the plane and headed to Vietnam.

Our flights went well, and we arrived in Saigon within five minutes of our expected arrival time. We were met at the airport by some of our relatives, including my precious mother. We hurried to my brother's house in Saigon and spent several hours visiting with family. We decided to spend the night in a nearby hotel to recuperate from jetlag.

The next morning, Saturday, April 29th, my brother took us by van to Ba To, about 20 miles from Binh Chau. This was where Pastor Quy's church was located. We spent the day with Pastor Quy, his family, and several of his elders. They gave us an update on the happenings of the previous few days. We were informed that, although the local Binh Chau government officials had all signed their approval for the home church and dedication, they kicked the petition upstairs to the provincial level, where the government officials were still taking our request "under consideration." This meant they forbid us to hold any type of dedication service. They even were so bold as to insist Pastor Quy was not to preach in the new building. If he did, they threatened to disapprove his petition, which meant he wouldn't be recognized by the government as a pastor. Pastor Quy stated he had lived over half his life waiting on the government to give him approval and this time he was going to do what God had put in his heart to do. Dennis and I agreed we must obey the will of God rather than the will of man.

*... We must obey God rather than men*

ACTS 5:29b AMP

Pastor Quy said the provincial officials had been getting nervous and asking a lot of questions in an attempt to discover what was going to take place on Sunday. Dennis and I had asked the Lord for wisdom concerning our visit to Binh Chau.

*If any of you lacks wisdom, he should ask God, who gives generously to all without finding fault, and it will be given to him.*

JAMES 1:5

We felt God was leading us to stay at a hotel in Ba To over the following few days. We would travel back and forth to Binh Chau. This way we wouldn't be drawing too much attention to our activities.

Sunday finally came. We woke up around two o'clock that morning and began a season of prayer. We continued to pray and study God's Word until seven o'clock. Then we went to Pastor Quy's church and attended the worship service. We rejoiced with our brothers and sisters in Christ in Ba To.

After the service, Dennis, Hiep and I left for Binh Chau to visit more family members before the dedication at two o'clock. When we arrived at Kim's house, we were told the provincial police had searched her house and the house of my other sister the night before looking for me, thinking I would be staying with them for the dedication. We thanked the Lord for giving us wisdom and leading us to stay in Ba To. After we visited for a few more minutes, the time came for us to see the new church. When we saw the church for the first time, tears of joy slipped down our cheeks. We knew this was much bigger than Dennis or me. It was God. He had built this physical church building, and even greater than that, He had built His Church of believers in Binh Chau.

Dennis and I didn't know what obstacles Satan might have in store for us that afternoon, but we felt completely at peace, knowing the same God who built His Church was in control of every situation in our lives.

More and more people filled the sanctuary. Someone counted approximately 160 people at the dedication service. Camonchua! (Vietnamese for "Thank You, Lord!") The government threats did not seem to detour anyone from coming.

The dedication started at two o'clock. We sensed the presence of God as His Word was proclaimed and His name glorified through testimony and song. Halfway through the service, the man who had previously given Lam and Mai a hard time began to make a little disturbance. Dennis and I got up and quietly led him outside to talk with him. While we were outside, the second obstacle showed up, a young man in his early 30s who identified himself as the official in charge of religious matters at the provincial level. He first started talking to Hiep, whose name the property is in. When she saw she wasn't getting anywhere with him, she brought him over to us.

Attempting to intimidate us, he began interrogating us. "What do you think you are doing? Don't you know what could happen to you because you are breaking the law?"

I stood upon the promises of God. I knew He was our Defender.

*But make up your mind not to worry beforehand how you will defend yourselves. For I will give you words and wisdom that none of your adversaries will be able to resist or contradict.*

LUKE 21:14, 15

I turned to him and said, "Shouldn't you be out there catching murderers or thieves who are causing so much trouble? We are a peaceful group who just want to worship our God."

He glared at me, and the words seemed to pour out of my mouth. "We worship the same God who made all of us and gives us everything we need. Even though you may not realize it, He loves you so much He sent His only Son to die for your sins that you might live eternally with Him. That is why, as Christians, we gather to celebrate what God has blessed us with in every situation."

I knew I hit a nerve when he mumbled back, "God didn't give me anything. I have worked hard for everything I have."

The Holy Spirit seemed to take over, and I asked him how much he would have if God took the air that kept him alive away from him.

He didn't like my response and continued to harass us. I felt a holy boldness well up in my soul. I motioned for one of the cameramen who was filming the dedication to come over. I asked him to film our discussion.

The young man looked shocked and stuttered, "You cannot allow him to film me because I have not given you permission."

I didn't let up and said, "I don't need your permission since you are on our property."

He left in a huff and warned us he was going to send his boss over to deal with us.

I gently replied, "We'll be right here if he wants to come by and talk to us."

Later some government officials drove by two or three times, but they did not stop. I felt they may have seen the angels God had positioned at the entrance and thought otherwise.

I was not speaking in arrogance, but in holy boldness like the apostles in the Book of Acts.

> .... *and they were all filled with the Holy Spirit, and they continued to speak the Word of God with freedom and boldness and courage.*
>
> ACTS 4:31b AMP

Pastor Quy had encouraged us to take advantage of the fact that we were Americans. The government is not as aggressive with American citizens as they are with the locals. The rest of the dedication went off without a hitch and was concluded by a catered dinner where all had a great time of fellowship.

When we finally arrived back at the hotel that evening, we realized we had only had three hours of sleep over the past 40 hours. We were amazed that we weren't even tired. We couldn't wipe the smiles off our faces as we reflected on where we were 14 years earlier. We were truly at the bottom of the pit and ready to give up, but Jesus passed by and reached down and gave us newness of life in Him. It humbled us that He would let us be a part of the dedication service and what God was doing in Binh Chau.

## ABOUT OUR FATHER'S BUSINESS

Dennis and I continued to be about our Father's business even after the dedication service. We attended events in Ba To and Binh Chau arranged by Pastor Quy and his staff. We attended Mr. Hai's 78th birthday party. Mr. Hai is an elder in Pastor Quy's church and was the first person to join his church over 14 years earlier. He had been a former member of the Communist Party and a guerrilla warfare fighter in the Viet Cong. When he became a Christian over 40 years ago, he was highly persecuted by the government, but he has served the Lord ever since. Another day I was able to witness to some ladies in the churches about some of my life's experiences. Before we left, we visited Tu Do, the Binh Chau Chief of Police who had given me a hard time the year before, and I ended up sharing my testimony with him.

## CONCERNS

One concern we all had was what the government would do when Dennis and I returned to America. We wondered if the new believers were strong enough to stand firm against intense government intimidation. We continue to pray God will strengthen Pastor Quy, his staff, and all the Christians in Vietnam. We pray specifically for each believer to stand firm in their faith and not fall prey to a spirit of fear.

*Now unto him that is able to keep you from falling, and to present you faultless before the presence of his glory with exceeding joy.*

JUDE 1:24 KJV

Over the next year, the Lord's hand was on the church, and it continued to bear fruit. Every obstacle of Satan was defeated to the glory of God.

# Chapter Twenty-three

# OPEN HEARTS
# AND OPEN DOORS

❧

In the summer of 2007, the Binh Chau church encountered a set-back. The leadership couple, Lam and Mai, made the decision to go back to Pastor Quy's church in Ba To. This left the Binh Chau flock without a shepherd. Pastor Quy, Dennis and I were very concerned. We began to pray about who would be the next shepherd to lead our brothers and sisters in their walk with the Lord. Pastor and Mrs. Quy agreed to temporarily take on these responsibilities. They would travel to Binh Chau three times a week to hold Bible studies and Sunday worship services. Dennis and I were burdened for the Quys because we realized they already had a full plate. (They have the duties of pastoring their own church and overseeing six other churches in the province.) We began praying God would raise up a pastor for Binh Chau.

The Lord began to deal with my heart about returning to Vietnam to help during this difficult transition. I felt like a wishbone pulled in two different directions. One part of me wanted to go, but another was afraid of stirring up governmental resentment toward the church. Our prayer had been to be able to put up the cross and sign for the Binh Chau church by the end of 2007. I didn't want to be a hindrance to fulfilling this request.

Early one morning, I found myself face down on the floor interceding to the Lord. I made a very unusual request. I normally wouldn't ask the Lord for these specifics, but I was desperate and didn't want to make any mistakes. I needed to know for sure if it was God's will for me to return to Vietnam at that time. There is a story in Judges that tells about another servant of the Lord named Gideon. He didn't know if the Lord wanted to use him to save Israel. When he prayed, he made a specific request of the Lord.

*Gideon said to God, "If this is right, if you are using me to save Israel as you've said, then look: I'm placing a fleece of wool on the threshing floor. If dew is on the fleece only, but the floor is dry, then I know that you will use me to save Israel, as you said."*

*That's what happened. When he got up early the next morning, he wrung out the fleece—enough dew to fill a bowl with water!*

*Then Gideon said to God, "Don't be impatient with me, but let me say one more thing. I want to try another time with the fleece. But this time let the fleece stay dry, while the dew drenches the ground."*

*God made it happen that very night. Only the fleece was dry while the ground was wet with dew.*

JUDGES 6:36–40 MSG

The God of Gideon is my God. I told the Lord I would return to Vietnam if He touched someone's heart to give me $5,000 for the airline ticket and money to help the church with their Christmas Outreach Program. Two weeks later, a woman called and asked for our tax exempt number because she desired to bless our ministry. A few days later Dennis opened a letter from her, and inside was a cashier's check for $5,000. I was dazed. The Lord had my attention.

Even though God had given me a clear sign, I still had some reservations. Dennis and I began to pray if it was God's will for me to go at that time, Pastor Quy would invite us to come. In October, we received a letter from Pastor Quy requesting that we come to Binh Chau to help with the church for the busy Christmas season. Dennis could not get away from work, but he and Cherée encouraged me to go. By answering this second prayer, God was making it clear that He had work for me to do in Binh Chau.

I was still concerned my presence could hamper the relationship between the church and the government. I decided to pray for one more sign: something that would "seal the deal" in my heart. I decided to pray about the supplies we needed for our Mercy Ministry during the Christmas season. We were hoping to distribute 2,000 pounds of rice to needy families. The approximate cost would be $2,500. I told the Lord if He really wanted me to go to Binh Chau, He would touch the hearts of His people and they would give generously to this ministry. We sent this request to Nancy Lupo, and she put it on our prayer chain. A few days later, when Dennis arrived at his Evangelism Explosion class, there was a letter on his table from one of the prayer chain partners. He opened the letter, and there was a check for $2,500.

*And my God will meet all your needs according to his glorious riches in Christ Jesus.*

PHILIPPIANS 4:19

It was very plain to see this trip to Vietnam was a "divine appointment." God had made it clear to me I was to walk through the door He had opened. I felt like I was experiencing what the prophet Isaiah spoke about.

*Whether you turn to the right or to the left, your ears will hear a voice behind you, saying, "This is the way; walk in it."*

ISAIAH 30:21

I contacted my family in Vietnam and let them know when I would be arriving. My sister told me that most of the church planned to meet me at the airport. I struggled with getting so much attention. Dennis and I enjoy working behind the scenes to make things happen. We try to avoid fanfare. It was my desire to quietly arrive in Binh Chau, but from the conversations with my family, it didn't sound like that was possible. I even asked some of my close friends to pray about this delicate situation. There was a woman in our church who heard my prayer request. She came to me and said, "Oh, honey, this is an honor. Let them do this for you." It became clear to me this was their way of thanking Dennis and me for helping them. They only wanted to do as the Bible teaches: Give honor to whom honor is due.

*Render to all men their dues. [Pay] taxes to whom taxes are due, revenue to whom revenue is due, respect to whom respect is due, and honor to whom honor is due.*

ROMANS 13:7 AMP

When I arrived at Tan Son Nhut Airport in Saigon, I was greeted by most of the Binh Chau Church and Mrs. Quy. It was such a joyous occasion. I began to thank the Lord with a humble heart for the love that surrounded me.

## MAMA'S GIRL

My mother and I had been through so much together. As I have grown older, I take long walks down Memory Lane and reminisce about my childhood. I have always loved my mother and missed her immensely, but as she has gotten older, it is harder for me to live so many miles from her. It had been almost two years since I had seen my mother. Her health was failing. During our two-year separation, she suffered a stroke and had broken her hip, leaving her bedridden. When we arrived in Binh Chau, I hurried to see her. Waves of emotion swept over us as I bent over her frail frame embracing her. She smothered me with hugs and kisses. I began to thank the Lord for allowing me to see my mother again. I spent the entire evening catching up with my family.

The next morning, I was hoping to catch up on my rest after the grueling flight, but God had a different plan. Church members started appearing at the door. Some brought their friends and neighbors. They wanted to hear more about Jesus. Throughout the day, I had many opportunities to share the Gospel with nonbelievers. Several prayed to receive Christ. At the end of the day, I gave God thanks for giving me the strength to be about my Father's business, even though I had not had much sleep for two days because of the long flight.

## PRAYER MEETING

The next day was Sunday. After the worship service, I asked Pastor Quy if it was okay to spend the night in the church with some of the church members. To eliminate interruptions, I felt the Lord wanted us to pray and fast throughout the evening. There were 19 hungry souls who joined me. We spent 24 hours praising God and lifting our requests to Him. We realized the government and powers of darkness weren't happy with all God was doing. We believed the words of Jesus in the Gospel of Mark.

*And he said unto them, This kind can come forth by nothing, but by prayer and fasting.*

Mark 9:29 kjv

## Specific Prayer Requests

We had several specific prayer requests as we began to travail in prayer.

- We asked the Lord to guide and direct the work during this transitional period.
- We pleaded with Him to raise up a pastor or Bible teacher to lead the Binh Chau flock.
- We prayed He would provide opportunities for each one of us to share the Gospel.
- We interceded for the Holy Spirit to make our spirits hungry and thirsty for truth.
- We bombarded Heaven and asked God to prepare the way for the cross and the sign to be put up on the church.
- We petitioned the Lord and asked that He open the door of training for the leadership of the church.
- We asked the Lord to grant us favor with the government officials.

A family in our group had a special prayer request. Their son, who was just 15, had run away from home two months before. We began to pray and asked the Lord to let this young man call home so his family would know he was all right. A holy boldness swept over me. I began to ask the Lord to let this boy return for Christmas. God answered our prayers, and this missing son called and arrived home on Christmas Eve. The promises of God are true. We can bring our needs before Him with great confidence and know He will help us.

*Let us then approach the throne of grace with confidence, so that we may receive mercy and find grace to help us in our time of need.*

Hebrews 4:16

Over the next two weeks, we continued to visit the homes of nonbelievers and those who had accepted Christ but were slipping back into old
ways. God answered our prayers and gave us favor and opportunities to
share the Gospel. The Lord was so faithful to draw and soften hearts. Many
prayed to receive Christ as their Savior. Some listened as we shared the Good
News of Jesus Christ, but they were not quite ready to make that commitment. This did not discourage us. We knew spiritual seeds had been planted
and some day those seeds would produce a bountiful harvest for the Kingdom of God. We just didn't realize how soon God would answer our prayers.
We invited everyone to the Christmas service and were thrilled when we
saw the ones who previously weren't ready to receive Christ walk through
the doors of the church. During the altar call, five of those dear ones stepped
forward and invited the Lord Jesus into their hearts. We rejoiced as we saw
before our very own eyes the fulfillment of the Great Commission.

*Then Jesus came to them and said, "All authority in heaven and on
earth has been given to me. Therefore go and make disciples of all
nations, baptizing them in the name of the Father and of the Son and
of the Holy Spirit, and teaching them to obey everything I have commanded you. And surely I am with you always, to the very end of the
age."*

MATTHEW 28:18–20

## GOD'S FAVOR

I was also able to meet with Mr. Tu Do, the Binh Chau police chief. He dis-
played a much friendlier attitude than he had the two previous years. I was
experiencing what the Bible teaches in Proverbs.

*When a man's ways are pleasing to the LORD, he makes even his ene-
mies live at peace with him.*

PROVERBS 16:7

The Lord allowed me another visit with the mayor of Binh Chau. During our conversation, she stated she had attended a Catholic church when

she was young, but had stopped. I knew the stringent rules and regulations of the Vietnamese government. Public officials take an oath that they will not join any religion while they are in office. This did not stop me from sharing the Gospel with her. She did not pray to receive Christ, but she sat quietly for an hour as I told her of Jesus' love for her. Her spirit was open, and she even seemed to agree with everything I said. I believe one day I will hear of her decision to be a believer in Jesus Christ.

## CHRISTMAS BLESSINGS

The Christmas service was a blessed occasion with around 150 people attending, including the government official who two years previously had threatened to keep me from returning to Vietnam if the building turned out to be a church. I am sure he was there to keep a watchful eye on what we were doing, but after the service he was very cordial and extended his hand in peace. He told me life had changed in Vietnam and times were different than when we first met.

Because of the generous support of God's people, we were able to give out wonderful gifts. We gave them out according to the needs of each family and believed God wanted us to obey the practical teaching found in 1 Peter.

*Everything in the world is about to be wrapped up, so take nothing for granted. Stay wide-awake in prayer. Most of all, love each other as if your life depended on it. Love makes up for practically anything. Be quick to give a meal to the hungry, a bed to the homeless—cheerfully. Be generous with the different things God gave you, passing them around so all get in on it: if words, let it be God's words; if help, let it be God's hearty help. That way, God's bright presence will be evident in everything through Jesus, and he'll get all the credit as the One mighty in everything—encores to the end of time. Oh, yes!*

1 PETER 4:7–11 MSG

The poverty in America is different than the poverty in Vietnam. The poorest of the poor in America are rich compared to the poor in Vietnam.

To help meet the basic necessities of the precious souls God sent to the Binh Chau work, we distributed medicine, noodle soup, cooking oil, sugar, milk, rice, money for medical expenses, clothes and fabric. Each little girl was given a teddy bear, and each little boy was given a truck. The children were so excited to receive new school supplies. After the gifts were handed out, we served a delicious dinner prepared by the ladies of the fellowship. I also had hired two women who were nonbelievers to help cook the meal. I had an opportunity to share the Gospel with them as we worked together that day. My heart filled with joy when one of these women came forward at the altar call that evening and asked Jesus into her heart.

Pastor Quy helped me meet with six churches and attend their Christmas services. I returned to Binh Chau for more fellowship, visitations and Bible studies. I hired a contractor to begin remodeling and repairing the church building. We removed the wall to expose the pulpit where the Word of the Lord was proclaimed. What a blessing when the baptismal pool was opened for those who gave their hearts to Jesus and desired to follow Him in believer's baptism.

## REPENTING AND REPAINTING

As the church was growing through souls repenting, we saw where the Lord's House needed some upkeep. We discovered that when it was painted in 2006 the paint had been watered down. This is a common practice in Vietnam, but now the church was in need of a new paint job. We sanded down the outside of the building and repainted. Also, church members had been sitting on plastic chairs, but now we purchased pews. The Binh Chau Church was shaping up and starting to look like a real church.

## SIGNS AND WONDERS

We had been earnestly praying for a number of months that the church sign and the cross would be in place by the end of 2007. Pastor Quy handed me some papers from the government stating we could gather in our building and call it the Binh Chau Christian Church. The paper had been issued in 2005, but the government had not signed it until April or May of 2007. Also, we had heard a governmental announcement over the town's loudspeaker system stating that Binh Chau now had a Christian church. My heart was encouraged. Based on these documents and a formal announcement, we decided to put up a temporary cross and sign for the Christmas service. For several days, no government official showed up or contacted us.

Early every morning, people came to see me at my sister's house. We visited, prayed, and sang hymns together. One morning my brother and I were sitting on the floor, drinking our coffee and discussing how we could have a permanent sign made for the church, when an unexpected guest showed up. He was from Saigon and used to live in Binh Chau. I had shared the Gospel with his wife two years earlier when the church was being built. His wife had accepted Christ at that time, but he had not. He did, however, attend the church until they moved to Saigon. Someone had told him I was in town, and he wanted to see me and let me know he had accepted Christ. While we were talking, he noticed our drawings and asked me what we were doing. I told him we were trying to design a sign for the church. You can imagine how my heart began to race when he announced he worked for a company that made and installed signs for commercial buildings. I asked him if he could make a sign for the church. He agreed to build a sign. I was jubilant. God had answered our prayer in His perfect timing. I contacted Pastor Quy and asked if it was all right to go ahead and order the sign and a cross since the government had recognized the church. Pastor Quy felt we should go ahead and get a permanent sign and cross put up.

## UNEXPECTED CROSS

Many times in life we have unexpected crosses. Situations arise that we weren't expecting. Simon of Cyrene didn't know that day when he was walking from the country that he would be forced to carry Jesus' cross.

*And they forced a passerby, Simon of Cyrene, the father of Alexander and Rufus, who was coming in from the field (country), to carry His cross.*

MARK 15:21 AMP

There are times in our lives, too, that we might be asked to carry an unexpected cross. Oh, let's carry it with the joy of the Lord, which is our strength.

*Then [Ezra] told them, Go your way, eat the fat, drink the sweet drink, and send portions to him for whom nothing is prepared; for this day is holy to our Lord. And be not grieved and depressed, for the joy of the Lord is your strength and stronghold.*

NEHEMIAH 8:10 AMP

God was blessing us as we went forth in His strength to provide for those who had nothing. Dennis and I have learned this one truth: When God starts blessing, the devil starts messing.

We had been rejoicing over the fact that there had been no government interference, but the very day the cross was delivered to the church, a government official stopped by and insisted we could not put the cross or the sign up. We explained to him about the official documents. He didn't budge. We asked him where we could go to get permission to put up the cross and the sign. We went on a wild goose chase. Every government office gave us a different answer. I was frustrated, but felt in my heart we should move forward. When we arrived back at the church it was almost dark, and the workers I had hired to put up the cross were waiting for instructions. Based on the documents that clearly stated we were recognized as the Binh Chau Christian Church, and trusting God's divine protection, we went ahead and installed the cross and the sign that night under the light of the moon and stars (and a little electricity). What a glorious sight to see the cross lifted high above the church! Hallelujah! God had answered our prayers that they be up by the end of 2007. Over the next few days, government officials requested the cross and sign be taken down, but the church leadership told them they could not comply. As of today, the cross and the sign remain. We give God all the glory. We pray the cross will be a landmark for future generations.

*Remove not the ancient landmark which your fathers have set up.*

PROVERBS 22:28 AMP

## SHOW ME THE CROSS

The day after the cross was lifted into place, a man from the nearby town of Nhu Lam drove by the church on his motorcycle. When he saw the cross, he stopped and told one of the workers at the church that God had healed him from some life-threatening injuries. He wanted to accept Christ. The cross going up reminded me of the scripture in John's Gospel.

*"But I, when I am lifted up from the earth, will draw all men to myself."*

JOHN 12:32 KJV

Jesus was drawing that man's heart to Himself. He returned the next day for Sunday morning service. Pastor Quy shared the Gospel with him, and he prayed to receive Christ. This was truly a "wink from Heaven" to remind us of God's glory and power.

A country pastor shared a story one Sunday morning about a little boy who was playing with his new puppy in his front yard. Suddenly, for no reason, the puppy darted down the street. The little lad loved his prized puppy and quickly followed him. Finally, after several blocks, the puppy stopped and let the little boy pick him up. The little boy was so happy to have his puppy safe in his arms, but then realized he was lost. Fear gripped him and he started to cry. About that time, a kind policeman walked around the corner. He saw the little boy crying, and he asked what was wrong.

"I'm lost," whimpered the little fellow.

"What's your name?" asked the policeman.

"Jimmy Joe Johnson."

"What's your address?" the policeman continued.

"I don't know my address, Mr. Policeman, but if you can get me to the church where the tall cross is lit, I can find my way home," the boy answered.

The policeman knew exactly what church the little guy was talking about, and soon the little boy was home safe and sound.

The country preacher continued, "Sometimes we are like that little boy. We find ourselves far from where God wants us to be. We wake up one morning and wonder how we drifted so far from the Lord.

Maybe you find yourself far from the Lord today. God has placed my story in your hands. He has sent me to tell you He loves you. His heart is lonesome for you and desires to have an intimate relationship with you. After you finish this chapter, maybe you would like to find a place to pray. Tell Jesus you are sorry. Confess your sins to Him, and then find a Bible-believing church. You will never regret following Jesus.

## SEE THE CROSS

*Have the winds of life blown dust into your eyes?*
*Dimming your vision – your day seems like night,*
*Then Hope calls from Calvary's Hill,*
*And Love's light reveals*
*That Calvary gives you back your sight.*
*Love reached through the corridors of time,*
*Bleeding a trail, then flooding souls with light,*
*The Rose wore the thorns,*
*Conquered death and more*
*The day our Champion crossed the finish line.*
*See the Cross with beams of mercy,*
*See the Cross – timbers of grace,*
*Crimson waters sing Redemption Story,*
*See the Cross – Your debt's been paid.*

—DIXIE PHILLIPS

It has been many years since our two children, Terri and Timmy, passed away. Satan meant to destroy our family, but Jesus passed by and comforted and strengthened us. We give thanks every day for all God has done in our lives. There is nothing in this world that compares to the relationship we have with Jesus. Satan wanted to completely destroy our future, but God had His hand upon us. The Lord would not let Satan's plans prevail.

*"For I know the plans I have for you," says the Lord. "They are plans for good and not for disaster, to give you a future and a hope."*

Jeremiah 29:11 amp

The day I knelt by our wingchair, my perspective on life changed forever. Even though I was hurting over Terri's terminal illness, Jesus gave me a deep faith in the biblical truth that God is in control. I was no longer a victim of my circumstances, but Jesus has made me a victor. The tragedies that broke our hearts were the very things that brought us to the foot of the cross. Through all of the heartaches, we came to know Jesus, and He was the only One who could help us get through such traumatic events.

## Redeemed by the Lamb

*Redeemed by the Lamb to love Him,*
*Redeemed by the Lamb to serve Him;*
*Redeemed by the Lamb to praise Him,*
*Redeemed by the blood of the Lamb.*
*When I knew Him not, He sought me,*
*With tenderness gently He brought me;*
*With His precious blood He bought me.*
*Redeemed by the blood of the Lamb.*
*Redeemed, how I love to proclaim it;*
*Redeemed, let the whole world exclaim it;*
*Redeemed by His love, I'm washed in His blood,*
*Redeemed by the blood of the Lamb.*

—Nancy Lupo

My friend, no matter what you are facing in your life today, Jesus is able to take your painful past and give you a bright future. Please don't let your painful past rob you of your future. Whenever Jesus' love touches a life, that life is transformed into a beautiful masterpiece. If you come broken, He will make you whole. Just give Him all the broken pieces of your life, and watch His love begin to work. You will be amazed by His miraculous touch.

He makes everything, even tragedies, work together for good to those who give their lives to Him.

> *And we know that all things work together for good to them that love God, to them who are the called according to his purpose.*
>
> ROMANS 8:28 KJV

# Chapter Twenty-four

# THE PRESENT

*Yesterday is history.*
*Tomorrow is a mystery.*
*Today is a gift.*
*That's why we call it the present!*

While I was in Binh Chau in 2007, I made a trip to a Christian bookstore in Saigon. After I purchased some Bibles and study materials, I began visiting with the owner of the bookstore and discovered he was a pastor and had a very fruitful ministry. During our conversation, he mentioned he also operated a Bible school that taught church leadership, discipleship and evangelism classes. I shared with him about the ministry in Binh Chau. He said he had heard of our ministry and extended an invitation for me to give my testimony at both the church and school. I told him I would pray about it, and as the days passed, I realized my time in Vietnam was limited. I felt I must keep my commitment to the Binh Chau fellowship. Later I returned to Saigon with some of the leadership from the Binh Chau church to tell the pastor I would not be able to share my testimony during this trip because of time restraints and previous commitments, but I assured him Dennis and I would love to come and speak on a future trip. He understood my dilemma, and our conversation turned to his school. The more he explained about the classes, the more I felt God putting in my heart this was exactly what the Binh Chau leadership needed. We prayed and stepped out in faith. I signed up six people for the 15-month training classes. I was trusting God to provide the financial support.

The leaders would go to Saigon two days a month for eight to twelve hours of classroom instruction each day, plus have three hours per day of homework assignments. There would be 24 lessons each month that must be completed before their next class session.

The cost was $75 per month for each student. This included $50 for the cost of the classes and $25 for transportation to and from Binh Chau. I felt it was important to reimburse the students for the pay they would lose from their jobs. These were very poor people who could not afford to go if they lost any wages. We were praying God would raise up people who would financially support these leaders. They needed this training so they could be effective in winning and mentoring souls in Binh Chau.

## THE SECOND LAM

Before I left, God answered another prayer. A Bible teacher, Lam, from Phan Rang, who used to attend Pastor Quy's church in Ba To, came to visit his son for Christmas in Ba To. Over several conversations with Lam, he agreed to come to work with the Binh Chau church. He had completed two years of seminary training and came highly recommended. What blessed me the most was his heart for the youth.

Two days before I returned to the United States, we spent another day of prayer and fasting. We thanked the Lord for all He had done for us and all He was going to do in the future. We asked for His shield of protection to surround the Binh Chau work and each member from any government interference. We could sense the Lord's nearness and felt in the depths of our souls that He heard the cries of our hearts.

*The Lord is near to all who call on him, to all who call on him in truth.*

PSALM 145:18

## MORE DECISIONS FOR CHRIST

I was blessed to visit a family where the husband was Catholic and the wife was Buddhist. They had three children and a giant altar stood in the middle of their home. On one side was a statue of Jesus, Mary and Peter. I glanced on the other side and immediately recognized the idols of ancestral worship. As I began to share the Good News of Jesus Christ with them, I was thrilled to see their hearts respond to Jesus' love. I prayed with them to receive Christ. As I stared at the altars, the Spirit of the Lord overshadowed me. I began to teach them from the Word of God about false gods and idols. Psalm 115 states:

> *Not to us, O Lord, not to us*
> *but to your name be the glory,*
> *because of your love and faithfulness.*

> *Why do the nations say,*
> *"Where is their God?"*

> *Our God is in heaven;*
> *he does whatever pleases him.*

> *But their idols are silver and gold,*
> *made by the hands of men.*

> *They have mouths, but cannot speak,*
> *eyes, but they cannot see;*

> *they have ears, but cannot hear,*
> *noses, but they cannot smell;*

> *they have hands, but cannot feel,*
> *feet, but they cannot walk;*
> *nor can they utter a sound with their throats.*

> *Those who make them will be like them,*
> *and so will all who trust in them.*

> *O house of Israel, trust in the Lord—*
> *he is their help and shield.*

*O house of Aaron, trust in the Lord—*
*he is their help and shield.*

*You who fear him, trust in the Lord—*
*he is their help and shield.*

*The Lord remembers us and will bless us:*
*He will bless the house of Israel,*
*he will bless the house of Aaron,*

*he will bless those who fear the Lord—*
*small and great alike.*

*May the Lord make you increase,*
*both you and your children.*

*May you be blessed by the Lord,*
*the Maker of heaven and earth.*

*The highest heavens belong to the Lord,*
*but the earth he has given to man.*

*It is not the dead who praise the Lord,*
*those who go down to silence;*

*it is we who extol the Lord,*
*both now and forevermore.*
*Praise the Lord.*

I taught them from the Word of God the importance of destroying the idols and removing them from their home. They were so hungry for truth and had an intense desire to please the Lord. We rejoiced together as the idols were taken down and destroyed. They now have a Bible study in their home and are active in the Binh Chau congregation.

*Josiah was eight years old when he became king, and he reigned in Jerusalem thirty-one years. He did what was right in the eyes of the Lord and walked in the ways of his father David, not turning aside to the right or to the left.*

*In the eighth year of his reign, while he was still young, he began to seek the God of his father David. In his twelfth year he began to purge Judah and Jerusalem of high places, Asherah poles, carved idols and cast images. Under his direction the altars of the Baals were torn down; he cut to pieces the incense altars that were above them, and smashed the Asherah poles, the idols and the images. These he broke to pieces and scattered over the graves of those who had sacrificed to them.*

2 CHRONICLES 34:1–4

## STATISTICS

As of December of 2007, around 125 souls had accepted Christ in the Binh Chau fellowship. They had 30 members who faithfully met for Bible study, 40 children who hear about Jesus every week, 10 youths who attended faithfully and 20 adults were meeting weekly for Bible studies. The work continues to grow, and we feel, as we invest in the training of the spiritual leaders, the best years are yet to come.

# Chapter Twenty-five

# WE'VE COME THIS FAR BY FAITH

*By faith we understand that the universe was formed at God's command, so that what is seen was not made out of what was visible.*

HEBREWS 11:3

ennis and I have enjoyed every mile of this journey since we have allowed Jesus to govern our lives. It has been an exciting life of faith. God has never failed to amaze us.

*My future is in your hands.*

PSALM 31:15a NLT

We are aware that we have more years behind us than we do ahead of us, but with whatever time we have left we want to be about our Father's business.

After the church in Binh Chau was built, Dennis and I felt a stirring in our souls to reach out to other nearby cities.

## GO

*And he said unto them, Let us go into the next towns, that I may preach there also: for therefore came I forth.*

MARK 1:38 KJV

Surrounding Binh Chau is a series of smaller towns. One of these villages is Bung Rieng. This was where my two uncles were gunned down by the Viet Cong when I was a little girl. This was also the hometown of the man who was riding his motorcycle, spotted the cross, stopped by the church and gave his heart to Jesus. Coincidental? Dennis and I don't believe in coincidence. We have experienced too many "divine appointments."

I felt the Spirit of the Lord speaking to me about another church plant in Bung Rieng. As I prayed about what the Lord had in store for the future ministries in this spiritually-neglected village, my heart broke when I remembered a previous phone call I had received from Binh Chau that continues to haunt me today. Some of the believers from the church had gone to visit the man who had given his heart to the Lord after seeing the cross on top of the church. He asked if they would visit some of his friends in Bung Rieng and tell them about Jesus. They went and had a wonderful visit, but were reluctant to share the Gospel with them. Three days later, one of the women they had visited died without knowing the Lord. I realized more than ever before that we must tell others while we can about the Good News of Jesus Christ. Today is the Day of Salvation.

*For God says, "At just the right time, I heard you. On the day of salvation, I helped you." Indeed, the "right time" is now. Today is the day of salvation.*

2 CORINTHIANS 6:2 NLT

## VALLEY OF DRY BONES

I asked Lam if anyone from Pastor Quy's church had ever attempted to evangelize in Bung Rieng. Lam informed me there were no Protestant Christians there. He said the town was spiritually dead.

I began to pray for Bung Rieng. One morning the Lord whispered, "Ezekiel 37!" to my soul. I opened my Bible up and began reading.

*The Lord took hold of me, and I was carried away by the Spirit of the Lord to a valley filled with bones. He led me all around among the bones that covered the valley floor. They were scattered everywhere across the ground and were completely dried out. Then he asked me, "Son of man, can these bones become living people again?"*

"O Sovereign Lord," I replied, "you alone know the answer to that."

Then he said to me, "Speak a prophetic message to these bones and say, 'Dry bones, listen to the word of the Lord! This is what the Sovereign Lord says: Look! I am going to put breath into you and make you live again! I will put flesh and muscles on you and cover you with skin. I will put breath into you, and you will come to life. Then you will know that I am the Lord.'"

So I spoke this message, just as he told me. Suddenly as I spoke, there was a rattling noise all across the valley. The bones of each body came together and attached themselves as complete skeletons. Then as I watched, muscles and flesh formed over the bones. Then skin formed to cover their bodies, but they still had no breath in them.

Then he said to me, "Speak a prophetic message to the winds, son of man. Speak a prophetic message and say, 'This is what the Sovereign Lord says: Come, O breath, from the four winds! Breathe into these dead bodies so they may live again.'"

So I spoke the message as he commanded me, and breath came into their bodies. They all came to life and stood up on their feet—a great army.

Then he said to me, "Son of man, these bones represent the people of Israel. They are saying, 'We have become old, dry bones—all hope is gone. Our nation is finished.' Therefore, prophesy to them and say, 'This is what the Sovereign Lord says: O my people, I will open your graves of exile and cause you to rise again. Then I will bring you back to the land of Israel. When this happens, O my people, you will know that I am the Lord. I will put my Spirit in you, and you will live again and return home to your own land. Then you will know that I, the Lord, have spoken, and I have done what I said. Yes, the Lord has spoken!'"

 Ezekiel 37:1–14 nlt

I began to claim that God's Spirit would breathe on the spiritually dead, dry bones of Bung Rieng.

## THREE GARDENS

As my heart was burdened for Bung Rieng, I thought of my two young uncles' premature deaths. A holy indignation filled my breast, and I began to see how God was in the restoration business. When sin came into the world, it was through a woman, but God had an antidote for the curse sin. Through another woman, a Savior was born.

Genesis begins with a tree in the Garden of Eden, where a woman ate of the forbidden fruit and the human race's Paradise was lost through Adam and Eve's disobedience. God's heart was broken, and He saw that mankind needed a remedy. He sent His one and only Son to restore the broken relationship. When Jesus was just 33, He prayed in another garden—Gethsemane—and won a magnificent victory through His obedience. If there had been no Gethsemane, there would be no hope of Heaven. Jesus was nailed to a tree on Calvary and began restoring the souls of men, women, boys and girls.

*Then Jesus went with his disciples to a place called Gethsemane, and he said to them, "Sit here while I go over there and pray." He took Peter and the two sons of Zebedee along with him, and he began to be sorrowful and troubled. Then he said to them, "My soul is overwhelmed with sorrow to the point of death. Stay here and keep watch with me."*

*Going a little farther, he fell with his face to the ground and prayed, "My Father, if it is possible, may this cup be taken from me. Yet not as I will, but as you will."*

*Then he returned to his disciples and found them sleeping. "Could you men not keep watch with me for one hour?" he asked Peter. "Watch and pray so that you will not fall into temptation. The spirit is willing, but the body is weak."*

*He went away a second time and prayed, "My Father, if it is not possible for this cup to be taken away unless I drink it, may your will be done."*

*When he came back, he again found them sleeping, because their eyes were heavy. So he left them and went away once more and prayed the third time, saying the same thing.*

*Then he returned to the disciples and said to them, "Are you still sleeping and resting? Look, the hour is near, and the Son of Man is betrayed into the hands of sinners."*

MATTHEW 26:36–45

*And when they were come to the place, which is called Calvary, there they crucified him.*

LUKE 23:33a KJV

Revelation closes with another tree: the Tree of Life. The first Paradise was lost, but the last Paradise is restored. This tree is reserved for those who obey His commandments. From the tree in the Garden of Eden to the tree Jesus died on, God has been restoring lives one soul at a time.

*Blessed are they that do his commandments, that they may have right to the tree of life, and may enter in through the gates into the city.*

REVELATION 22:14 KJV

*Then the angel showed me the river of the water of life, as clear as crystal, flowing from the throne of God and of the Lamb down the middle of the great street of the city. On each side of the river stood the tree of life, bearing twelve crops of fruit, yielding its fruit every month. And the leaves of the tree are for the healing of the nations.*

REVELATION 1:1, 2

## FULL CIRCLE

God creates full circle moments in our lives. Moments of healing the past hurts and winning victory over the defeats Satan has attempted to bring our way. Sometimes our spiritual ears become dull and we cannot hear what the Spirit is saying, but as I reflected on the pain I had endured as a child when my two uncles' lives were snuffed out, I knew God was desiring to restore something that had been damaged in my soul and also, take back the land for the Kingdom of God. Could it be God was asking us to plant a church in Bung Rieng?

Dennis and I began to pray. One day our phone rang and we were introduced to a Vietnamese missionary pastor. He had traveled to Laos, Cambodia and Thailand planting house churches. My nephew had told him about us and the Binh Chau work. The young pastor asked if there was anything he could do for the village of Bung Rieng. I asked him to travel there and check the spiritual temperature of the town. He and his wife took a road trip to Bung Rieng. They visited a man who was an old friend of our family. After hearing the Gospel for the first time, this man and his son prayed to receive Christ. As the pastor shared his desire to plant a church there, the new convert offered a small piece of property to build a house on.

I couldn't help but rejoice at how God was moving. I remembered how Satan attempted to destroy my life, my family and my marriage. He was almost successful, but Jesus passed by and changed my destiny. Satan meant it for evil, but God meant it for good. The town where I experienced such emotional trauma and hopelessness was now the place where God's Spirit was showering down hope and healing for all who believed.

*As for you, you thought evil against me, but God meant it for good, to bring about that many people should be kept alive, as they are this day.*

GENESIS 50:20 AMP

## BLEEDING HEARTS' CLUB

I am a charter member of the Bleeding Hearts' Club. My heart was hemorrhaging for many years, and I didn't know how to get the bleeding to stop until Jesus touched me. There was another woman who suffered with an issue of blood for 12 long years. She heard that Jesus was passing by. She pressed through the crowd and touched the hem of His garment and her bleeding stopped.

*A woman in the crowd had suffered for twelve years with constant bleeding. She had suffered a great deal from many doctors, and over the years she had spent everything she had to pay them, but she had gotten no better. In fact, she had gotten worse. She had heard about Jesus, so she came up behind him through the crowd and touched his robe. For she thought to herself, "If I can just touch his robe, I will be healed." Immediately the bleeding stopped, and she could feel in her body that she had been healed of her terrible condition.*

*Jesus realized at once that healing power had gone out from him, so he turned around in the crowd and asked, "Who touched my robe?"*

*His disciples said to him, "Look at this crowd pressing around you. How can you ask, 'Who touched me?'"*

*But he kept on looking around to see who had done it. Then the frightened woman, trembling at the realization of what had happened to her, came and fell to her knees in front of him and told him what she had done. And he said to her, "Daughter, your faith has made you well. Go in peace. Your suffering is over."*

Mark 5:24–34 nlt

If you are reading my story today and you have a bleeding heart, Jesus has sent me to tell you He can stop the bleeding and heal your broken heart. God sent Jesus to this earth to heal the brokenhearted and set the captive free. He sent Jesus to heal your broken heart.

*The Spirit of the Lord is upon me, because he hath anointed me to preach the gospel to the poor; he hath sent me to heal the brokenhearted, to preach deliverance to the captives, and recovering of sight to the blind, to set at liberty them that are bruised.*

Luke 4:18 kjv

## You Cannot Drink Grapes

Oswald Chambers writes in his devotional *My Utmost for His Highest*, "If we are ever going to be made into wine, we will have to be crushed—you cannot drink grapes. Grapes become wine only when they have been squeezed."

Brokenness seems to be God's tool of choice to make us "wine." Broken dreams, shattered relationships, devastating losses, fragmented homes and wounded hearts are the experiences in life God will use to take us from the natural to a life in the supernatural, where He receives all the glory and honor.

Dennis and I have allowed God to squeeze the "grapes of affliction" we have experienced in our lives. He has taken our sufferings and produced a sweet, fragrant wine. Everywhere we go, we see spiritually dehydrated souls who are dying for a drink. We pray our story and the "wine" He has produced in our lives will be useful in quenching the parched lips of the thirsting world around us.

If you're thirsty today, He invites you to come and drink from His well. If you have any prayer needs, please feel free to contact us at:

camonchua@comcast.net

*But those who drink the water I give will never be thirsty again. It becomes a fresh, bubbling spring within them, giving them eternal life.*

JOHN 4:14 NLT

# A Peek Behind the Scenes

*From the tribe of Issachar, there were 200 leaders of the tribe with their relatives. All these men understood the signs of the times and knew the best course for Israel to take.*

1 Chronicles 12:32 NLT

As Dennis and my family in Vietnam began to discern what God wanted to do in Binh Chau, and we spent time seeking the Lord for His will and guidance, we began to understand in the Spirit the direction God was leading us—and it was exciting! Prayers were being answered daily. The Holy Spirit was speaking into our hearts exactly what ministries we were to start in Binh Chau. In this final section, we wanted to share with our readers a "peek behind the scenes," the inside scoop on how God led and opened doors for what began as a "call" to its fulfillment.

The following pages are letters we received from Pastor Quy and other helpful information that will give each reader insight into what life is like in Binh Chau and the ministries we have implemented to meet the physical and spiritual needs of the precious souls we have been called to serve. We've also given a brief introduction before each letter to clarify what was transpiring at the time.

## First Letter

In the summer of 2004, Dennis and I spent a month in Vietnam gathering information on what we could or couldn't do according to the Vietnamese government about planting a church in Binh Chau. We then returned home and shared this information with the Missions Committee at our church in

Tucson. Beginning in February of 2005, Catalina Foothills Church started financially supporting our ministry to Vietnam. We wrote Pastor Quy a letter asking him to give us a breakdown of how this monthly support of $200 would be spent to start the church plant in Binh Chau so we might share this with our church. This letter is Pastor Quy's response to our request.

*April 15, 2005*

*Dear Mr. and Mrs. Spencer and the Servants of the Lord in His Church, in the Name of Jesus Christ,*

*We thank the Lord. Since the beginning of this year, 2005, until now, the Lord has been with our church and has filled us with much joy and peace.*

*How are both of you doing? Well, I hope. How about your church? I hope everything is well and joyful.*

*About us here in Vietnam, we had a four-day meeting of prayer and worship in Saigon. In attendance at that meeting were Mr. and Mrs. Thomas Stebbins, Mr. and Mrs. Peter Norris Nanfelt —the head of Evangelic Gospel United and Pastor and Mrs. Nguyen Anh Tai of the Vietnamese Christian Church in the United States. They all taught the Word of God to us at the meeting. I wish you were here to rejoice with us, Mr. and Mrs. Spencer—and the people in your church who have a heart and concern for the work of the Lord in our church in Binh Chau.*

*I thank God the past two months. We have begun the first steps of His work in Binh Chau. The first decision was choosing the right people to go to Binh Chau. God has blessed us with three people: Mr. Tam, who lives in Binh Chau, and Lam and Mai, a husband and wife from my church in Ba To. They are willing to go to Binh Chau. Lam will teach the weekly adult Bible study, and his wife, Mai, will teach the weekly children's Bible study. Tam and Lam will share the worship service on Sunday.*

*In the children's Bible study, we have some who are believers and some who are not. They are at the stage where we have to get them warmed up. Please pray that God will work in their hearts to strengthen them to come together full of zeal and faithfulness to Him.*

*As for the financial support your church is giving us, I pay the people who are going to Binh Chau to teach 1,500,000 Vietnamese or 100 U.S. dollars each month. With the other 100 U.S. dollars, I help the servants of God in three other small towns. I give Elder Dong, Elder Minh, and Mr. Quang each 250,000 Vietnamese or 16 U.S. dollars each month to help support their work in these three towns. I use 750,000 Vietnamese or 48 U.S. dollars each month for Mercy Ministry for the churches I oversee, and I pay a translator 100,000 Vietnamese or 5 U.S. dollars each month for their work.*

*This is all I have done for the church in Binh Chau and the church in Ba To. If anything I do is not pleasing to you and your church, please let me know so I can improve on it. Please pray for God's work in Binh Chau. I thank you, Mr. and Mrs. Spencer and your church, for praying for us and supporting us.*

*Pastor Nguyen Dinh Quy*

## SECOND LETTER

In July of 2005, Dennis and I returned to Vietnam for a month to work with the home church in Binh Chau and Pastor Quy. We held Bible studies and visited with the brothers- and sisters-in-Christ in Binh Chau. God also gave us many opportunities to share the Gospel. Unfortunately, we discovered the government had learned of the land we had purchased in Binh Chau the summer of 2004 for a possible church site. They had passed a law stating no one could build in that area. We returned to the United States a little disappointed, learning how fickle the government could be, but also trusting God to open another door. Pastor Quy had tried to e-mail us, but our computer had crashed and we weren't able to receive the messages. He then wrote us this letter to check on us and give us an update of what had happened with the church in the month of August 2005.

*September 1, 2005*

*Dear Mr. and Mrs. Dennis and Mai Spencer, in the Love of our
Savior, Jesus Christ,*

*In the past, I have e-mailed you, but I have not received your
answer yet. I wanted to know if you got home OK. I called your sister Hiep to ask her how you are all doing.*

*Over here we are all doing OK. The Lord has blessed the church
in Binh Chau, and more people are gathering to worship and rejoice
in the Lord. The children especially are very faithful in their fellowship and study. This past Sunday, August 28, about 7:30 p.m., we
had a program to evangelize the nonbelievers in my church in Ba To.
God blessed the church in Binh Chau to rent a bus to bring nonbelievers to the program that day. Four people from Binh Chau and
four people from Ba To received Christ as their Lord and Savior. Hal-
leluiah! Thank God! In the eighth months, eight souls came to Christ.*

*We ask you and the Church, our brothers and sisters, to keep us
in prayer, that God will give us the strength to keep going out to tell
people about the love of the Lord and His Name. Please pray God
will give us favor. We wish God would give you the opportunity to
come back to Vietnam to help us strengthen the church in Binh
Chau and to witness to the people of Binh Chau.*

*I hope to hear from you all and your church. Please send my
regards to your pastor and all those serving the Lord. I pray that
God's love and favor will be upon your pastor and all the servants of
the Lord and His church.*

*In the loving Blood of Christ the Savior,*
*Pastor Nguyen Dinh Quy*

## THIRD LETTER

Pastor Quy wrote this letter to make sure we were safe from Hurricane Katrina. They had heard of the devastation the hurricane had caused and did-
n't know if we were involved in it. He also wanted to ask us to return to
Vietnam to help with the church plant in Binh Chau. He saw how God had
used us when we were there in July, and we had talked then about return-

ing as soon as we could to continue meeting and visiting with the people in Binh Chau. God was starting to draw people to Himself, but Jesus tells us what the problem is in the Gospel of Matthew.

*Then he said to his disciples, "The harvest is plentiful but the workers are few."*

MATTHEW 9:37

*September 14, 2005*
*Dear Mr. and Mrs. Spencer and family, in the Name of our Precious Lord and Savior, Jesus Christ,*

*I hope the Lord has given your family peace and joy. We heard about Hurricane Katrina and were worried about you. We called Hiep to ask if your family was safe from Katrina.*

*Will you please give my regards to your pastors and the church? We thank God with all our hearts, knowing both of you and your church are praying and encouraging us to serve the Lord in my country.*

*In August, the eighth month, God blessed us with a total of twelve people coming to know the Lord. We had four nights of evangelism meetings. The brothers and sisters in Binh Chau rented a van for transportation to drive some of their friends and family to my church so we could share the Gospel with them. This month in Binh Chau, we had a woman named Phung accept the Lord. Her husband, Mr. Kim, is Korean. We just baptized nine people on Sunday, September 11th.*

*We ask that you and your church pray for the people here as many of their hearts are hard. In the field of Binh Chau, we need a harvester to send out, but we have not found one yet. We have few people who are able to teach the people to make them strong and grow in the Lord. On behalf of the Church, I would like to invite you and your wife to come back to work with our church and the church in Binh Chau.*

*Dear Mr. and Mrs. Spencer and your church, we really hope to have a room in our church in Ba To to welcome guests from far away places and make it convenient to serve the Lord here. So when we invite guests to come to my church in Ba To, they will have a place for teaching and resting. You and your husband came to visit us, but we can not ask you to stay because we have no room. We would like to build a room at the door to our house 4 meters long and 3 meters wide and 4.5 meters high; a total of 12 square meters. The cost would be 5,000,000 Vietnamese or over 300 U.S. dollars. We ask you and your church to pray for us.*

*I will stop now. I hope to see you soon and will share more with you then. I pray for peace and new strength of the Lord all Mighty in your calling. I pray for your family and all the brothers and sisters in the Church.*

*Respectfully and sincerely,*
*Pastor Nguyen Dinh Quy*

## FOURTH LETTER

This letter was written to give to our congregation at the Catalina Foothills Church after I had spent two months in Binh Chau working with the church. Pastor Quy wanted to express his appreciation and give our church a little more information about the churches he oversees. During my two months there, God opened door after door to show His love for the people in Binh Chau. Many people came to Christ despite government opposition. God also opened the door for us to purchase another piece of land, and construction of the church building was under way.

*November 30, 2005*
*Dear Pastor, Pastoral Staff, Ministries Staff, and all of the Lord's Children in the Presbyterian Church in Tucson, Arizona,*
*First of all, on behalf of God's church in Xuyen Moc district, we'd like to send to you and your families our warm regards. May God bless you and your ministries.*
*We were very happy because you were interested in praying for our church, especially because you supported the building of the Binh*

*Chau church house, our branch church, as well as sending Mrs. Spencer to come here to preach the Good News to the Binh Chau area and other places. Thank God for her mission. She led a lot of people in this place to the Lord.*

*We'd like to tell you some more about the Binh Chau church. In the past, this church had a lot of people who believed in God, and they often gathered to worship God in Christian homes, but because of their hard life, they didn't gather to worship God regularly. Gradually, they lost their faith. Our mother church frequently sent the worker of the church there to visit and look after them. But they still didn't return to worship God. We think Mrs. Mai Spencer is the Christian who is full of God's grace. She came there and used the Lord's words to help them, and they become stronger and are eager now. Mai Kha's house, where the church gathered to worship God, is crowded now. We need another place. Maybe, through some photos taken, you can understand some more about this place.*

*When we are writing this letter to you, the Binh Chau church house is being built. We think when you come to visit us next year, it will perhaps have already been built. But there is one thing that makes us anxious. That is the church in Binh Chau is growing and spreading thanks to Mrs. Mai's witness and these new Christians haven't grown up yet in the faith. We really need Mrs. Mai to visit and look after them. We expect that you will send her to return here soon.*

*We would like to tell you some more information about our church so that you know it well and will pray for it. It was set up in 1990. The mother church is in the center of Xuen Moc district, Ba Ria, Vung Tau province, South Vietnam. Total Christians are about 550. We have four branches (or sister churches). They are Binh Chau, Hoa Hiep, and Bao Lam churches. They are names of the villages of Xuyen Moc district, and every place is about 20 kilometers from the mother church. Two of those three church houses were built or is being built. But Hoa Hiep church house was only built temporarily with light material. It is now decayed and waiting for*

*rebuilding. (We have some photos of this church taken by Mrs.*
*Mai.)*

  *In addition, we are planning to set up a new branch church at*
*Hoa Hoi village that is about twelve kilometers away from the*
*mother church. There are about 80 Christians there. So we will have*
*one mother church and four sister churches around. However, we*
*still have some difficulties because of the local government. This will*
*be told clearer by Mrs. Mai. We wish you will help us with prayer*
*and support to rebuild the church house that was decayed so that the*
*Lord's children here will have a better place to gather for worship-*
*ping God.*

  *Last of all, May God be with you and your ministries.*

  *Love in Christ,*
  *Pastor Nguyen Dinh Quy*
  *Chairman of the Church*

## FIFTH LETTER

This letter was sent to us to ask us and our church to pray for the many
needs of the growing church in Binh Chau and Pastor Quy's additional
churches. Pastor Quy also wanted to officially invite us, Kathryn Farris, Pastor Matt, and others from our church here in Tucson to come to Vietnam
and help with the work of the Binh Chau church. Pastor Matt had expressed
an interest in going to Vietnam to help teach the men of the church, but
he would not be permitted to teach at the church unless the government
officially recognized the Binh Chau church. Pastor Quy felt the government
was close to recognizing the church, but this actually did not happen until
a few months later.

*Xuyen Moc  5/10/2007*
*Dear Mr. and Mrs. Dennis and Mai Spencer, precious in our Sav-*
*ior, Jesus Christ,*
  *On behalf of the church of Xuyen Moc and Binh Chau, I say*
*hello to you and your precious family and the whole body of Christ*
*in the church in Tucson (Catalina Foothills Church). Thank you so*

*much for remembering us in your prayers, interceding for us, and
sharing in the good work of the Lord in all six churches in Huyen
Xuyen Moc province, including the church in Binh Chau.*

*We rejoice because the churches have been very fruitful, despite
many difficulties, to overcome. We are so blessed. We ask that you all
continue to pray for us, that the Lord will help us to overcome the
difficulties still before us in doing the Lord's work here. Please pray
for the following:*

- *That God will bless us to lead 200 souls into His kingdom in
  2007.*
- *That the government will recognize the church in Binh Chau
  and the church in Tan Lam.*
- *That the transfer of the deed to the land in Binh Chau
  would be approved by the government.*
- *That God would open the doors for us to preach the Good
  News in two new towns, Bung Rieng Nhu Lam and Bong
  Trang. The population of these two towns is 14,000 with no
  Christian church there.*
- *That the organization and the funding of the summer Bible
  schools will go well. The youths will go to the central mountain city of Dalat, and the young children will come to the
  Mother church in Xuyen Moc (Ba To). We are expecting 115
  children to attend in Xuyen Moc. The financial cost will be
  12 million Vietnamese (800 U.S. dollars).*
- *That the ceremony organized by the Evangelical Church of
  the South to have the government officially ordain Pastor
  Quy (after 14 years of applying) and recognize five of six
  churches (Binh Chau being the only exception) be scheduled
  soon. \*\*\*\*In a phone conversation with Pastor Quy after this
  letter was received, this event was scheduled for June 29,
  2007. Pastor Quy invited us to the ceremony, but we were
  unable to attend. \*\*\*\**
- *That the church in Binh Chau would be able to purchase the
  remaining land next to the church (approximate cost: 35,000*

U.S. dollars) to develop as a conference center for all Christian churches in that region of Vietnam. This land could provide a future home for a school for children in the area to learn God's way to be able to serve in God's Kingdom, a mercy ministry to meet the needs of many poor people and to open the door for evangelism, to teach and train the young leaders of the future churches in God's Word, and many more uses for God's work.

That the Mother church in Ba To would be able to purchase an additional five meters of land next to the church to extend the church to have room for growth and fellowship. The church is now very small. The sanctuary is only six meters wide by fourteen meters long with the entrance into the church only two meters wide and thirty-two meters long. The church building is old, and when it rains, it is damp and the air is polluted. It is very hot, and many of us get sick.

On behalf of the church, I wish to invite Mr. and Mrs. Dennis, and the lady friend of Mr. and Mrs. Dennis (Kathryn Farris), Pastor Matt and his wife, and any of the brothers and sisters who have supported us and have a heart for the Lord's work to come to our church. Please come and share God's Word with us and especially train the ones to go out and witness to nonbelievers. Train us to be on fire to be good disciples for Jesus.

Dear Mr. and Mrs. Dennis, when I find out the date for the ordination, I will let you, your pastors, and your church in Tucson know.

I am sending this letter to you by way of an American pastor who has been in Vietnam teaching and is now returning home. I write this letter so you can pray for us and know of the work of the Lord here. Thank you for your love for us. I should end this letter now.

I pray that God would be glorified forever and His love and peace and prosperity be in you and your family. Amen.

Nguyen Dinh Quy
Senior Pastor

## INTERESTING FACTS ABOUT BINH CHAU

**Where is Binh Chau?**

Binh Chau is located approximately 100 miles east of Ho Chi Minh City (formerly Saigon). It takes between two and three hours to drive by car or bus due to heavy traffic and poor road conditions.

**What is the population of Binh Chau?**

The town of Binh Chau and several surrounding smaller towns and villages consist of about 30,000 people.

**Are there any tourist attractions in Binh Chau?**

Binh Chau is located on the South China Sea and contains many beaches of white sand. In recent years, it has become a major tourist attraction due to the development of a natural hot springs area into a resort—complete with hotels and recreational activities.

**What are the occupations of the residents of Binh Chau?**

The people of Binh Chau are mostly fishermen, farmers or small shop owners. It is a poor community where many residents make only an average of two dollars or less a day in wages.

**What is the religion of the people of Binh Chau?**

There are approximately 25 Protestants, between two and three hundred Catholics, and the rest are Buddhists, who practice ancestral worship, and even witchcraft and voodoo. To our knowledge, over 99.9 percent do not know about Jesus. As far as churches, Binh Chau has a large Buddhist temple located on about three acres of land and a Catholic church also located on three acres of land.

**What is the education level in Binh Chau?**

Most are poorly educated because, as children, they had to work to help support the family, or their parents could not afford to send them to school. Most parents there today want to see their children go to school, but many still cannot afford to do so. It costs about $100 per month to send each child to a good school. When you make between 40 and 60 dollars a month and have more than one child, it is a difficult, if not impossible, task.

**What is the lifestyle in Binh Chau?**

Fishermen are away from their families for days or weeks at a time out on the sea. Farmers put in long days working their fields. They work hard, but also play hard, as smoking, drinking and gambling are embedded in their culture. Because the parents are working hard to survive from day to day, many children are left to take care of themselves or each other. There are few activities to keep children busy and out of trouble. In many cases, they are exposed to smoking, drinking and gambling at a very early age, which makes them vulnerable to the wrong crowd.

## MERCY MINISTRY

*Religion that God our Father accepts as pure and faultless is this: to look after orphans and widows in their distress and to keep oneself from being polluted by the world.*

### JAMES 1:27

There is a strong hesitancy in some churches in Vietnam to meet the physical needs of the people in fear that people will come to the Lord in order to continue to receive food, clothing, money or medical assistance from the church. While this may be a possibility in some cases, we believe it is very hard for someone to be receptive to the Gospel of Jesus Christ when they are struggling to provide food, clothing and shelter for their families from one day to the next. Jesus not only gave the people the Bread of Life for their spiritual needs, but also fed them fish to meet their physical hunger. Because of the culture, lifestyle, lack of educational opportunities, and more, many people in Binh Chau are in need of both spiritual and physical help.

In the fall of 2005, Mai was working with the church in Binh Chau. They had 37 precious souls pray to receive Jesus as their Lord and Savior. Three of those families were in need of assistance, and Mai focused on helping them meet their daily needs through some of the funds of God's people. The following is a testimony of the impact Mercy Ministry made on one family.

Mai went to visit a family of six. There was a mother, father and four children in Binh Chau. The husband is a fisherman and goes out to sea a month at a time on a fishing boat. It is very dangerous and hard work. In fact, he was supposed to be out to sea when Mai went to visit, but he had gotten sick and came ashore to get medication and then was to return to his boat. However, he returned late and his boat had already left, so he returned home. We saw the hand of God in this. Mai learned that sometimes the family actually runs out of food before the husband returns from his long month at sea. When this happens, they resort to searching for wild green leaves and coconuts for food and stay curled up inside their home—what we would call a shack. The wife was the first to accept Christ, then her husband, and then all four of their children. Mai gave them some money for food and also enough for the wife to start a little business to help provide for the family when the husband is out to sea. This family was practicing Buddhism and dabbled in voodoo and witchcraft. Their home was full of idols. The husband told Mai before she left that he would pray about getting rid of all the idols in his house. After Mai returned to the States, Lam informed her the man had indeed taken all the idols out of his house and destroyed them. And the testimony gets even better. Lam also told us this family led another family of six to the Lord and that family destroyed all the idols in their house, also. They are all currently attending Sunday worship services and the Bible studies. They are getting ready to be baptized in water.

We believe this story confirms that there is a place for Mercy Ministry in Binh Chau. We pray God will provide the funds to help those in dire need in Binh Chau, not only to have their spiritual needs met, but also their physical needs, too.

## CHILDREN'S MINISTRY

*Jesus said, "Let the little children come to me, and do not hinder them, for the kingdom of heaven belongs to such as these."*

MATTHEW 19:14

When we went to Binh Chau in June of 2004, we found they were holding Sunday worship services in a home, but only two or three adults were attending. There were no programs for the children. Because of the sinful lifestyle and the culture, many children are neglected and exposed to smoking, drinking, gambling and drugs. The adults were so hardened in their ways, and many were not receptive to the Gospel of Jesus Christ. We began to pray. God put it in our heart that the focus should be on the children and the future generations. By God's grace, the children's parents would come to know Him. We stood on the Word of God.

*......a little child will lead them.*

ISAIAH 11:6b

We visited with Pastor Quy from Ba To and asked him if he was willing to send some people from his church to Binh Chau to help start weekly adult and children's Bible studies with financial support from our church in the USA. Pastor Quy said this would be possible. When we returned to our home in Tucson, Arizona, we presented this information to our congregation. They generously agreed to help support the outreach effort to Binh Chau, and in February of 2005, Pastor Quy sent Tam, Lam and Mai to Binh Chau on a weekly basis to hold Sunday worship services. They also have started some much-needed adult and children's Bible studies.

When we returned to Binh Chau in July of 2005, we attended Sunday worship services, which were being held in a home. We also attended the Tuesday night children's Bible study and the Friday night adult Bible study. There were ten children in attendance, and they were full of energy and eager to learn about the Word of God.

Lam and Mai were riding a motorcycle from Ba To to Binh Chau each Tuesday night. They made numerous trips around town on their motorcycle transporting their students to class. Then they would teach the children and, after the meeting, drive back to Ba To late at night. Their love for and dedication to the children warmed our hearts. As they diligently taught the Word of God to the children, they made it exciting and fun. They had to be very creative and come up with their own ideas because they had no teaching materials.

We returned to Tucson in August 2005 and shared all we had witnessed in Binh Chau. Almost immediately Pastor Quy began to send us letters requesting we return to help with God's Work in Binh Chau. We prayed about whether Mai should return so soon and God answered our prayers. Catalina Foothills Church offered to pay for the plane trip to Vietnam, and other members of our congregation gave financial support to purchase training materials and Bibles. We were able to purchase two sets of felt board figures that Pastor Quy, Lam and Mai had requested for the children's ministry.

In October 2005, Mai arrived in Binh Chau for seven weeks, and started working with Pastor Quy, Lam, and Mai, visiting families in the area. During Mai's visit, she saw the children's Bible study class increase from 10 children to 30. The felt board figures were a great tool in making the Bible stories come alive to the children. They also played games and handed out prizes for scripture memorization. One girl who was 11 was given her first birthday party. It was a joyous time of fellowship in the Lord. Mai wishes everyone could have seen the twinkle in the eyes of the children as they experienced the love of God. We thank God for touching the people's hearts at our church who made this trip possible through their financial support.

In phone conversations recently with Lam and Mai, they reported the children's Bible study class has now grown to 42 students per week. Their ages are from five to thirteen. They now have 11 young people to start a youth ministry on Tuesday evenings. Great is His faithfulness! Lam teaches the children, and Mai teaches the youth.

We are so grateful that God has allowed us the privilege of serving Him through this ministry. The needs are growing, but the workers are few. Please pray that God will raise up laborers to teach and disciple these precious souls.

*But when he saw the multitudes, he was moved with compassion on them, because they fainted, and were scattered abroad, as sheep having no shepherd.*

*Then saith he unto his disciples, The harvest truly is plenteous, but the labourers are few;*

*Pray ye therefore the Lord of the harvest, that he will send forth labourers into his harvest.*

(MATTHEW 9:36–39 KJV

Please also pray that God would provide the funds to purchase a van to transport all the precious little ones to and from the Bible studies.

We rejoice in all God is doing in the hearts and lives of the children. These wee ones are like wet cement, and now is the time to shape and mold their little hearts for Jesus. We hope to capture the hearts of the children for the King.

*From the lips of children and infants you have ordained praise.*

PSALM 8:2a

## LITTLE ONES TO HIM BELONG

The Lord led us to have our first Vacation Bible School June 19-23, 2008, in Binh Chau. We realize, more than ever before, we must sow into the hearts and lives of the children of Vietnam. It may take time, but eventually God is going to give a bountiful harvest of souls through our investment.

The first morning of Vacation Bible School, Lam was up bright and early praying. The children were to be picked up and brought to the church for opening prayer and given a schedule of the events for that day. Breakfast would be served between seven and eight o'clock, before the activities began. Lam waited anxiously for the children to arrive, but by eight o'clock, not one child had shown up. Lam went into his room, fell to his knees, and began to cry out to the Lord. "You called me to come to Binh Chau to serve You here, but what have I done wrong? Where are all the children? I need Your help, Lord. I can't do this alone."

Around nine o'clock he walked outside to the entrance of the church and peered down the road in both directions, but saw no children. His heart was broken. Then, in the distance, he spotted a boy with a backpack over his shoulder walking towards the church, a sister and brother tagging along behind him. Behind them was a long line of more children with backpacks. Lam began to praise God for answering his prayers. God spoke into the depths of his heart. "Lam, you are not alone. I am with you, and here are My children."

Victory was in the camp. Lam's tears of sorrow were now tears of joy. He wanted to run down the street and hug each little one who was coming to Vacation Bible School.

As the children got closer, they started running towards Lam shouting, "Hi, Uncle Lam. We know we are late, but no one came to pick us up. We had to walk. Can we still come in and pray and sing and go to Bible school?" Lam answered joyfully, "Yes, you can. Let's do it!"

Forty children walked to the church in Binh Chau to attend their first Vacation Bible School. Their excitement and enthusiasm filled the church. Even though they were a couple of hours behind schedule, they were still able to complete all the activities planned for that day.

All of you who partner with us are helping change Vietnam one soul at a time. We cannot think of anything more important. When we get to Heaven, the only thing we can take with us are the souls of men, women, boys and girls. Everything else we leave behind. May God help us win souls for His Kingdom.

*Only one life so soon will be past.*
*Only what's done for Christ will last.*

We would love to hear from you. If you'd like to partner with us, please contact us at:

Dennis and Mai Spencer
Jesus in Vietnam Ministries
E-mail: camonchua@comcast.net
Website: www.Jesusinvietnam.com